HumAnimal

Posthumanities
Cary Wolfe, Series Editor

(continued on page 312)

HumAnimal

RACE, LAW, LANGUAGE

Kalpana Rahita Seshadri

posthumanities **21**

University of Minnesota Press

Minneapolis

London

Published by the University of Minnesota Press
111 Third Avenue South, Suite 290
Minneapolis, MN 55401-2520
http://www.upress.umn.edu

Library of Congress Cataloging-in-Publication Data
Seshadri, Kalpana Rahita (also Kalpana Seshadri-Crooks), author.
    HumAnimal : race, law, language / Kalpana Rahita Seshadri.
       (Posthumanities; 21)
    Includes bibliographical references and index.
    ISBN 978-0-8166-7788-7 (hc : alk. paper)
    ISBN 978-0-8166-7789-4 (pb : alk. paper)
    1. Philosophical anthropology. 2. Silence (Philosophy). 3. Feral children.
I. Title. II. Series: Posthumanities; 21.

    BD450.S399 2011
    128—dc23   2011040193

Printed in the United States of America on acid-free paper

For Amma
and
Robert

Contents

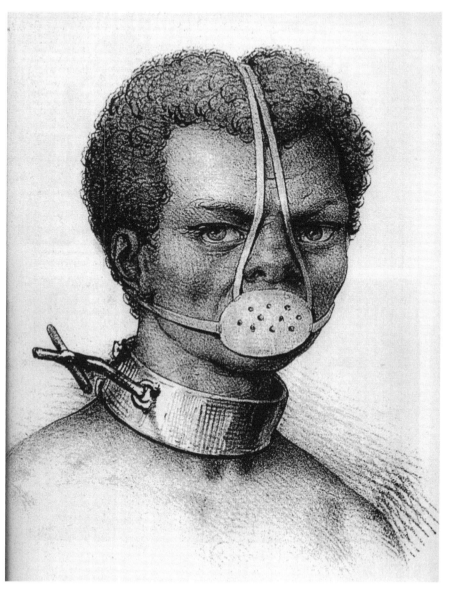

Jacques Etienne Arago. *Castigo de Escravos*, 1839. Museu Afro Brasil (São Paulo).

What This "Book" Is About

THIS BOOK AIMS TO MAKE A CONTRIBUTION TO THE PHILOSOPHY OF race and racism in terms of the questions raised in studies of animality and human propriety. It explores the practice of racism as dehumanization to argue that the deprivation of speech that characterizes the inhuman is a political realm where the exercise of power can meet its potential neutralization through the very silence to which the inhuman is assigned. By the term "power," I refer to Foucault's genealogy of power in terms of sovereign, disciplinary, and biopower. If we understand modern discriminatory practice as a functioning of what Foucault terms biopower, we can immediately discern that what is termed "racism" is synonymous with the practice of dehumanization, whereby the victim is disqualified from being a full member of the elite company of human beings. It has often been observed that dehumanization occurs through the instrumentalization of the sole and sacrosanct dividing line between human and nonhuman—that is, language or, more properly, the *logos* as meaningful and credible speech. The other is silenced—rendered speechless as a mute beast undeserving of human sympathy or recognition. However, insofar as language as such refers to both speech and silence, dehumanization as the privation of speech raises a series of questions: How is the concept of humanness (as being in logos) articulated with power? How can power be discerned as the exercise of a decision on what is and is not human? How should language be approached in the context of power? How does power instrumentalize language, and can the two be separated? Can the withholding (rather than the availability) of speech open the space of the political? Are there perhaps political and ethical possibilities in the relation between silence and power? What does it mean to discern silence as the power of language, rather than the language of power?

Following Foucault and Agamben, my premise is that the practice of dehumanization depends on the logic of a power that can decide on the value of a given life. Such a decision works fundamentally to exclude the other from the realm of human intercourse, which can be achieved only by denying access to speech and, of course, law. In fact, the *locus* of power's decision on life is the conflation of language and law, while the *exercise* of power is the withholding of access to the law–speech nexus in order to consign the other to silence. In other words, power is what it is because it presupposes the union of law and language, and it does what it does by separating a part of language (silence) from the law. This is a scenario that is endemic to extreme states of violence, such as genocide or strategic neglect, where the protection of the law is withheld or denied. In such a scenario, the trinity of law, language, and humanness not only opens the abyss of silence to which it consigns the inhuman but also, above all, exposes itself as thoroughly and merely conditional in its functioning. Thus, if a certain liberation of language from the law can be countenanced, does this not also promise the neutralization of power?

In order to expand on this hypothesis and explore the themes of law and language, the argument is made simultaneously in several different registers—namely the political, theoretical, and narrative. In writing this book, I have been like a thumbless potter working at the wheel, unclear about the shape of what might emerge from the clay under my hands. As the wheel spins and the clay waxes and wanes, the odds of it being misshapen, asymmetrical, unconventional, and unregulated are high and yet one hopes it may be available to some use. Whatever it may be, it has insisted on appearing, and now responsibility for the work of these missing fingers must be fully assumed. I have learned an incalculable amount over the years from the brilliant philosophers at Boston College and elsewhere, whose lectures and texts have been humbling and chastening in ways that inspired me to at least try. I freely acknowledge an unrepayable debt to Professor John Sallis, whose lectures I attended from 2006 through 2008, and to Fr. William (Bill) Richardson SJ, whose blessing and gentle words of encouragement meant more to me than he could have ever bargained for. Kelly Oliver has been like a lighthouse—the distant beacon urging me to safe harbor. I owe many thanks to Andy Von Hendy for remaining interested in my ideas through all the changes, Judith Wilt for very firmly nudging me to let go of the manuscript and contact a publisher, and my wonderful and painstaking students for sticking with me through two courses on *Of Grammatology* and "Derrida and Agamben on Law and Sovereignty." But above all, to Professor Richard Kearney, I feel a deep and inexpressible sense of gratitude. With great generosity of heart, he and Anne gave me the courage I sorely lacked to reflect and write. To these and other philosophers—especially my collies Frege and Russell, their cousin Maisie, and Norbu the cat eternal—as well as to every biped and quadruped in my family, I only wish this book, its cover and pages, all its words, stories, and pictures were deliciously edible so it could provide a fulfilling thank-you feast for all the noisy peace they continue to provide.

The Trace of the Political

THIS PROJECT TAKES THE RISK TO DISCERN THE PREVALENCE OF what can be termed nonsovereign power, a power without right, as that which empties the legitimized power of disciplines and law (moral and juridical). The risk lies in thinking of the practice and prevalence of such neutralizing power as the temporal spacing that is constitutive of all named identities—what Derrida indicates as "trace" or the play of *différance*—thereby disclosing it as the site of the biopolitical. Despite the differing historicity of the biopolitical perspective from the deconstructive, and the difficulty of bringing the interrogation of presence (or oneness) to bear on the analytics of power conceived as fractal, the shape of this inquiry is wholly conditioned by Derrida's long-standing and relentless engagement with the self-presence and purity of the concepts informing what is said to be proper to the human being as distinguished from the so-called animal. By biopolitical, I refer to a modality of power, which Foucault theorizes as characteristic of "state racism" or a discourse of "care" (the state's care of its population), which is exercised as a decision over the life that is and is not worth saving or living.

My understanding of power in relation to race draws on Foucault's genealogy of modern power as characterized by "what might be called power's hold over life . . . the acquisition of power over man insofar as man is a living being" (Foucault, *Society Must Be Defended*, 239–40). Further in this same lecture of 17 March 1976, he says,

> The specificity of modern racism, or what give it its specificity, is not bound up with mentalities, ideologies, or the lies of power. It is bound up with the technique of power, with the technology of power . . . We are dealing with the workings of a State that is obliged to use race, the elimination of races and the purification of the race, to exercise its sovereign power. The juxtaposition of—or the way biopower functions through—the old sovereign power of life and death implies the workings, the introduction and activation, of racism. And it is, I think, here that we find the actual roots of racism. (258)

As the originally canceled origin, the trace, which is the spatializing of time and the temporalization of space, inhabits and haunts every living entity, thereby rendering its self-presence as a dissimulation of what in fact produces it—namely, a temporal composite of a succession of marks in space on a page. The identity of the living subject, in other words, is always written, inscribed by and in a space/time. For Derrida, the trace is not only "prior" but also the condition of all conditions of possibility, be they sensible or transcendental intuitions. It is the mark of the "living in life." What, then, does it mean to say that this self-canceling and instituted origin, which is nothing if not the necessity of temporal movement, is also the site of biopolitics? Why situate the contemporary struggle of biopolitics at the level of a critique of traditional ontology? How can it be said that the stakes of biopolitics (which are the effects of a historically marked discourse of power/knowledge) are best disclosed through the logic of the trace?

The two perspectives (biopolitics and deconstruction) achieve a synthesis in Agamben's political theory. For Agamben, who develops the concept of biopolitics, the decision on life (a process of animalization) derives from a political ontology that founds itself on an ancient structure of sovereignty. Agamben's analysis of the paradoxical structure of sovereignty as a form of power that is essentially sustained by and harbors anomie—as evidenced by its potentiality to suspend the law and create lawlessness (state of exception)—suggests that anomie is properly the trace of the *nomos*. Here, in this space where the trace of the law as anomie is both its suspension and its violent force, Agamben locates a genuine and immanent political possibility—namely, the neutralization of the force of law, an event that he variously delineates as a species of worklessness or nonsovereign power. There is a decisive value to interpreting Agamben's analysis of sovereign power in terms of the deconstructive trace: it enables a narrowed inquiry into the relation between law and language. The suspension of the law (anomie, trace, state of exception) can now be parsed as the suspension of speech (right, subjectivity, humanity)—a site where the silence opens the political. To reintroduce this analysis into the discursive terrain of contemporary race politics has the effect of reradicalizing the function of the trace with regard to human/animal propriety. Thus, it appears that any investigation of the logic of race for a revised political ontology requires some contiguity or an impure synthesis of biopolitics and deconstruction.

Derrida elaborates the logic of the trace in varied disciplinary contexts and thereby proliferates a vast lexicon (*différance*, writing, pharmakon, gift, hospitality, democracy, justice, etc.) that refers to singular events that disclose nonpresence. This project takes its point of departure from the ontological and political context of what Derrida terms *la bête*, which can be understood as the trace that renders undecidable the attributes of speech and life in the polis as proper to man. In a parallel yet displacing move, Agamben's apprehension of sovereignty's self-division (between constituting and constituted power) as indicative of a secret anomie within law and right locates power (over life) not in self-presence but in the operation of *différance*. In other words, keeping in mind the necessary coimplication of law and language, the problem of sovereign power must be thought as the potentiality of spacing to divide and separate (and manage) life: the state of exception as the *trace* of the law. To follow the workings of power as the appropriation of temporal spacing is also to translate the trace into the terms of potentiality. By rigorously privileging the thought of potentiality in its survival beyond its actualization, Agamben thereby gradually brings into view a power without right that does not so much differ and defer the power of decision and division as it altogether empties it of all significance. The consequence of this displacement is not minimal. If the operation of *différance* is the potentiality that is always held in reserve—the power that invariably spaces and temporalizes—and remains unexhausted by the sovereign decision, then what is thrown open to question by this displacement of the trace is the necessity of the powerful concomitance between language and law. In other words, if violence as anomie or exception is the trace of the structure of sovereignty and its deployment of the law, and if this structure can be neutralized, then language is liberated from a necessary implication in power. What is language that is not implicated in law, sovereignty, and its capacity for violence?

The pretheoretical motivation of this inquiry was to think through what it might mean to outfox the norms by which life is governed and managed in the contemporary global context. The juxtaposition of deconstruction and biopolitics delivered this pursuit to the aporia of a logic where not only does sovereignty dissimulate presence (and vice versa) but nonpresence, or the trace, is disclosed as nothing but differentiated powers. *HumAnimal* engages the logic of the displacement of the trace into the thought of potentiality by focusing on the spacing between law and language through the figure of silence. More specifically, the question is whether the figure of the animalized brute (neither properly human nor animal) can exercise a power of silence. Throughout, the attempt is not only to apprehend silence as the emptying power within language—in other words, a political potential that dislocates the overlay of language by the law—but more important, to disclose the spatial temporality of such power as quintessentially ethical.

Part I attempts to detail the process of arriving at this argument by first situating the questions within the context of the philosophy of race and studies of animality. Listen: It may all be very well to exhibit the insubstantiality of racial categories as ontological essences, but it is another to address the practice of race as an "ism"—that is, as the violent extirpation of human or animal identity (or propriety) that was never fully possessed to begin with. Furthermore, the political task of conceptualizing resistance on the terrain of impropriety means that it must be discerned as immanent to power. Thus, after delineating the broad problematic and the reasoning that led to its construction, and specifying the use of certain recurring terms, "First Words on Silence" turns to the question of silence as a manifestation of this impropriety and aims to understand its role as immanent to language. As a theme and a device, literature has, of course, claimed ownership of the signifier "silence," and it has done more to dislodge its adhesion to any given signified by rendering it the element of the literary within literature. However, given the genealogy of literature and its unspeakable secret, as discussed by Derrida, and the "work" that a certain unspeakable silence does in a novel such as J. M. Coetzee's *Foe*, I attempt, in the next chapter, to distinguish the appearance of a certain neutralizing power held by the slave from what binds the discipline of literature to a discourse of contract. But in what sense does such silence sever language from the law (be it of literature or right)? And what are the political implications and theoretical consequences of making such distinctions? The inevitability of these questions demands focused attention to the approaches that Derrida and Agamben assume toward the law and its relation to language. This chapter, entitled "Law, 'Life/Living,' Language," however, privileges the question of power as biopower and the commitment to its neutralization through nonsovereign silence. The next chapter in turn privileges the relation between Derrida and Agamben in terms of the deconstruction of presence. What, I wondered, do Agamben's writings say about the metaphysics of presence and logocentrism? Would it be fair to say that Agamben engages in a serious parody of deconstruction?

These inconclusive elucidations (or obfuscations) of Derrida and Agamben on law and language, silence and power, raised for me other related questions pertaining to singularity and silence and seemed to partition the project along the lines of the political in the first part and a reflection on the ethical in the second.

"The Wild Child: Politics and Ethics of the Name" pursues Derrida's ethical injunction to a certain silence in the context of hospitality in relation to an extreme figure outside the law—the so-called feral child that haunts the nature/culture dichotomy. To refrain from questioning, and to encounter the ethical decision in and through a discernment of the inherent violence of naming, what do these agonistic experiences disclose about the proper name and its relation to the law and, more pointedly the "good name" of a child that has no name? This inquiry into the wild child is carried over into the next chapter to the context of scientific naturalism as a discipline of naming.

In the last chapter, "HumAnimal Acts: Potentiality or Movement as Rest," it is the mute physical body of the acrobat that appears to turn cartwheels around the machine of the law to confound its workings. This body, it seems, requires that it be situated at the threshold between identities, concepts, even philosophical traditions, and best shows itself in relation to Agamben's appropriation of Aristotle's concept of potentiality. This joyful body of the rigorous acrobat redefines space and time by disclosing the stillness that resides in action. To contemplate this body, I suggest, is to perceive that it can embody the very power of language beyond the law's purview. As a modality of what Foucault might term the "care of the self," which refers to practices that are necessarily anomic and exceptional, agile movement, if practiced thoughtfully, recalls living beings—humAnimals—to their essential capacity for happiness.

I. Language and Silence

The Mute Prince

Once, a much-longed-for heir was born to the powerful and wealthy king, Sakka of Benares. There was great rejoicing throughout the kingdom. When the baby was one month old, he was dressed in fine clothes, fed sweetened milk, given the name Temiya (for he was born on a rainy day), and placed on the king's lap to witness his father's great power as he held court. Four criminals were presented to him. The king ordered the first to be put to death, the second to be imprisoned for life, the third to have his body impaled, and the fourth to have his eyes put out. The babbling baby was speechless with horror at the king's power. Later, as he lay in his crib, wondering how he could avoid the fate of becoming a cruel king himself, he heard a voice advising him to be mute, to use his capability to not move or speak. And so it was that the little infant prince, to repudiate his inheritance and his father's power, gathered his own within himself and resolved to remain speechless and unmoving. As he grew up, many were the devices, some clever, some stupid, and some outright cruel, that were used to rouse the prince from his infancy. But to no avail. Exasperated, the king called in the soothsayers for an answer, who, to cover their ignorance, said, "The prince is a danger to you and your kingdom. Have him taken out by the western gate, out of the kingdom, and once outside, dig a grave, have him killed and throw him into it." The king, believing in this threat to his body and his kingdom, called his old servant Sunanda and entrusted him with the duty to take the boy out of the kingdom and kill him. The servant, with a heavy heart, escorted the prince to the city gates and, once they were outside the kingdom, stopped in a quiet place and began to remove all of the prince's royal clothes and insignias. Temiya the prince felt as though a great rock had fallen from his back. He was at last banished from the kingdom and had lost all rights to his inheritance, and to the city itself. Thereupon he rose for the first time in his life, flexed his arms and legs, turned to Sunanda and spoke in a hitherto un-heard language that, like the clear rain, rang of speechlessness and silence. The humble Sunanda was astonished by this miracle, but fully grasping from the brilliance radiating from Temiya's face that he was what he knew not, the servant hurried back to the city and informed the king. Sick to his heart of his own bloody right, powerful Sakka wept for his own law and his subjects. In the end, the king and the city came to think that they, too, should learn to find a way out of the city toward that form of life beyond the law and its violence. Thus began the hope of an exodus from sovereignty. But Sunanda could not trace the road he had taken, and they could not find their way to that place where the prince had gone. To this day, the king and the city are yet seeking that way to a coming community.

First Words on Silence

It is no longer possible to think in our day other than in the void left by man's disappearance. For this void does not create a deficiency; it does not constitute a lacuna that must be filled. It is nothing more, and nothing less, than the unfolding of a space in which it is once more possible to think.

—Michel Foucault, *The Order of Things*

Our age does indeed stand in front of language just as the man from the country in [Kafka's] parable stands in front of the door of the law.

—Giorgio Agamben, *Homo Sacer*

THE DISCIPLINARY CONTEXT

In 2003, the Animal Rights group PETA (People for the Ethical Treatment of Animals) launched an ad campaign using 60-ft. panels that juxtaposed photographs of Jews in concentration camps with those of caged animals in a crowded factory farm. The caption paraphrased the Yiddish writer Issac Bashevis Singer's famous line from the short story "The Letter Writer," namely: "To Animals, All People Are Nazis." Allusions to the "eternal Treblinka" set off an outcry of protest, leading the highest court in Germany to rule the ads as offensive. In the United States, the Anti-Defamation League and the NAACP (in reference to lynching and animals) also protested the linking of animal slaughter and anti-Semitism/racism. What is made evident by this debate is not so much the confusion over ideas about human dignity, but the deep gulf between the political commitment to social justice (achieving equality, dignity, respect) and the philosophical inquiry into life and the living (problems of identity, propriety, death). The fact that today, in the absence of any moral authority, it is only juridical law and the discourse of rights that can provide a flimsy bridge across these two domains should give us pause. For what does it mean that the concerns of social justice and the contemplation of life can encounter each other only within the discourse (if not the court) of law? Among all contemporary thinkers, it is certainly Jacques Derrida who has troubled most over this question.

In an interview with Elizabeth Roudinesco in *For What Tomorrow*, published in 2001, Jacques Derrida, responding to a question about animality and the proposal to extend human rights to nonhuman great apes, says,

> The "question of animality" is not one question among others, of course. I have long considered it to be decisive (as one says), in itself and for its strategic value; and that's because, while it is difficult and enigmatic in itself, it also represents the limit upon which all the great questions are formed and determined, as well as all the concepts that attempt to delimit what is "proper to man," the essence and future of humanity, ethics, politics, law, "human rights," "crimes against humanity," "genocide," etc.
>
> Wherever something like "the animal" is named, the gravest, most resistant, also the most naïve and the most self-interested presuppositions dominate what is called human culture (and not only Western culture); in any case they dominate the philosophical discourse that has been prevalent for centuries. (Derrida, *For What Tomorrow*, 62–63; 106)[1]

For those familiar with Derrida's writings, it is an unsurprising statement, since the interrogation of what is "proper to man" can be said to form one of the central axes of the project of deconstruction. Derrida's declaration on animality followed on the long seminar (reportedly a ten-hour lecture) that he gave a few years earlier at Cérisy-la-Salle entitled "The Autobiographical Animal," since published as *L'animal que donc je suis*.[2] Almost as though in response to Derrida's more explicit attention to the animal in the 1990s, a new subfield of animality studies has emerged. In the past few years, several anthologies and monographs, particularly within contemporary philosophy, have appeared that question and trouble the frontier between the human and the animal.[3] While the perspectives have been varied, and address the question of the animal as it emerges in the work of one or the other thinker or school of thought, they have together engendered an important field of study based on their shared premise that the task confronting contemporary thought today is the critique of the unquestionable and impassable separation between human and animal as the foundation of common sense. These important studies are interdisciplinary in the best sense. Utilizing the resources of contemporary researches in primatology, animal intelligence, animal communication, and language, they raise the great questions and engage the limits placed on their thinkability within the philosophical tradition.

Adjacently, for those critics who situate themselves within what can be termed broadly the philosophy of race, this subfield of animality studies may appear to open up new resources. Given that the latter is inextricably concerned with difference in terms of the *a priori* privilege granted to the norm of humanness and undertakes an ontological critique of that norm, it shares with race theory a broad predilection for an analysis of the discourses of power and exclusion. Since Peter Singer's *Animal Liberation,* there has been a plethora of work treating species bias, or what has come to be termed *speciesism.*[4] Most studies on animality justifiably focus their attention on the exploitation of the nonhuman animal and contribute to our thinking about race and its political effects by way of analogy or homology. In other words, we can discover the origins of the practice of racial dehumanization in our long history of managing the nonhuman animal world. We are invariably led to discern a strict colonialist homology or similarity between our exploitation of nature and animals and of "inferior" peoples. Yet the exchange between those who work on questions of race and those who concern themselves with animality and human propriety has been minimal. No doubt, this is attributable to the fact that the concepts of "race" and "animal" are anthropological/political and ontological categories, respectively, and are therefore tacitly indifferent, if not exclusive, of each other. For those preoccupied with the historical outcomes of the discourse of race, questions regarding the ontological basis of racial identity can appear to serve as a distraction from the practical problems at hand. It is well known that race identity, like gender, is a construction that is nevertheless, to use Judith Butler's useful phrase, a "constitutive constraint" (Butler, *Bodies that Matter,* 1993) with very real political effects. The urgent task as perceived is to deal with those effects. On the other hand, those concerned with the question of the animal are necessarily focused on the instability of the categorical opposition between human and animal. While historical and political issues are perceived as being equally urgent, these issues, as Derrida suggests, arise as global, even transhistorical, problems pertaining to the "most self-interested presuppositions [that] dominate what is called human culture (and not only Western culture)" (Derrida, *For What Tomorrow*, 62–63; 106).

The fact is that even though both fields are concerned with ethical and legal presuppositions that govern the determination of norms and standards, there are some caveats that remain due to the weakness of the analogy between the perceived opposition that governs the categories human and animal and the relational difference of white and nonwhite that subtends the system of race. In *The Claim of Reason*, Stanley Cavell suggests that this perceived weakness of analogy has more to do with a core indefiniteness regarding what is meant by the analogy to begin with. Invoking the context of the U.S. Southern slave system, he writes, "It is sometimes said that slaveowners do not see or treat their slaves as human beings, but rather, say, as livestock; some slaveowners themselves have been known to say so . . . But does one really believe such assertions? My feeling is that they cannot really be meant. Of course the words mean something; they are not spoken at random. In what spirit are such words said?" (Cavell, *Claim of Reason*, 372–73).

By expressing disbelief with regard to the analogy, Cavell is of course not disavowing racism. On the contrary, by slowing down the work of identity that analogy can sometimes too quickly produce, Cavell forces us to reckon with what in fact is really meant and held as a belief by the slaveowner. "What he really believes," Cavell suggests, "is not that slaves are not human beings, but that some human beings are slaves . . . [T]his man sees certain human beings as slaves, takes them for slaves" (375). In other words, the slaveowner assumes that what is, because it is, is right. In fact, the slaveowner may or may not consider his slaves to be lesser than certain other whites in terms of intelligence, industry, or beauty. Thus

> He means, and can mean, nothing definite. This is a definite frame of mind. He means, indefinitely, that they are not purely human. He means, indefinitely, that there are kinds of humans . . . He means, indefinitely, that slaves are different, primarily different from him,

secondarily different from you and me. In the end he will appeal to history, to a form, or rather to a way of life: this is what he does. He believes exactly what justice denies, that history and indefinite difference can justify his social difference of position. He need not deny the supremacy of justice; he may be eloquent on the subject. He need deny only that certain others are to be acknowledged as falling within its realm. (Cavell, *Claim of Reason*, 376)

Cavell's argument suggests that the racist not only harbors a core "indefiniteness" but that this indefiniteness has also something to do with purity and justice. In other words, it seems that the racist is one who is able to extend the principles of justice only to those who are properly human. This is not a point that Cavell pursues. Instead, it is the fact that such a wrong belief can be held and that such injustice can be countenanced that exercises his moral judgment. In a memorable phrase (one that Cora Diamond refers to in her wonderful essay), Cavell terms this a form of blindness—"soul blindness." The slaveowner does not "see" the slave as a human being like himself. However, Cavell also suggests that insofar as the slaveowner is content to enslave other human beings and demands specific forms of servitude and obedience from them, he is in fact already treating them as "more or less human" (376). That is, what he demands of his slaves differs vastly from what he demands of his livestock. "When he wants to be served at table by a black hand, he would not be satisfied to be served by a black paw. When he rapes a slave or takes her as a concubine, he does not feel that he has, by that fact itself, embraced sodomy . . . He does not go to great lengths either to convert his horses to Christianity or to prevent their getting wind of it" (376). All of this, no doubt, points to a "fact" of sorts, regarding the slaveowner's assumption of the slave's minimal humanity, but there are certain consequences to deploying it as a premise for an understanding of racist belief and practice.

First of all, such a premise leads one to lament the ascription of impurity to the slave, while necessarily leaving intact the association of humanness with a certain purity/propriety as well as the general structure of hierarchical thinking. The moral implication is that the analogy with the animal, as an inferior life form, is always to be abhorred. Second, to establish as a logical premise the social fact that the slaveowner tacitly acknowledges the humanness of his slaves is necessarily to avoid or ignore as problematic all those ways in which the slave is treated and regarded exactly as the slaveowner and slave trader regard and treat livestock. What remains untouched here in the examination of belief is the practice and production of inhumanity. These consequences to Cavell's argument provide some insight into the caveats that remain between those interested in race and those who are focused on the question of animality.

While thinkers of animality share similar concerns with race theorists—namely, the problems of discrimination, bias, and mistreatment—they are, however, differently positioned within what might be called our shared moral universe. The bottom line can be stated simply as pertaining to the poles of humanism and antihumanism. Antiracist work finds its justification within the parameters of humanism, whereas speciesism is nothing if not a radical critique of humanism as unjustified anthropocentrism. Thus, in contemporary modernity the universal norm declares race discrimination, be it speech or action, to be illegal; however, the idea that speciesism can be legislated out of existence is an impossible one. In other words, contemporary criteria for what counts as moral, sane, and rational make the assertion of intrinsic human inequality and defense of social discrimination universally impossible, let alone illegal. The same is not true for those interested in countering speciesism, whose norms are still a work in progress. This is not only because the thinker of animality will invariably interrogate the propriety of species difference and thereby trouble some of the humanist certainties that govern the discourse of race and antirace, but also because he/she will invariably have to confront foundational norms that organize social and ethical community. Thus, these critics face the additional burden of ethical persuasion regarding the validity of their concerns and interests. It is not easy to encourage the average consumer of fried chicken or even the philosopher of biopolitics who enjoys "eating well" to care about the treatment of poultry in a factory farm. Care and concern invariably turn into finite quantities, with never enough to go around beyond narrow human interest. It requires the greatest skills of moral persuasion to overcome the quantification of responsibility and expose it for what it usually is: namely, an alibi for custom and habit. Thus, the philosophical task of formulating coherent arguments and developing a sound logic to defend their moral perspective appears more crucial when the object is to problematize fundamental norms governing the value of nonhuman animals. This situation has led Cora Diamond (2008)[5] to suggest that the deflection (a term she borrows from Stanley Cavell) of an authentic response to an appalling concrete condition into the correctness of moral argumentation testifies to the difficulty of reality and philosophy's difficulty with it. While I agree with Diamond that animal philosophy suffers from an undue investment in argumentative correctness, my sense is that the tyranny of propositional correctness rules the thought of difference anytime and anywhere, thereby tethering the thought of difference to the separation between clearly demarcated entities. As I understand it, Derrida's assertion that the question of the animal marks the parameters of our thinking about crimes against humanity, such as slavery, genocide, and so on, strongly implies that both discourses are governed by the same unspoken logic. My sense is that Derrida here is not advancing an analogy between racism and speciesism; rather, he is interested in the difficulty of thinking (species) difference in relation to our conception of (expressive) life. Perhaps it is time we acknowledged that we cannot do anything at all about the appalling ways human beings treat other human beings or animals without rethinking and renewing our norms, presuppositions, platitudes, and morals with regard to life and what is living.

THE PROBLEMATIC: PRESENCE VERSUS POWER

Doing something about the mistreatment of humans or animals usually means a recourse to legislation and law enforcement. Though the discourses of animality and race are distinguished in terms of ethical norms, they nevertheless share a strong and similar interest and faith in the law, which they call upon to redress wrongs through the formulation and assertion of legal subjectivity. Insofar as the speciesism approach has evolved most fully within the purview of animal rights advocacy, it belongs to the major political lineage of rights discourses, just as race theory when it speaks of degradation often confines itself within the purview of human rights. While important questions are raised in both arenas, less attention has been devoted to issues that arise at their intersection—issues that powerfully implicate the structure of juridical law, thereby displacing the question of responsibility as well as any possible resolution. To note this contamination of the law in the very issues that it authorizes itself to adjudicate is to find oneself at the door of law—"before the law" in a very specific sense.

Inquiry into the political effects of race, as I have already noted, has not been much impacted by questions about animality. Despite Cavell's view regarding the core vagueness of perceiving humans or even parts of humans in (de)gradable terms, the fact remains that there is a concrete practice associated with it that entails representing and using certain others as mute animals or, more precisely, as less than animals—brutes that are a source of labor and, increasingly, genetic and other organic raw material. In other words, the threshold between human and animal is the point of desubjectification, and resolution of the problem cannot lie in strengthening the separation between the two entities. What is called for is attention to practices of "animalization," as the particular and strategic deployment of what is universally held as the fundamental separating border between human and animal. And this border is of course the long-standing view of human language as the divine voice of the logos, with its essential semantic and structural elements of syntax and recursion, founded upon the inseparable correlation of sense to sound, as having no analog among other species.[6] The task, in other words, is twofold: on the one hand, to tenaciously question the logocentric presumption that generates the brick-solid border between human and animal and, on the other, to analyze the plasticity of this border within the discursive regime of race as an instrument of power that engenders the abject experience of animalization. This entails oscillating between registers of inquiry—from the deconstruction of the metaphysics of presence to the genealogy and analytics of power. Such a movement requires forging or discerning links between logocentrism and biopower with a view to grasping the stakes of animalization. How is language, as the unique property of the human being, deployed as a modality of animalization, desubjectification, racism, and so on? Simply, it entails technologies that serve to deny and exclude the other from the use of language and thereby to render this other into a brute.

The premise here is that a core element of contemporary bio-politics, as a mode of what Foucault terms "state racism," is its ability to deploy language itself as an "apparatus" or a *dispositif*. The site of animalization or brutalization is primarily one where language as representation and legitimate speech becomes inaccessible. This site is marked by an absence of any semantic structure. It is effectively a mute space—a pocket of semantic failure or "silence" that marks the limit of the discourse of rights. It is the prevalence of this nonsemantic site—the *effect* of biopolitics—that this project aims to discern as also the *cause* of a radical disturbance that empties and confounds power. To pose the question differently, when power uses a concept of language to silence the other, to render this other a wretched hybrid of human and animal (consider Saladin Chamcha's fate at the hands of the police in Rushdie's *The Satanic Verses*), is there, however, a possibility that in turn silences or further neutralizes power? And can we think of this possibility as nonsovereign power?

To clarify the theoretical underpinnings of this inquiry, the particular and small challenge that this project sets for itself is to refuse the presupposition that institutional power is invariably and only a dissimulation of presence, of wholeness and indivisibility. Rather, by focusing on the "how" of power, it also attends to power as exercise, as the process of division and separation, to appear as paradoxical topos of the inside-out. Briefly, my theoretical hypothesis is as follows: For Derrida, sovereign power, through the concealment of origin, is always figured as wholeness, purity, auto-affection, oneness, simultaneity, and indivisible presence. As he says in his seminar on *The Beast and the Sovereign,* "the concept of sovereignty will always imply the possibility of this positionality, this thesis, this self-thesis, this auto-position of him who posits or posits himself as *ipse, the (self-) same, oneself*" (103).[7] The work of deconstruction is to expose the dissimulation of presence, to disclose the dependence of the full or totalized entity on the other, and to mark this dependence or contamination as the irreducibility of temporality as spacing or the trace of an absence. The inscription of the other renders the self-same an impossibility. In *Of Grammatology*, Derrida delineates the *historicity* of power as follows:

> [T]he very sense of power and effectiveness in general, which could
> appear as such, as meaning and mastery (by idealization), only with
> the so-called "symbolic" power, was always linked with the disposi-
> tion of writing; that economy, monetary or pre-monetary, and graphic
> calculation were co-originary, that there could be no law without the
> possibility of trace . . . all this refers to a common and radical possibility
> that no determined science, no abstract discipline, can think as such.
>
> Indeed, one must understand this *incompetence* of science which is
> also the incompetence of philosophy, the *closure* of the *episteme* . . . This
> common root, which is not a root but the concealment of the origin and
> which is not common because it does not amount to the same thing ex-
> cept with the unmonotonous insistence of difference, this unnameable
> movement of *difference-itself*, that I have strategically nicknamed *trace*,
> *reserve*, or *difference*, could be called writing only within the *historical*
> closure, that is to say within the limits of science and philosophy. (93;
> 141–42)

Though the trace, *"un blanc textual* [the blank part of the text]"
(Derrida, *Of Grammatology*, 93; 142) sustains and makes appear the disciplines of power as pure and true acts of logos, whose order and creative potency are served by the obsequious scribe, the disclosure of
this (non)origin as writing can be said to bring to a closure the epoch
of power as presence. The trace sustains as it threatens power as presence. In his later works, Derrida places more pressure on the political
valence of this logic. Elaborating on the term "autoimmunity," which
Derrida introduces into his lexicon of *différance* in some of his later
works, (such as *Rogues*), Michael Naas writes, "'Autoimmunity,' that
'illogical logic,' as Derrida put it, that turns something against its own
defenses, would appear to be yet another name, in some sense the last,
for what for close to forty years Derrida called 'deconstruction'" (Naas,
"One Nation," 18).[8] Naas further clarifies the valence of the term for
any theory of sovereignty:

> Deconstruction is at work in texts and discourses, but also, as be-
> comes clear in texts such as *Rogues*, in structures and organizations, in
> nation-states and international institutions, in every *autos* that tries to
> maintain its sovereignty, its autonomy and power, by immunizing itself
> against the other. Hence autoimmunity is not *opposed* to immunity but
> is, as it were, secreted by it; it is a self-destructive "force" produced by

the immunizing gesture itself, a weak force that undoes the force or power of sovereignty. (Naas, "One Nation," 34)

In other words, while the germ of self-infection of the absolutely immune entity is as much immanent to it as it is heterogeneous, nevertheless, the self-infection, insofar as it wrecks the defense system, is perceived as a counterforce to power. The point of departure is, of course, the classical notion of sovereignty as indivisible, unshareable, and unspeakable. To quote Michael Naas again,

> Derrida agrees with thinkers of sovereignty from Plato and Bodin to Carl Schmitt who argue that sovereignty is essentially *indivisible* and *unspeakable*. In its essence without essence, sovereignty must be unshareable, untransferrable, undeferrable, and silent, or it "is" not at all. Sovereignty can thus never be parceled out or distributed in space, deferred or spread out over time, or submitted to the temporality and spatiality of language. As soon as sovereignty tries to extend its empire in space, to maintain itself over time, to protect itself by justifying and providing reasons for itself, it opens itself up to law and to language, to the counter-sovereignty of the other, and so begins to undo itself, to compromise or autoimmunize itself. (Naas, "One Nation," 21)

However, if we train our focus on the analytics of power (which entails understanding power as exercise), as Foucault recommends, and note that it is but a decentered network where it is always already more than one, then the logic of the self-same undone by its own other gives way to the play of *différance* as the very site of the political—of power and struggle against. Insofar as contemporary power does not pretend to be one but functions by unmasking itself, the tactic of opposition can no longer be one of exposure but perhaps a neutralization of its functioning.

The site of contention in the conceptualization of power as dissimulation of presence or power as deployment of difference emerges around the question of technology. According to Derrida, the disclosure of the logic of writing and the trace brings a certain epoch of power and knowledge to closure, as the history of writing dispenses with

> concepts that habitually serve to distinguish man from other living beings (instinct and intelligence, absence or presence of speech, of society, of economy, etc. etc.), the notion of *program* is invoked. It must of course

be understood in the cybernetic sense . . . It is an emergence that makes the *grammè* appear *as such* (that is to say according to a new structure of nonpresence) . . . If the expression ventured by Leroi-Gourhan is accepted, one could speak of a "liberation of memory," of an exteriorization always already begun but always larger than the trace, which, beginning from the elementary programs of so-called "instinctive" behavior up to the constitution of electronic card-indexes and reading machines, enlarges difference and the possibility of putting in reserve: it at once and in the same movement constitutes and effaces so-called conscious subjectivity, its logos, and its theological attributes. (Derrida, *Of Grammatology*, 84; 125–26)

The history of writing, therefore, discovers the history of life (whether it is animal, human, or plant) itself as a process of "exteriorization" of technology, the program, or difference. The future of "man," then, is completely open. But, clearly, such "liberation of memory," the making appear of the *grammè*, prescient as it is about our increasingly webbed world, is not commensurate with any "liberation" from or dissipation of the effects of power. In reference to the problematic aspects of animalization, the question that must necessarily be raised here is how to think of the contemporary *dispositifs* of power that subjugate and govern through the making appear of the *grammè* understood as ordering. Undoubtedly, this question entails a shift in critical registers (from Derrida to Foucault), even as the problem turns around the machine of contemporary biopower, which governs and manages life as difference. The question is whether power or force can be characterized in any way as "centric" in its functioning or appearance.[9] And if force is founded on the disclosure rather than the concealment of difference, is it then not indifferent to the deconstruction of presence? As technology, how can power be metaphysical?

More specifically, for Agamben, who extends the analysis of biopower to the *nomos*, sovereignty is analyzed in its autoimmunity. In the introduction to *Homo Sacer,* he writes,

Carl Schmitt's definition of sovereignty ("Sovereign is he who decides on the state of exception") became a commonplace even before there was any understanding that what was at issue in it was nothing less than the limit concept of the doctrine of law and the State, in which sovereignty borders (since every limit concept is always the limit between two concepts) on the sphere of life and becomes indistinguishable from it. (11; 15)

What is the implication of situating sovereignty not at a fortified center but at a limit, to apprehend it as a limit concept located at a point of undecidability between life and law? The point of departure here is not the sovereignty of the self-same, but the sovereignty that exhibits its own paradoxical topology in its *exercise* as being neither properly inside nor outside the law. Agamben's reference is to that aspect of sovereignty where "the particular 'force' of law consists in this capacity of law to maintain itself in relation to an exteriority" (Agamben, *Homo Sacer*, 18; 22). Thus, if contemporary power is characterized by the law deploying its own trace of lawlessness as the state of exception where the law works through its own suspension, then the site of the political and ethical decision is necessarily situated in this space-time of the law's suspension. The counterforce as imagined by Agamben through Benjamin would be not to restore oneness to the law, and thereby shore up power, but to neutralize power by rendering the law suspended *and* not in force.

More narrowly in this project, I approach modern racism as dehumanization or "animalization" (i.e., as the manipulation of the impropriety between human and animal through the withholding of language as speech, which is necessarily also an expulsion from law and society). If, as Agamben suggests, the "force" of law is its capacity to suspend itself—to withhold itself as sovereign silence—then the work of alterity or resistance in this biopolitical scenario will be neither simply heterogeneous nor autogenous to this suspension and silence. Rather, a certain other silence appears to neutralize the exercise of power as the play of difference at the limit between law and lawlessness, norm and exception, speech and silence, human and animal. Where the figures of desubjectification are concerned, my sense is that to focus only on their social and political causes (to answer the questions why and how did it happen) cannot disclose the stakes of what is held as an unquestionable certainty (i.e., the subtractability of life, or the supposition that life as such can be subtracted from the living). How did life come to be an object of power? What is at stake in maintaining the norm of life as precisely tractable? These questions once again allude to Foucault's genealogy of power—that is, the shifts in emphasis among sovereign, disciplinary, and biopower, and its extension and reinterpretation by Agamben, particularly in *Homo Sacer.* In his theorization of sovereignty as a limit concept, a form of biopower that targets life, Agamben underlines a powerful and suggestive homology between the figure of the sovereign and the delegitimized figure of the lawless *(homo sacer)* that is isolated or extirpated from the circle of the law, thereby exposing it as mere life to a completely arbitrary violence. What the sovereign and the outlaw share, he suggests, is such a subtracted life as the intimate link between violence and law expressed in the topos of being an included exclusion or an excluded inclusion. Derrida as well remarks on the uncanny proximity of the sovereign to the beast, but for him such proximity does not imply the capture of bare life as the secret kernel of the law as norm. In other words, the proximity does not bespeak the origin of force and legitimacy as the undecidable difference between law and life. Thus, Derrida does not grant the sovereign exception a necessary status in the genesis or structure of the law. At best, what can be said is that for *le souverain* to set himself above the law is analogous to being *une bête* without the law and only exposes the difference within the *auto-nomy* of sovereignty. For Agamben, on the other hand, the disclosure of such a proximity between the sovereign and the *homo sacer* constitutes the core of his critique of the law's inescapable violence. Agamben writes,

> [T]he state is founded not as the expression of a social tie but as an untying *(déliason)* . . . The tie itself originarily has the form of an untying or exception in which what is captured is at the same time excluded, and in which human life is politicized only through an abandonment to an unconditional power of death. The sovereign tie is more originary than the tie of the positive rule or the tie of the social pact, but the sovereign tie is in truth only an untying. And what this untying implies and produces—bare life, which dwells in the no-man's-land between the home and the city—is, from the point of view of sovereignty, the originary political element. (Agamben, *Homo Sacer*, 90; 101)

To clarify the practical direction of this project, though Agamben's analysis of the structure of sovereignty as biopolitical power, where life is separated as a target of government and decision, is one of my guiding threads, my intention here is not to further delineate or elaborate the appalling historical aspects of such reduced lives, or even to analyze the epistemological foundations of such procedures of diminishment. Rather than gather evidence regarding the appearance and procedures of power, this project focuses on the possibilities that arise within regimes of domination to effectively annul, neutralize, or escape power in the very moment of its exercise. Two recent works can here be cited as providing concrete instantiations of such evasion: James Scott's monumental history *The Art of Not Being Governed,* about Zomia, the hill territory roughly including the borders of several South Asian and Southeast Asian countries where communities outside the framework of nation-state sovereignties have emerged, and Rebecca Solnit's *A Paradise Built in Hell,* on the communities that form in the state of exception that ensue after disasters hit, such as Hurricane Katrina, which broke the levees in New Orleans in 2005.

Terminology: Trace, Animalization, Apparatus
Trace and Silence
The site of struggle with power invariably takes place *within* the opening or interval effected by the law's own self-suspension, and this site is best understood as a "spacing," in the sense that Derrida alludes to most famously in "Différance" also as the trace.[10] By spacing, Derrida does not merely indicate the gap that ensues between two full entities. In a footnote to his interview with Jean-Louis Houdebine in *Positions,* he emphasizes the importance of the gerund and thus the event aspect of the term:

> Spacing is a concept which also, but not exclusively, carries the meaning of a productive, positive, generative force. Like dissemination, like *différance* it carries along with it a *genetic* motif: it is not only the interval, the space constituted between two things (which is the usual sense of spacing), but also spac*ing*, the operation, or in any event, the movement of setting aside. This movement is inseparable from temporizatio n-temporalization . . . and from *différance,* from the conflicts of force at work in them. It makes what is set aside from itself, what interrupts every self-identity, every punctual assemblage of the self, ever self-homogeneity, self-interiority. (Derrida, *Positions,* 106–7)

In *Of Grammatology*, Derrida provides perhaps the most rigorous exposition of the concept of the trace and spacing in the context of an extended discussion of the phonological (the valorization of speech over writing) prejudice that governs Western metaphysics. The relevance of this prejudice is, of course, not a purely academic matter—for Derrida shows that it is the very foundation of the ethnocentrism (of phonetic writing) that engenders the ontological separation of the properly human versus the animal and the properly literate societies versus the peoples without writing or history. For my purposes here, generalized writing, as Derrida discovers it, opens a text of silence. He writes,

> *Spacing* (notice that this word speaks the articulation of space and time, the becoming-space of time and the becoming-time of space) is always the unperceived, the nonpresent, and the nonconscious. *As such*, if one can still use that expression in a non-phenomenological way; for here we pass the very limits of phenomenology. Arche-writing as spacing cannot occur *as such* within the phenomenological experience of a *presence*. It marks *the dead time* within the presence of the living present, within the general form of all presence. The dead time is at work . . . Constituting and dislocating it at the same time, writing is other than the subject, in whatever sense the latter is understood. Writing can never be thought under the category of the subject; however it is modified, however it is endowed with consciousness or unconsciousness, it will refer, by the entire thread of its history, to the substantiality of a presence unperturbed by accidents, of to the identity of the selfsame [*le propre*] in the presence of self-relationship. (Derrida, *Of Grammatology*, 68–69)

For Derrida, the pursuit of generalized writing as the inescapable inscription of the other within the same ("the world as space of inscription, as the opening to the emission and the spatial distribution of signs, to the regulated play of their differences, even if they are phonic" [Derrida, *Of Grammatology*, 44]) leads essentially to the disruption of the opposition between "nature and institution, of *physis* and *nomos* (which also means, of course, a distribution and division regulated in fact by *law*)" (Derrida, *Of Grammatology*, 44). In other words, if writing is all there is where language is concerned, there is no natural relation between thought and *phonè* that is also not contaminated by the instituted trace of the sign. This means that the so-called natural relation has always already been regulated by law as its outside. Language and law are coextensive. There is no part of language that is not always already instituted, conventionalized, submitted to the protocol of the sign as representation and repetition.

The specific value of attending to silence rather than writing as play of difference (or, for that matter, invisibility or the unconscious), can here be clarified. If, as Derrida says, law (*nomos*) regulates the relation between nature (*physis*), as the realm of the animal, and meaningful language (*logos*), as the realm of man, then we can ask what the relation is between *a-logos,* or that aspect of language that is not meaningful, and the *nomos.* Would it not be *a-nomos*—not regulated by law? And can silence be discerned as that anomic aspect of logos? No doubt, this question can be posed only after taking into account Derrida's observation in his reading of Rousseau that "it is toward the praise of silence that the myth of a full presence wrenched from difference and from the violence of the word is then deviated" (Derrida, *Of Grammatology*, 140; 202). That silence can serve power, however it is conceived, as presence or difference, is well known. But insofar as powerful silence functions as a mode of refusal (of difference or the law), it opens a space for opposition.

Let us recall that silence is necessarily absence as well—the mark of death within language. As a modality of generalized writing, silence can legitimately be understood as that which inserts itself between law and language. As a function of language that does not signify, silence neutralizes the conventionality that cements language and law by signifying nothing. It is the dead space within the time of the law. Thus, I hazard that the spacing of species impropriety would perhaps be structured by a chiasmus—one that emerges between the opposed pole of human on the one hand and animal on the other and the opposed pole of language at one end and law at the other. I warrant that to parse this indistinct zone of mute silence and the inhuman would entail a significant disclosure of the (contingent) relation between language and law. To mark and refer to the exceptionality of this spacing, I shall deploy a neologism—namely, "humAnimal," preferably without even an indefinite article in order to prevent humAnimal from being assimilated to a bounded space, a representable object, an identity, a concept, or even a name. In the context of brute silence, it can perhaps only mark a blip, a hole, or, more properly, an orifice, an opening in language.

As I discuss in the next chapter, the spacing of humAnimal can be necessarily discerned and traced only by a spectral language, by a tongue that has been severed—like that of Friday in J. M. Coetzee's novel *Foe*. And as Susan Barton, the would-be narrator of his story, says, this tongue can only tell what "is properly not a story but a puzzle or hole in the narrative (I picture it as a buttonhole, carefully cross-stitched around, but empty, waiting for the button)" (Coetzee, *Foe*, 121). In a sense, this project is akin to cross-stitching around a hole—an A-shaped slash that can open and close the weave of power that separates and unseparates human and animal.

I capitalize the A in humAnimal in solidarity with the "gross spelling error" that Derrida declares is the necessary passage in any writing about and within writing—a violation that governs and regulates writing (Derrida, "Différance," 131). Perhaps this aggravating error resonates with the trace of that unresonating letter that Derrida indicated as that "which remains silent, secret and discreet as a tomb," a graphic pyramid, a stone with an inscription that "is not far from announcing the death of the tyrant" (Derrida, "Différance," 4). In one sense, this runs counter to Derrida's insistence that the trace "is not announced by any capital letter. Not only is there no kingdom of *différance*, but *différance* instigates the subversion of every kingdom" (Derrida, "Différance," 22). But insofar as my letter arrives in the spacing between two kingdoms—the animal kingdom and the sovereign and lawful human kingdom—it serves not as *itself* but as a graphic buttonhole that not only calls into question the human and the animal[11] but also attends to power's confounding of the two. Thus, without undertaking the limitless task of interrogating the proper as such with regard to man and animal, the site of animalization or species impropriety is here approached as the effect of power that nevertheless harbors the possibility of its arrest. As this possibility is not any particular thing but only a semantic absence; we can only attempt to listen for it. As Susan Barton, who at the end of the novel dreams of gliding into the wreck on the ocean floor, says, "it is for us to open Friday's mouth and hear what it holds: silence, perhaps, or a roar of a seashell held to the ear" (Coetzee, *Foe*, 142).

Animalization

Animalization refers to that indistinct zone of the inhuman where life is rendered brute. The term that Derrida seems to prefer is beast, or *la bête*, which in French has the additional resonance of *bêtise*, or stupidity. In his seminar *La bête et le souverain*, volume 1, Derrida says, "it is never said of the beast that it is *bête* [stupid] or bestial. The adjective, epithet, attribute *bête*, or 'bestial' are never appropriate for animal or beast. *Bêtise* is proper to man (or even to the sovereign qua man)" (Derrida, *Beast and the Sovereign*, 104).[12] In what does the *bêtise* of the *bête* lie? Derrida suggests that it lies first and foremost in life itself (Derrida, *Beast and the Sovereign*, 240) but, more pertinently, as the element of the political in human life. Not only must man as a political animal appropriate animality and prevail over it but he must also participate in the said animality: "Political man as superior to animality and political man as animality" (Derrida, *Beast and the Sovereign*, 50). As an example, Derrida discusses Machiavelli's advice to the sovereign to possess a "double nature," to be half man and half beast, and to further bifurcate the beast into fox and lion (Derrida, *Beast and the Sovereign*, 129). In other words, "recognizing that sovereignty is divisible, that it divides and partitions, even where there is any sovereignty left, is already to begin to deconstruct a pure concept of sovereignty that presupposes indivisibility. A divisible sovereignty is no longer a sovereignty, a sovereignty worthy of the name, i.e. pure and unconditional" (Derrida, *Beast and the Sovereign*, 115). The itinerary of such a deconstruction of sovereignty, then, follows from the more fundamental interrogation of the notion of the animal, a term that refers to a vast diversity of sentient life in the singular as a simple category that is opposable to the human being, whose propriety is marked by his relation to the logos.

Derrida analyzes the philosophical ground of this common-sense opposition in his analysis of Descartes's theory of animals as automatons: "According to many philosophers and theoreticians, from Aristotle to Lacan, animals do not respond."[13] The identification of the limit of the animal, Derrida discovers, prevails even in the ethical thought of Levinas and the antinormative theory of Lacan. In the latter's *Rome Discourse* (1953), Derrida argues, this limit is determined in "the most dogmatically traditional manner, fixed within Cartesian fixity, within the presupposition of a code that permits only *reactions* to stimuli and not *responses* to questions" (Derrida, *Animal That Therefore*, 122; 168). The force of Derrida's reading, then, falls on the categories of reaction and response, as it does on other terms and concepts (such as lying, forming societies, etc.), that sustain the human/animal opposition. It once again bears remarking that, for Derrida, sovereignty and the power it wields are entirely founded upon indivisibility, and thus his target as always is on the dissimulation of oneness and self-identity by sovereignty and power. While this powerful exposure of sovereignty's hybrid ontology is of utmost importance for any conceptualization of a counterforce, it is also necessary to acknowledge that the production of hybridity can be deployed as a strategy of power. In other words, while the deconstruction of the sovereign's purity to disclose his animality has the effect of exposing the lie of indivisibility, the production of hybridity as technology of power cannot be ruled out. The shift in emphasis here is small but not insignificant. When Derrida speaks of power's capacity to degrade and dehumanize, his analysis proceeds to detect the underlying logic of purity and exclusion. Discussing Lacan's view that only human beings are capable of cruelty, which is defined as causing one's fellow person to suffer, Derrida says that "comes down to giving exorbitant credit to this value of fellow" (Derrida, *Animal That Therefore*, 152). He goes on to ask how we recognize the "fellow" and what form we require that fellow to have in order to be taken as a being to which we are responsible. More pointedly, he asks,

> But does one only have duties toward man and the other man as human? And, above all, what are we to reply to all those who do not recognize their fellow in certain humans? This question is not an abstract one, as you know. The worst, the cruelest, the must human violence has been unleashed against living beings, beasts or humans, and humans in particular, who precisely were not accorded the dignity of being fellows (and this is not only a question of profound racism, of social class, etc., but sometimes of the singular individual as such). (Derrida, *Animal That Therefore*, 155)

In this analysis, power is discerned in its exercise as the practice of assigning identity and asserting identification. The other is not a fellow because it is not properly human like oneself. To undo this "self" by discovering its metaphysical nonfoundation would constitute the prime political task as conceived by deconstruction. However, to press the analysis further on the side of the other—the one who is denied personhood—is necessarily to ask how fellowship becomes political. In other words, it is to ask how power emerges from the recognition of the instability and indeterminacy of all identity as endlessly divisible.

For instance, the aforementioned deconstruction of the response/reaction opposition as pertaining to man and animal, respectively, can also serve as an exercise of power to produce the hybrid figure of the brute. The folklore of contemporary life says that the brutishness of a brute is manifest when it does not speak or respond. If this extreme view of animals has been supplanted today by the widespread validation of companion and service animals, and the efforts of conservationists and animal ethicists, the underlying logic nevertheless survives in the rhetorical field of the brute. Animals may suffer cruelty; that they have a range of emotional expression may now be recognizable, but the capacity of brute life to suffer is questionable. Whether it is a dispensable laboratory rat or faceless populations—terrorists, crowds, and so on—such entities react instinctively, either passively or with terrifying violence. To be rendered brute, then, is a fate that is undoubtedly endured by nonhuman animals as well when they are treated as though they were nonsentient creatures, merely numerical entities that constitute a species population, or forcibly humanized as spectacle. In other words, the process of rendering a living creature into something indistinct, neither human nor animal, namely a brute, is founded on power's ability to manipulate the indeterminacy that haunts all identity. It is this manipulation of life and its forms that is suggestively termed by Agamben in *The Open*[14] as "animalization," or a zone of indistinction.

Agamben approaches this zone as that which must be discerned and thought through in its functionality (i.e., how does it work and what is it for?) in order to grasp the human being as the subject who realizes himself or herself in the historical process. To continue on the track of that subtle but consequential shift in emphasis from Derrida, for Agamben, the in-between zone of human-animal is the default of a primary ontological procedure: the incessant operation by which the properly human is distinguished and separated from animal. Anyone familiar with Agamben's works will recognize the motif of separation and conflation as the operative strategy that informs his philosophical anthropology of power—specifically, biopower. Agamben's account of biopower in its institutional manifestation as biopolitics develops Foucault's genealogy by identifying it as a fundamental ontologic that organizes the history of the subject. The strategy of articulations and caesurae that Agamben discerns in its concretion in every social formation is thus analyzed in terms of the "ungovernable" remnant that it produces. For Agamben, then, it is this strategy of articulation and separation that is seen to propel the very movement of history. Significantly, this caesura, Agamben suggests, runs first and foremost within man.

Referring to Kojève's ruminations on the form of completed humanity at the end of history in the context of his lectures on Hegel, Agamben says,

> For in Kojève's reading of Hegel, man is not a biologically defined species, nor is he a substance given once and for all; he is, rather, a field of dialectical tensions always already cut by internal caesurae that every time separate—at least virtually—"anthropophorous" animality and the humanity which takes bodily form in it. Man exists historically only in this tension; he can be human only to the degree that he transcends and transforms the anthropophorous animal which supports him, and only because, through the action of negation, he is capable of mastering and, eventually destroying his own animality. (Agamben, *The Open*, 12; 19)

The analysis and critique that Agamben offers apropos this incessant procedure of self-separation is ethically and politically consequential. He suggests that this so-called motor of history by which man humanizes himself through the negation of his animality is fundamentally biopolitical in its effects. As he elaborates in *Homo Sacer*, the separation of the properly human as legal, lawfully recognized subject from the inhuman or animal as the unrecognized and lawless is the foundation upon which political violence and right are installed. Simply put, sovereignty (characterized as it always is by the perfect self-circularity of its own accountability, or unconditionality to use Derrida's term) exercises the power to dissolve this separation between the lawful and the lawless simply by suspending its own rule. In these political "states of exception," humans are "animalized" in the sense that they are exposed to arbitrary violence. It is in this sense that the machine by which humans humanize themselves and progress in history is a biopolitical one.

In *The Open*, Agamben elaborates that the "anthropological machine functions as an apparatus or a *dispositif* of man's own creation by and to which he binds himself. Situating this compact and efficient machine on the platform of language as erected by naturalists and linguists who argued that human beings are distinguished from animals by their capacity for language," Agamben writes,

> Insofar as the production of man through the opposition man/animal, human/inhuman, is at stake here, the machine necessarily functions by means of an exclusion (which is also already an inclusion.) Indeed, precisely because the human is already presupposed every time, the machine actually produces a kind of state of exception, a zone of indeterminacy in which the outside is nothing but the exclusion of an inside and the inside is in turn the inclusion of an outside.
>
> On the one hand, we have the anthropological machine of the moderns . . . it functions by excluding as not (yet) human an already human being from itself, that is by animalizing the human, by isolating the non human within the human: *Homo alalus* or the ape-man. And it is enough to move our field of research ahead a few decades, and instead of this innocuous paleontological find we will have the Jew, that is, the non-man produced within the man, or the *néomort* and the overcomatose person, that is, the animal separated within the human body itself.
>
> The machine of earlier times works in an exactly symmetrical way. If, in the machine of the moderns, the outside is produced through the exclusion of an inside and the inhuman produced by animalizing the human, here the inside is obtained through the inclusion of an outside, and the non-man is produced by the humanization of an animal: the man-ape, the *enfant sauvage* or *Homo ferus*, but also and above all the slave, the barbarian, and the foreigner, as figures of an animal in human form. (Agamben, *The Open*, 37; 42–43)

In order to grasp the crux of Agamben's critique of the anthropological machine by which man registers his historicity, it is necessary to look briefly at the way in which he conceptualizes the Foucauldian "apparatus," or *dispositif*.

Apparatus or the Dispositif

In his essay "What Is an Apparatus?" Agamben interprets Foucault's term as pertaining above all to a network of relations between heterogeneous elements such as discourses, institutions, laws, and so on that arise at the crossroads of power and knowledge (2; 7).[15] Acknowledging that the term refers to a set of expedient practices and mechanisms evolved to deal with some sort of an urgency, Agamben goes on to show that the term has not only epistemological but also profound ontological implications.[16] He suggests that once we grasp the theological genealogy of the term as pertaining to divine economy[17]—the division of God into the sovereign father and the Son as the executor of his household—we can discern the apparatus as the practicotheoretical thing that separates "being and action," ontology and praxis (Agamben, "What Is an Apparatus?", 16; 25). Thus, insofar as the apparatus is merely an instrument of management separated from being, it is nothing if not a pure technology of subjectification. In other words, it is any given technology that has the power to capture and control the most quotidian and intimate habits and thoughts of a living being. Anything, Agamben says, can be a *dispositif* if it captures, intervenes, or shapes life—including language.

The problem that Agamben identifies with the *dispositif,* then, is not so much that it exists, but that today technology is not only ubiquitous but absolutely indifferent about its power to subjectify. Agamben reminds us that in Foucault's conception of discipline, disciplinary power invests a certain subject position on the basis of a self-negation, the paradigm being perhaps Augustine, who in his *Confessions* negates his former self but by appropriating that negated self through speech thereby acquires a new subjectivity. Foucault's prime example is Bentham's Panopticon—the open prison with a high watchtower that forces the prisoner to internalize the regulations and surveil himself. Thus, the process of submitting to the apparatus of a given regime meant that it produced for you a new subjectivity out of a negation. "The split of the subject performed by the apparatus of penance resulted therefore, in the production of a new subject, which found its real truth in the nontruth of the already repudiated sinning I" (20; 30). What, then, does it mean for the apparatus to not care whether the living entity in question finds its "truth" or not in its negated part? In other words, the new technology continually negates but does not make it possible for a new subjectivity to arise out of it. Perhaps another way to understand the current situation is that today, technology subjectifies and desubjectifies with equal zeal, so much so that the distinction between subjectification and desubjectification (control and noncontrol) is eroding. The consequence of technology creating a zone of indistinction between intervention and nonintervention is that the subject as such, who is the effect or the residue of a certain struggle with or resistance to the apparatus, is dispersed. According to Agamben, the *dispositifs* that together make up a great machine of governance are today on a manic course, incessantly separating and collapsing being and action, natural and political.

Perhaps more suggestively in *The Open*, Agamben diagnoses the particular *dispositif* of man's historicity, the anthropological machine, as idling. He reminds us that today the epoch of historical tasks assigned to a people as their destiny has once and for all come to an end in the cinders of the world wars. No doubt, to say that the machine appears to be idling is also to say that the state of exception (negation) has become the norm and a permanent one. Thus, in the contemporary situation we witness the political giving way to the dominance of the economic. Humans now take their own animality as an object, which they seek to govern through new technologies (medical, biological, statistical, etc.) that manage brute life. Thus, in *The Open*, Agamben's analysis of the historicity of man as dependent on the workings of the anthropological machine is fundamentally concerned with the possibilities that open up in the inevitable idling of that machine.

This project is concerned with one small but key aspect of that field of possibilities, and that is silence. If the sovereign state of exception is the site where the law falls silent, it is here in this withdrawal as power that the possibility for an altogether other power is cleared. It is necessary to turn, then, to silence itself not so much to define it, which would be impossible given that it is nothing, least of all a concept, but to situate it and ask after its endless guises and ruses. HumAnimal silence is above all evasive, but it is necessary to consider how it is so in relation to the *dispositif* of language. Where is silence within the mousetrap of language and meaning?

LANGUAGE AS SILENCE

Silence as Text

As a process by which life is consigned to a zone that is neither properly human nor animal, animalization refers to a way of being that is fundamentally without access to meaning—an asemantic space or a site of speechlessness that does not yield to proper representation or translation. However we might conceive such muteness or asemanticism (as literature, as nature, as the body, etc.), we cannot fail to acknowledge that they each nevertheless constitute a text where something withholds or withdraws itself from meaning. Nothing further can be said about these contexts if not for the fact that such texts may yet constitute a kind of *writing* that may not accede to speech at present meaning but nevertheless appear at the level of the signifier where the signified is suspended, even absent. In other words, these texts function as modes of indication without expression. Such priority of indication also informs and marks the distinction that Roland Barthes makes in his influential essay "From Work to Text,"[18] which answers the question of what a text is and its reference to something that exceeds any form of binding. Here, Barthes proposes seven elements that distinguish the text from the work, and while each of these proposals is extremely pertinent to any attempt to think through the status of muteness or silence within language, the following clarifies how we can view muteness as a text that is constituted when it is traversed:

> The Text is plural. This does not mean just that [it] has several meanings, but rather that it achieves plurality of meaning an *irreducible* plurality. The Text is not coexistence of meanings but passage, traversal; thus it answers not to an interpretation liberal though it may be, but to an explosion, a dissemination. The Text's plurality does not depend on the ambiguity of its contents, but rather on what could be called the *stereographic plurality* of the signifiers that weave it (etymologically the text is a cloth; *textus*, from which text derives, means "woven"). (Barthes, "From Work to Text," 76)

In other words, we can hazard that silence or muteness, insofar as it is "held in language" (Barthes, "From Work to Text," 75), belongs to language not as communication and meaning but as structure that is necessarily without a center and can never be closed. Where the mute text of animalization is concerned, there is no question of mistaking it for a work. It is always overlooked, and yet it is not nonexistent. Its elements are always open to being woven by each one of us into a text. In other words, the disclosure of the text is an event, not an interpretation. Given the resistance of this text to objectivity, it becomes incumbent upon the inquirer to formulate a question that will not aim at determining what is unspeakable. Thus, perhaps we can at best ask something like the following: can that which is *unspeakable* have a possibility of its own—a possibility, even a power, in the sense that it lets what is *unsayable* appear? I take my cue here from the introduction to *Languages of the Unsayable,* where the editors, Sanford Budick and Wolfgang Iser, invoke the context of "negative gestures" in literary, philosophical, and historiographical texts, and pose two questions: "Is there some power of dissemination or articulation that is inherent in the negative gestures themselves? To what extent might the phenomenon called 'negativity' be an agent in bringing about such dissemination, thereby allowing the unsayable to speak for itself? . . . Once we have encountered the limits of the sayable, we must acknowledge the existence of 'unsayable things' and by means of a language somehow formed on being silent, articulate that which cannot be grasped" (Budick and Iser, *Languages of the Unsayable,* xi–xii).[19]

Silence as Discourse

Silence is far from being a simple term. A great loquacity surrounds it as a philosophical, juridical, and literary concept, which renders impossible any attempt to sketch its history. However, the kind of silence that this project attempts to track requires clarification and specification in terms of context, if not essence. Where animalization is concerned, silence, or a certain muteness (or *bêtise*), emerges as an effect of power through a procedure of exclusion from discourse. On the other hand, silence, I hypothesize, is a possibility that power cannot govern, and though it undoubtedly emerges within its force field, it is distinguishable from muteness as a counterforce, a force of annulment. In the following, I turn first to Foucault's concept of silence in the context of epistemology, where silence is imposed through a procedure of exclusion (i.e., it appears as muteness), but silence in Foucault can also function as a corollary to power. However, as Wendy Brown has shown, the notion of silence as a counterforce is not absent in Foucault and can be extrapolated from his work.

In his inaugural lecture "Discourse on Language"[20] at the Collège de France in 1971, Michel Foucault describes three groups of exclusion that operate within language that serve to police, manage, or neutralize the proliferation of discourse. His hypothesis, as he describes it, is "that in every society the production of discourse is at once controlled, selected, organized and redistributed according to a certain number of procedures, whose role is to avert its powers and its dangers, to cope with chance events, to evade its ponderous, awesome materiality" (Foucault, "Discourse on Language," 216). He goes on to describe these procedures as follows:

1. The rules of exclusion that include prohibition. The motivation here is what Foucault terms "the will to the truth" and involves the strategy of separating reason from folly.
2. Internal rules "where discourse exercises its own control" (Foucault, "Discourse on Language," 220), as in commentary, the author function, and the organization of the disciplines.[21]
3. Rules that mandate the proper use of discourse by establishing qualifications, a fellowship of discourse, and doctrinal conformity.[22]

Foucault suggests that the constraints placed on discourse in order to elide its reality are largely enabled by three themes: the philosophy of the founding subject; a philosophy of what he terms "originating experience," where things reveal themselves to us in a reading; and, in an even more complex move, the theme of universal mediation, which posits everything as logos. This is not the place to discuss these observations in depth; however, the tasks that Foucault sets for current thinking following from these analyses are of immediate relevance to our pursuit. He writes that the tasks necessitate that we "question our will to truth; to restore to discourse its character as an event; to abolish the sovereignty of the signifier" (Foucault, "Discourse on Language," 229). But once these principles of regulation have been discovered, what, Foucault asks, should we affirm? What are the implications?

> Should we affirm that a world of uninterrupted discourse would be virtually complete? . . . The existence of systems of rarefaction does not

imply that, over and beyond them lie great vistas of limitless discourse, continuous and silent, repressed and driven back by them, making it our task to abolish them and at last to restore it to speech. Whether talking in terms of speaking or thinking, we must not imagine some unsaid thing, or an unthought, floating about the world, interlacing with all its forms and events. (Foucault, "Discourse on Language," 229)

The importance of this statement perhaps could not be exaggerated. Nor can the difficulty and the complexity of the undertaking Foucault recommends we engage ourselves in, which is nothing less than negotiating a way between two pieties. It entails on one hand that we recognize the limits of the familiar ideology that protests suppression and silencing with the singular aim of restoring the silenced to discourse—the political piety of giving voice—and on the other that we remain skeptical of the ideology of the unsaid as the ineffable, that which partakes in the mystical plenitude of silence, the piety of the transcendent. How does one successfully negotiate between the impulse to restore everything to speech or posit the deep interiority and heterogeneity of the unsaid? The choices that we are usually presented with are either to regard silence as the effect of discursive repression or to valorize it as a pristine state beyond and outside the reach of mundane discourse and language. In one case, speech is valued as freedom as opposed to powerless silence; in the other, silence is valued as pure presence opposed to the banal worldliness of speech. What would it mean to not oppose speech and silence, but to see each as immanent in language and to each other? What are the implications of positing such an interrelation for a critique of normalization or discursive regulation? My sense is that the specific question of formulating an appropriate ethical disposition apropos animalization, which clearly produces a condition of desemanticization or muteness, exceeds the humanist politics of restoring to speech or resemanticization. However, the reasons for repudiating the presumption that putting everything into speech and breaking every silence is the one and only road to freedom requires a justifying argument. What are some alternatives to the great countertradition of (what can be termed as) the politics of silencing?

In an essay entitled "'In the Folds of Our Own Discourse': The Pleasures and Freedoms of Silence,"[23] Wendy Brown addresses the dominance of confessional modalities of speech in feminist and other discourses of resistance. Critiquing what she aptly phrases "compulsory feminist discursivity and the presumed evil of silences" (Brown, "'In the Folds,'" 187) and venturing to open a fresh perspective on the relations among "silence, speech, and freedom," Brown offers an insightful reading of a well-known passage from Foucault's *History of Sexuality,* volume I. The following is her quotation and gloss. The Foucault passage is as follows:

> Discourses are not once and for all subservient to power or raised up against it, anymore than silences are . . . Discourse transmits and produces power; it reinforces it, but also undermines and exposes it, renders it fragile and makes it possible to thwart it. In like manner. Silence and secrecy are a shelter for power, anchoring its prohibitions; but they also loosen its hold and provide for relatively obscure areas of tolerance. (100–101)

In this passage, Foucault suggests that both discourse and silence can be deployed on the side of or against power's prohibitions, but Brown's emphasis falls on the last part of the quotation, on the "obscure areas of tolerance" that are cleared by silence and secrecy. She writes,

> Silence, as Foucault affirms it, then, is identical neither with secrecy nor with not speaking. Rather, it signifies a relation to regulatory discourses, as well as a possible niche for a practice of freedom *within* those discourses. If, as Foucault insists, freedom is a practice (as opposed to an achievement, a condition, or institution), then the possibility of *practicing* freedom inside a regulatory discourse occurs in the empty spaces of that discourse as well as in resistance to the discourse. Moreover, silence can function as speech in both ways at once. (Brown, "In the Folds," 188)

If silence, as Brown suggests, is not identical with itself but is something that is practiced within discourse, it is incumbent upon us to inquire into its appearance, its repetition in its difference from identity. It may be more apropos to say, following Brown's observation, that though refraining from speech can itself be discursive and function as speech (pro- and contra- power), perhaps silence is that which is not identical with not speaking. In other words, it is whatever remains in discourse that is neither simply speech nor taciturnity (muteness) and is in an oblique relation to regulation and resistance as opposition. If it is indeed somehow the very possibility of the practice of freedom, surely we must ask how we can effect silence as "the empty space" within discourse, and also how we can proliferate silence as silence—as what Agamben specifically terms "inoperativity,"[24] or neutralization. The task is to conceive silence, then, not as a signifier of defiance or abstinence, but as an empty space, where the regulatory power of discourse is nullified. The temporality of silence can only be expressed in the subjective, as that of immanence, and therefore of a power that is the power of conservation rather than exhaustion, of neither presence nor absence, but both. Silence, then, is a temporality that can only be thought of as condensed moments of the past and the future that are immanent within the present spaces and moments of discourse. Focusing for the moment only on that aspect of nondiscourse that is contra-power and not a shelter for it—*in fact, let us affirm that insofar as power is by nature loquacious, it can be taciturn but cannot be really silent*—surely, we must also ask if the difference between taciturn resistance and silence (as inoperativity) does not also refer us to the difference between emancipation and freedom? For surely, if we equate freedom not only with free speech but also with the "right to remain silent," then we invariably inscribe freedom as possible only within legal discourse, guaranteed to someone who is a legal entity, a modern subject of rights. Considering that the enslaved function as the very paradigm of animalized brute life, and are therefore precisely those for whom the law does not function, and who have the right neither to speak nor to remain silent, who, in Hannah Arendt's famous words, do not have "the right to have rights,"[25] it makes no sense to circumscribe freedom to the guarantees of the law. In general, the law can grant taciturnity and thereby make available a place for refusal, even opposition, but perhaps silence is not merely the deployment of resistance as opposition and, though it is engendered by the law, it is that which also renders it inoperative.

Let us, then, turn to the question of the "impossible" rather than the forbidden or the unspoken. Is silence distinguishable as silence? What can be said about silence that silence itself does not already say?

Silence as Nothing / Zero / Absence

Semantically, silence functions as a noun and a verb. Consequently, as a phenomenon it engenders innumerable definitions and approaches. As a noun, it can refer to existential conditions—anything from aphasia and autism to melancholia, dying, contemplation, mysticism. Silence can be an attribute (silence of something) or a condition (silence in). As a transitive verb, silence as the process of silencing or remaining silent usually alludes to a context of authority, right, and law. Given the plethora of silences and the loquacity of the discourses that accompany them, a useful point of beginning an inquiry into the topic is provided by Dennis Kurzon's *Discourse of Silence*. Kurzon's approach is that of a linguist and a pragmatist. Kurzon's premise is that silence is meaningful, but in order to decode that meaning one must broaden linguistic analysis to take account of nonverbal communication (Kurzon, *Discourse of Silence*, 5). Thus, he proposes to arrive at "a type of communicative competence with regard to silence within a semiotic framework, especially as a study in pragmatics" (Kurzon, *Discourse of Silence*, 23).

Kurzon distinguishes between meaningful and meaningless silence by deploying the criterion of intentionality. He establishes intention not in terms of psychological intention or, for that matter, the phenomenological (transcendental) intention. He begins instead with a brief discussion of the function of the zero sign as indicative of an absence that is nevertheless of morphological and lexical value. Kurzon cites Jakobson's essay on the morphology of the "Zero Sign," where Jakobson analyzes zero as a linguistic sign in modern Slavic languages.[26] While "nothing" is not a linguistic sign (Jakobson, "Zero Sign," 7), and therefore is not subject to linguistic analysis, zero clearly has a value, if a negative one. The relation of zero to silence as a linguistic signifier lies in the meaningful absences that operate at several linguistic levels, as, for instance, in the nominative "sheep," which is a zero number, or "dog," which is zero semantic feature insofar as it does not indicate gender. These unmarked features in the morphology of languages, Kurzon suggests, can be regarded as the forerunners of meaningful silence in language. Though Kurzon, rather surprisingly, does not cite Saussure, it is well known that the significance of the notion of zero in linguistics (as Jakobson himself acknowledges [151]) was first put forward by the Geneva School, particularly by Saussure and later by Charles Bally. In the chapter on "The Role of Abstract Entities in Grammar," Saussure emphasizes that the zero sign cannot be regarded as a positive sign. He writes, "to think that there is an incorporeal syntax outside material units distributed in space would be a mistake. In English, *the man I have seen* apparently uses a zero-sign to stand for a syntactical fact which French expresses by que 'that' (*l'homme que j'ai vu*). But the comparing of the English with the French syntactical fact is precisely what produces the illusion that nothingness can express something. The material units alone actually create the value by being arranged in a certain way" (Saussure, *Writings in General Linguistics*, 139).[27]

Implying that Saussure and Jakobson's categories have been superseded by modern research, Kurzon argues that it is important to distinguish zero value as signifier from zero value as signified, despite the fact that Saussure (as Jakobson acknowledges) had clearly pronounced that "language is satisfied with the opposition between something and nothing" (Saussure, *Course in General Linguistics*, 86). In other words, nothing must be opposed to something. Only when there is the presence of an absence, in the sense that either the signifier or the signified has an accompanying propositional element, can the zero be meaningful. Nonsense words and nonsemantic words also have a zero value, but insofar as the signifier and the signified here both have zero value, such words are meaningless. The fact that zero signified and signifier—a staple of some forms of poetry and art such as the Dada movement—can be intentional is not a phenomenon that interests Kurzon, as it cannot translate into meaning. "For silence to have meaning in the linguistic sense, the speaker must have an intention—hence a zero signifier has an utterable signified, a meaning that may be uttered in words" (Kurzon, *Discourse on Silence*, 8).

Though Kurzon claims that silence, if it is to be considered meaningful (and implicitly worth researching), must be communicative *activity* (i.e., it is intentional like speech), he nevertheless holds speech and silence to be opposed. In other words, in a given speech act, silence cannot co-occur with speech in the same instance. There must be an alternation. Thus, silence must be distinguished from nonverbal communication (i.e., gesture, expression, etc.) as the latter can co-occur with speech. Kurzon further introduces the question of acoustic activity. Interestingly, while he agrees with Fernando Poyatos[28] that silence contrasts with speech in being nonacoustic, he nevertheless balks at the idea that silence can be paired with stillness, as noise can with movement. Since this scheme implies that stillness means inactivity and speech activity, it contradicts the notion of silence as activity, "a speech act in the form of a modal utterance" (Kurzon, *Discourse on Silence*, 16). Kurzon argues that, insofar as silence produces signs, it is inactive only in a proxemic sense, having to do with distance. "Silence, then, is non-verbal communication proper because it may alternate only with speech, and does not accompany it in the communicative behavior of one individual within one speech event, as do other co-verbal devices . . . So intentional silence is in contrast to speech, and unintentional silence to noise" (Kurzon, *Discourse on Silence*, 18).

Given that the present project aims to think through the silence that shadows or haunts animalization (humAnimal) as a remnant that cannot be governed by *dispositifs*, a strict adherence to this linguistic approach can be limiting. Moreover, to consider silence as empty spaces within discourse and as the practice of freedom, we cannot presuppose the necessary intentionality of silence. Nevertheless, it provides us with some useful criteria and a set of manipulable lexican terms: the relevance of pairs such as intentional/nonintentional, zero signifier/utterable signified, and movement/stillness.

A more philosophical approach to silence, one that aids the movement of this inquiry, is provided by Bernard Dauenhauer's *Silence: The Phenomenon and Its Ontological Significance*.[29] In his meticulous and formalistic study, Dauenhauer distinguishes four types of silences. The first is active performance, to be distinguished from muteness. He writes,

> The difference between muteness and silence is comparable to the difference between being without sight and having one's eyes closed. Muteness is simply the inarticulateness of that which is incapable of any sort of signifying performances. A man cannot be absolutely and permanently mute unless he can be completely and permanently

unconscious. Unlike muteness, silence necessarily involves conscious activity. But precisely because silence does involve conscious activity, the occurrence or nonoccurrence of passively or spontaneously encountered noise, of itself, can neither prevent nor produce silence. (4)

By this characterization, it appears that muteness is a negation of speech, whereas silence is its contrary and therefore a positive act. The other three types of silence are intervening silence (in other words, the pauses and alternations with speech); fore- and after-silence, which pertain to breaks between sound phrases; and deep silence, referring to "silence of intimates, liturgical silence, and the silence of the to-be-said" (Dauenhauer, *Silence*, 16–17). These initial distinctions are then examined with reference to private and public discourses, which help establish the complex manifestations of silence. Dauenhauer then undertakes an intentional analysis of silence, where he shows the problems associated with defining the noematic element of silence as simply a question of abstinence from all the possible motivated utterances that could be employed. Since this implies that abstinence is a positive performance, insofar as it refrains from determinate expressions, the question then turns on the problem of "how can I silently intend the nondeterminate?" (Dauenhauer, *Silence*, 57). Dauenhauer goes on to inquire about the status of silence in relation to prepredicative and predicative expression and to conclude that there is a necessary and originary silence, which is the condition of possibility for *expression* as such. It is a silence that "detaches one from absorption in spontaneous, pre-predicative experience" (Dauenhauer, *Silence*, 59) and should be understood not as spontaneous performance but as an act—an act of detaching and severing. Thus, rather than regarding silence as abstaining, Dauenhauer suggests that there is not a determinate intentional object in each and every silence. Rather, *"some occurrences* of silence . . . involve no determinate noematic phases"* (Dauenhauer, *Silence*, 60; emphasis added). Ultimately, then, silence, given its great internal heterogeneity, is best grasped as "not the correlative opposite of discourse, but [that which] rather establishes and maintains an oscillation or tension among the shared levels of discourse and between the domain of discourse and the domains of nonpredicative experience" (Dauenhauer, *Silence*, 82). In the latter sections of the book, Dauenhauer mounts a strong argument for the ontological significance of silence as that which discloses "the preeminence of the indeterminate in man" (Dauenhauer, *Silence*, 175). Silence, he suggests, appears as "a grounded phenomenal manifestation of the irreducible tensions at play in the intersection of man and world" (Dauenhauer, *Silence*, 174) or indetermination and determination. However, neither man nor the world are wholly such—that is, indeterminate and determinate, respectively. Rather, silence appears in the tension in the intra- and interplay of these elements and thereby affirms the dyad of syntheses as the locus of being (Dauenhauer, *Silence*, 142).

Foucault, Kurzon, and Dauenhauer each offer perspectives on silence that clarify different aspects of the phenomenon. While both Kurzon and Dauenhauer agree that silence is intentional and active, they part ways on the issue of determinate and indeterminate expressions. Foucault, on the other hand, regards silence as a correlate of power. A given discursive regime can produce unintentional and indeterminate silences, but silence can equally contest the determinations of power, both intentionally and unintentionally. Wendy Brown's interpretation of Foucault's notion of silence as "empty spaces" within discourse and as the practice of freedom also suggests silence itself as being indeterminate—between intention and nonintention, activity and stillness. There is no question that, for Foucault, silence can no more be attributed to intentional consciousness than discourse. If it is language that speaks the subject, then no doubt silence unspeaks the subject by eventuating a hiatus within discourse.

The place of silence, then, is both within and without language—a site of the inhuman, it is also the site where the traditional dichotomies (human/animal, sovereign/outlaw) and the traditional pairs (law/language, belonging/name, mind/body) find their mediation through the inoperativity of an active stillness.

TWO

The Secret of Literary Silence

The animal, what a word!
—Jacques Derrida, *The Animal That Therefore I Am*

[T]he aptitude for the *logos* . . . and logocentrism is first of all a thesis regarding the animal, the animal deprived of the *logos*, deprived of the *can-have-the-logos*.
—Jacques Derrida, *The Animal That Therefore I Am*

THE ABOVE EPIGRAPHS PROPOSE A PROJECT—THE TASK OF INQUIRing into what Derrida terms "limitrophy." "Limitrophy is therefore my subject. Not just because it will concern what sprouts or grows at the limit, around the limit, by maintaining the limit, but also what feeds the limit, generates it, raises it, and complicates it. Everything I'll say will consist, certainly not in effacing the limit, but in multiplying its figures, in complicating, thickening, delinearizing, folding, and dividing the line precisely by making it increase and multiply" (Derrida, *Animal That Therefore*, 29). Following Derrida, then, the "limitrophy" of this chapter is the difference within silence as the limit of language. Insofar as silence is not opposed to speech, this limit (silence) cannot be one; the frontier between speech and silence is not a uniform and unbroken line. In the context of the indisputable abyss that separates human and animal, Derrida suggests that

> instead of asking whether or not there is a limit that produces a discontinuity, one attempts to think what a limit becomes once it is abyssal, once the frontier no longer forms a single indivisible line but more than one internally divided line; once, as a result, it can no longer be traced, objectified, or counted as single and indivisible. What are the edges of a limit that grows and multiplies by feeding on an abyss? (Derrida, *Animal That Therefore*, 30–31)

Turning now to the domain of literature and the role of silence as the limit that defines the literary, we encounter questions that differ markedly from the limit that haunts the language of law. Attending only to the language of literature and its limit in this chapter, my point of departure here is the much-theorized notion of the literary as an element that sustains itself, feeds upon, and feeds the border between the sayable and the unsayable that marks literature. Derrida's discussion of literature's silence as the "secret" not only discloses the element of the literary, but also exposes its unexpected foundation in the covenant and contract. Far from an anomic element within the language of literature, the literary as the secret and silence within literature is here fully submitted to sovereignty and the law. However, there is an added complication: it is not only that the literary element is the kernel and the limit, the constitutive silence around which literature expresses itself, but also that, true to its nature as difference, it is itself internally divided. The task here is to consider Derrida's theory of the secret silence of literature founded on an unspeakable covenant (i.e., as the constitutive ethical element of the literary text) in relation to the mute silence of humAnimal, which refuses every conceivable contract, be it human or divine.

These questions about edges of silences that feed upon the abyss find a textual playground in J. M. Coetzee's novel *Foe,* which thematizes and performs muteness and silence at multiple levels. Derrida's theory of silence as the secret of literature here discovers another abyss. However, before I turn to *Foe* and Friday's severed tongue, let us consider briefly a dominant critical method in which the unsayable has been attested to in the context of literary interpretation.

CANONICAL SILENCE AS THE LITERARY

It will be freely acknowledged that silence is not only a literary phenomenon but also a theme that generates an extensive critical literature. What is more, the genre of literature that classifies itself as the progeny of silence is accorded considerable canonical prestige. In "Silence and the Poet,"[1] George Steiner writes that "the election of silence by the most articulate is, I believe, historically recent ... It occurs, as an experience obviously singular but formidable in general implication, in two of the principal masters, shapers, heraldic presences if you will, of the modern spirit: in Hölderlin and Rimbaud" (Steiner, *Language and Silence*, 46–47). In this context, it is in fact customary to cite a series of proper names such as Mallarmé, Joyce, Beckett, Blanchot, Kafka, Bataille, and Celan as representatives of a contemporary poetic and literary sensibility. As my limited references indicate,[2] the theories and studies that have developed around this kind of hyperliterary literature are equally extensive.

For instance, the Marxist philosopher Pierre Macherey is well known for calling attention to the tacit dimension of every literary text. In *A Theory of Literary Production*,[3] he suggests that the critical enterprise begins with the recognition of the unsaid, the necessary incompletion of every work. "The recognition of the area of shadow in or around the work is the initial moment of criticism" (Macherey, *Theory*, 82). However, the critic's function is not to complete the work, since the incompleteness of the work is "so radical that it cannot be located" (Macherey, *Theory*, 84) but merely displayed. Thus, "the speech of the book comes from a certain silence, a matter which it endows with form, a ground on which it traces a figure. Thus the book is not self-sufficient; it is necessarily accompanied by a *certain absence*, without which it would not exist" (Macherey, *Theory*, 85). Furthermore, a work has the tendency to conceal its own silence. If the moment of absence is the origin of the work, the text nevertheless succeeds in disavowing that absence, thereby presenting itself as a totality. The task of the critic, Macherey proposes, is to bring this absence into presence, to make the silence speak. "Can we make this silence speak? What is the unspoken saying? What does it mean?" (Macherey, *Theory*, 86). Proposing, then, a hermeneutics of silence within the field of literary criticism, Macherey's theory gives rise to some of the richest rereadings of numerous literary traditions informed by feminist, antiracist, and social class concerns, so that the omissions, the elisions, the ellipses, and so on acquire new and concrete meanings.

However, Macherey is not at all suggesting that critics become forensic experts of literature. On the contrary, he warns that to posit a "fundamental veracity, a plenitude of expression" as the cause of the division between spoken and unspoken risks capture by the real snare of language: an assumption of "its tacit positiveness" (Macherey,

Theory, 89). Thus, Macherey proposes that "to know the work, we must move outside it" (Macherey, *Theory,* 90) and that we must be able to pose the question of the ineradicable margin, the *a priori* silence from which the text emerges simultaneously with the question of the unspoken, the visible and the invisible, and so on. Only then, he writes, will it be "possible to trace the path which leads from the haunted work to that which haunts it" (Macherey, *Theory,* 94).

Where the mute silence of humAnimal is concerned, the text in question is not a specific kind of speech but rather nonspeech or muteness. If the task of the literary critic is to disclose the text as concealing a silence (based on the premise that texts have a propensity to conceal their absence), then the point of departure is of course utterance. However, does the inverse necessarily follow, whereby if one is confronted by a brute silence then one must presuppose that muteness as concealing an utterance? In other words, can we assume that muteness has a propensity to conceal speech? This is no doubt the assumption that informs the very word "mute." The mute lack speech, which can be traced to a cause of some kind: censorship, violence, domination, trauma, confusion, and so on. Thus it is that one speaks of "giving voice" to the poor, the discriminated, the forgotten, and so on.[4] The importance of these studies cannot be overstated; however, to presuppose an opposition between muteness and utterance and its significance would be to fall prey to what Derrida terms the lure (*le leurre*) of presence insofar as the opposition aims to turn the silence into meaningful utterance, thereby sloughing off the textuality of the text. The question perhaps should be reformulated into something like the following: if every text is shadowed or haunted by an absence, then is the "text" of muteness itself not haunted by silence? What is a silence that does not so much transcend the opposition between speech and (its absence) but rather testifies to their mutual contamination? Is it that such a silence, insofar as it escapes the fundamental opposition of speech and silence or culture and nature, human and animal, by implicating one in the other, appears then as a certain *muteness* that discloses (humAnimal) *silence*?

In short, I suggest that the question of silence in relation to the indistinct zone of humAnimal will not lend itself to an easy assimilation into the contemporary canon. This difference is genealogical in the sense that humAnimal silence cannot avow a shared filiation to the theological and political legacy of Western literature. In other words, insofar as the prestigious silence of contemporary literature emerges from a certain tradition of what counts as literary, this tradition necessarily excludes the muteness of the inhuman. In the context of speech and writing, muteness signifies a privation, and is marked as the absence of language. If literary silence transcends the opposition between speech and muteness, humAnimal silence neutralizes that opposition. However, the question is not by what rigorous criteria canonical and humAnimal silence can and should be distinguished. It would be futile to pursue such criteria—for neutralization indicates the deactivation of criteria of separation. The relation of humAnimal silence to literature differs from the rarefied silence of avant-garde literature and art, fundamentally in terms of genealogy. Speech may well be haunted by silence, but what does it mean to say that muteness, too, harbors silence? To indicate this (im)possibility, and to mark a genealogical difference from avant-garde literature and art, I turn in the latter part of this chapter to the severed tongue of the slave Friday in Coetzee's novel *Foe*. In the following, instead of reviewing the prolific theories pertaining to artistic subjectivity and the performance of canonical silence, I take up Derrida's "Literature in Secret,"[5] where the literary sustains itself around a silence that marks the implication and partnership of sovereignty and law in its secret.

The Secret of Silence

In his rich and suggestive analysis of the theological genealogy of literature—or the literary text—Derrida situates its emergence squarely within the Abrahamic tradition of the promise as covenant and its secret. Derrida begins his inquiry into the literary not by asking after the meaning of any given well-known work with a signatory author, but by traversing the text of a not-meaning—a text that is not even a sentence but a fragment, or a phrase: *"pardon de ne pas vouloir dire"* (translated as "pardon for not meaning [to say]"). This anonymous (completely meaningless) phrase that asks for forgiveness for not meaning, for not signifying, provides Derrida with a jumping-off point to state his leading question. Invoking the terrible secret of the sacrificial demand that Abraham was bound by God to keep, Derrida writes, "Does the secret of some elective affinity therefore ally the secret of the elective Covenant [*Alliance*] between God and Abraham with the secret of what we call literature, the secret *of* literature and secrecy *in* literature?" (Derrida, *Literature in Secret*, 121; 163). In three brief and terse chapters, Derrida develops a complex argument that discloses the literary secret (the secret *of* and *in* literature) as that of a patrimonial covenant founded on an aporia of forgiveness that is both mutual as it is self-directed and "narcissistic" (Derrida, *Literature in Secret*, 145; 192). Reading the Abrahamic ordeal alongside Kierkegaard's *Fear and Trembling,* Derrida suggests that the secret is itself a secret "that is not one" (Derrida, *Literature in Secret*, 132; 176). Not only is God's demand (for Isaac as *holocaustum* or burnt offering) one about which Abraham must remain silent, but the demand and its abrupt recantation is itself secret insofar as Abraham simply does not know or understand, since it is not at all shared with or by God. Furthermore, the secret itself is simply a test to see how far Abraham can go in keeping the secret (Derrida, *Literature in Secret*, 129; 172–73). And this fact of the undecidable secret, its being more than one, Derrida suggests, "announces literature" in the Western tradition "as though the essence of literature, in its strict sense, in the sense that this Western word retains in the West, were essentially descended from Abrahamic rather than Greek culture" (Derrida, *Literature in Secret*, 132; 177).

But what is the connection between the undecidable secret and the sentence fragment (*"pardon de ne pas vouloir dire"*) or for that matter of either to the literary? There is, of course, no single or proper answer, but it seems to pertain to a hidden forgiveness within what Derrida terms the "secretless secret" (Derrida, *Literature in Secret*, 133; 177) and its indeterminable context. Something in the phrase, as well as God's recanting of his terrible demand, hangs suspended "up in the air" like a "meteorite" (Derrida, *Literature in Secret*, 139; 185). With this concrete metaphor, Derrida deconstructs the phenomenon as such (and consequently of God's self-presence) through the rhetoric of mutual and self-forgiveness. And this deconstructibility in some sense is the opening of the literary and of a legacy.

Literature is allied to the secret because it emerges from what is suspended (e.g., meaning, truth, the word, a determinate context, a proper signatory and addressee) and therefore can only be read and interpreted as a sign. God withholds the meaning of the demand as he withholds the demand itself by recanting—*as if* to say *"pardon de ne pas vouloir dire."* Calling attention to his frequent deployment of the "as if" construction, Derrida says in a salient moment of reflexivity, *"As if*—I often say 'as if' by design, as if I didn't mean (to say) what I am saying, and that would constitute the entry of revelation into literature . . ." (Derrida, *Literature in Secret*, 151; 199–200). God does not strike Abraham with his terrible demand; he withholds it, and in glimpsing in the blink of an eye the suspension, which hangs "up in the air" *as if* it were a meteor, Derrida is led to say, "literature will have been meteoric. Like secrecy. A meteor is called a *phenomenon*, such as appears in the brilliance or *phainesthai* of light, produced in the atmosphere. Like a type of rainbow" (Derrida, *Literature in Secret*, 139; 185). This withholding that is also his secret forgiveness is like a meteor in that it is a sign in the shape of a meteor—a rainbow. Derrida invites us to read the rainbow as God's signature of the covenant—a writing that inaugurates literature as a "crypt" of forgiveness. The rainbow, Derrida says later in the text, is an *aide-mémoire* or mnemonic, a sign in the world, a mnemonic technique that will no longer have the merely spontaneous form of a living and auto-affective memory" (Derrida, *Literature in Secret*, 153; 202).

But the withholding is itself is at least double. What is also withheld as if it were a secret is the scene of forgiveness. Abraham begs God's forgiveness for having obeyed him, just as God by recanting acts as if he were asking for forgiveness—from himself. It is this double-bottomed secret of forgiveness that leads to a reading where God himself is "more than one."

Derrida undertakes this audacious move to deconstruct the sovereign God of monotheism by first disclosing the *différance* in any scenario of forgiveness. Forgiveness possesses an aporetic structure whereby "one doesn't forgive someone who is innocent" (Derrida, *Literature in Secret*, 137; 182) any more than one can without guilt forgive the unforgiveable, and this is despite the fact that only the latter (i.e., the unforgiveable) can enter into the transaction of forgiveness. In other words, the acts of forgiving and exculpating, Derrida suggests, are mutually exclusive, thereby exposing the split within the sovereign act of the pardon. As Derrida says, "One of the causes of this aporia of forgiveness is the fact that one cannot forgive, ask, or grant forgiveness without this specular identification, without speaking in the other's voice. Forgiving by means of this specular identification is not forgiving, because it doesn't mean forgiving the other as such for an evil as such" (Derrida, *Literature in Secret*, 137; 183).

This structure of specular identification implicit in any act of forgiveness is observable in another moment in Genesis (8:21–22) when God seems "to repent, to express regret or remorse" (Derrida, *Literature in Secret*, 141; 187) for having cursed the earth and sent the flood from which Noah and his family alone are exempted. Shortly thereafter appears the meteor—a rainbow that carries the pledge of a covenant that God makes not only with Noah but all living creatures. It is at this point, then, that Derrida locates a certain excess in God. It appears that by recanting, or regretting his actions, by going back on himself, God also asks for forgiveness. As if to say "*pardon de ne pas vouloir dire*" or "pardon for not meaning (to say)." But here we are faced with a rich irony. What does it mean for God to recant and thereby implicate himself in the structure of forgiveness? As Derrida writes, "For if God were to ask for forgiveness, of whom would he ask it? Who can forgive *him* for something, a misdeed (the question of 'what')? Or forgive *it*, itself (the question of 'who'), the fact of having sinned? Who could forgive *him* or forgive *it*, if not himself? . . . This question of the plea, this prayer for forgiveness to be given, seeks its undiscoverable location on the edge of literature . . ." (Derrida, *Literature in Secret*, 142; 189). This structure is perhaps taken to its modern limit in Kafka's *Letter to My Father,* where Derrida says we encounter "a forgiveness that is named, requested, and granted as soon as it is named, a forgiveness so originary, a priori, and automatic, in short so narcissistic that one wonders whether it really took place, outside of literature" (Derrida, *Literature in Secret*, 145; 192).

However, Derrida also cautions the reader against a too hasty translation of God's retraction as regret, remorse, or repentance (Derrida, *Literature in Secret*, 146; 194). Instead, he recommends that we attend first of all to the covenant with Noah. What interests Derrida is the fact that God seems to recant or repent or regret his actions twice—the first time causes the flood and the second "interrupts it"—so that it is as if "Noah is twice forgiven. On two occasions he finds grace. As though the Covenant between father and son could be sealed only through a repetition, a double coming-back, the coming back on oneself of this retreat or retraction" (Derrida, *Literature in Secret*, 147; 194). A necessary repetition, then, is at the core of God's covenant, insofar as this covenant is founded on God going back on himself. "This 'God' has the attribute of being able to recall (himself), and to recall to himself that what he did was not necessarily well done, not perfect, not without fault or flaw. That would be the (hi)story of 'God'" (Derrida, *Literature in Secret*, 147; 195).

To recant, Derrida suggests, is inseparable from a plea for forgiveness. In other words, the covenant is a complex of repetition (as recantation) and therefore of forgiveness, which can only be asked of the other or of oneself, both of which must imply specular identification. In other words, Derrida detects a moment of hetero-affection in God (!). Interestingly, however, he refuses to attribute a simplistic atheistic value to this powerful event of deconstruction. Instead, this hearkening to the unnameable trace within forgiveness that founds as it unfounds (because we simply cannot know "who grants it to whom, *in the name* of whom and of what" [Derrida, *Literature in Secret*, 151; 200]) and confounds the covenant can only be read as the history *of* God:

> It is written or addressed to the name of God. Forgiveness comes to pass as a covenant between God and God through the human. It comes to pass through the body of man, through the flaw that crosses through man [*à travers le travers de l'homme*], through man's evil or fault, which is nothing but his desire, and the place of the forgiveness *of* God, according to the genealogy, inheritance, and filiation of this double genitive. Saying that forgiveness is a history *of* God, an affair between God and God—and we humans are found from one end to the other of it—provides neither a reason for nor a means of dispensing with it. (Derrida, *Literature in Secret*, 148; 196)

What is secret, then, is the trace *of* God's forgiveness, and also God's forgiveness *as* trace, which testifies to a multiple splitting, splintering of being as presence or sovereign oneness as such. It is this productive moment of dissemination that then comes to legitimate and invest the core of man's dominion over beast and the relation to the literary text.

In Derrida's ingenious reading of the literary secret, the dissemination engendered by the silent forgiveness has everything to do with the question of sovereignty. For when God makes a pact, a covenant with Noah and his loved ones, he also foreswears the destruction of life: "neither will I again smite any more every thing living, as I have done" (Genesis 8:21–22; Derrida, *Literature in Secret*, 141; 188). Nevertheless, in confirming the covenant with Noah, Derrida points out that God also grants man's absolute sovereignty over the world. In other words, what we have here is a sharing, even a splitting of sovereignty: "a terrifying sovereignty, whose terror is at the same time felt and imposed by the human, inflicted on the other living things" (Derrida, *Literature in Secret*, 152; 201). Once again, it is a structure of specularity, for as is clarified in Genesis 9:1–7, "in the image of God made he man." And in the renewal of this covenant with Abraham, we once again witness the structure of a double forgiveness before and after the sacrifice of Isaac.

Where or how, then, does the literary enter into this deconstructive schema of the covenant organized as it is around a doubled and secret forgiveness or hetero-affection that implicates sovereignty? This is by far the most consequential piece of Derrida's layered argument, and he expounds on it only in the last few pages of the essay by iterating a single leap over all the instances of forgiveness and renewals back to what he calls the "absolute axiom." This axiom refers to God's demand as a demand not so much for the sacrifice of Isaac as the demand for secrecy itself. Derrida underlines that God's demand can only be understood as the demand to maintain the absolute singularity of the relation that can admit of no third party—"the absolute exclusivity of the relation between the one who calls and the one who responds" (Derrida, *Literature in Secret*, 154; 203). To respond to this secret demand for secrecy, wherein Abraham may not confide in anyone even the fact of his vexed complicity in an unspeakable secret, a pure secrecy that doubles back on itself, is to be "ready to sacrifice everything" (Derrida, *Literature in Secret*, 154; 203). Significantly, for Derrida, this is the moment of the "absolute *desacralization* of the world" (Derrida, *Literature in Secret*, 154; 203), for the secret that there is a secret, he says, cannot be said to be anything, least of all sacred. It may be, he suggests, *saint* (translated as holy) but not *sacré* (translated as sacred). Derrida is here alluding to the distinctions made in different ways by Durkheim and Levinas between the concept of *saint* or the holy as the sense of the numinous and *sacré* or the sacred as something with religious purpose that stands in opposition to the profane. Literature arises, then, in this moment of "profanation" (not secularization) as that which desacralizes the holy by repeating "the sacrifice of Isaac, stripping it bare, delivering to and exposing it to the world" (Derrida, *Literature in Secret*, 154; 203). In other words, by speaking of the secrecy of the secret, literature betrays the holy word. Such is the legacy of the covenant—its very renewability contains within itself the flaw of the betrayal of the singular secret "face-to-face" relation to God. Thus, in Abraham's response to the other, his responsibility is to endure what is at bottom a secret without a secret. Derrida writes,

> In order for that to be, nothing must be said and everything—at bottom at the bottomless depths of the bottom—must mean (to say) nothing. "Pardon for not meaning (to say) . . ." In short, the secret to be kept would have, at bottom to be without an object, without any object other than the unconditionally singular covenant, the mad love between God, Abraham, and what descends from him. His son and his name.
>
> In the case of what descends from him, however, the singularity is sealed but *necessarily betrayed* by the inheritance that confirms, reads, and translates the covenant. By the testament itself.
>
> What would literature have to do with the testamentary secret of this "pardon for not meaning (to say)" . . . with the inheritance of this promise and this betrayal, with the forswearing that haunts this oath? What would literature have to do with a forgiveness [*pardon*] for the secret kept that could be a "pardon for not meaning (to say) . . . ?" In other words, in what way does literature descend from Abraham, in order to ask forgiveness for its broken oath? "Pardon for not meaning (to say) . . ." Is literature this forgiveness that is requested for the desacralization, what others would religiously call the secularization of a holy revelation? Forgiveness requested for the betrayal of the holy origin of forgiveness itself? (Derrida, *Literature in Secret*, 156; 205; emphasis added)

With these series of questions, Derrida then locates the secret *of* literature and the secret *in* literature as the forgiveness that ruptures the singularity of the holy covenant by calling for both responsibility and betrayal. Literature, in other words, desacralizes by repeating and exposing the singularity of the relation with the other. As an ironic patrimony with a structure of inheritance as betrayal, literature is disclosed as the ultimate covenant of the antifoundation. Adopting the language of a legal document, Derrida articulates in a series of six clauses that begin with "whereas" (*"attendu que"*) literature's doubled and deconstructive (i.e., infinite) responsibility: namely, its right as fiction to say everything and nothing, while exonerating itself from responsibility before political and civic law, to a so-called reality, and extreme autonomy as freedom, while at the same time committing itself to an infinite responsibility to the singular event, being properly phenomenological if not realistic, and submitting to an extreme heteronomy of context and convention. The literary covenant then concludes with the following:

> Be it understood that literature surely inherits from a holy history within which the Abrahamic moment remains the essential secret (and who would deny that literature remains a religious remainder, a link to and relay for what is sacrosanct in a society without God?), while at the same time denying that history, appurtenance, and heritage. It denies that filiation. It betrays it in the double sense of the word: it is unfaithful to it, breaking with it at the very moment when it reveals its "truth" and uncovers its secret. Namely that of its own filiation: impossible possibility. This "truth" exists on the condition of a denial whose possibility was already implied by the binding of Isaac.
>
> Literature can but ask forgiveness for this double betrayal. There is no literature that does not, from its very first word, ask for forgiveness. In the beginning was forgiveness. For nothing. For meaning (to say) nothing. (Derrida, *Literature in Secret*, 157; 208–9)

Literature, then, is a betrayal of the "necessary betrayal" insofar as it disavows its own abyssal genealogy. However, the denial of its "filiation" with the secret forgiveness at the heart of the covenant is also a way of maintaining the double structure of the secret—the double betrayal. In a sense, we could even say that literature covers over the splitting of God's sovereignty and auto-affection—his self-division and his shared power. It simultaneously conceals as it discloses the covenant. It is in these plural senses that silence is a literary phenomenon or is constitutive of the literary as a tradition: on the one hand, literature is that which must necessarily disclose the demand for secrecy and singularity and, on the other, it also obfuscates this necessity as inheritance. This double structure of disclosure and concealment is the ambivalent legacy of literature that Derrida suggests is founded in the figure of suspension and withholding as the repetitive trace of recantation and forgiveness.

Insofar as Derrida's argument uncovers the conditions of possibility of the literary as internal differentiation, the question arises whether and in what sense the silence of the interstice between human and animal can be said to share in this legacy. Can it be simply assumed that humAnimal silence partakes of the ironic patrimony of the holy covenant? And if so, how should its essential muteness be parsed in relation to the betrayal that is literature's loquacity concerning the singularity of the relation with its own responsibility? Can humAnimal silence be fully subsumed under the sign of literary inheritance, improper though such inheritance might be? Can we continue to entertain the hypothesis that it may in fact signal a point of exit from (God's) sovereignty? Let us turn, then, to one of the most spectacular silences recorded in the literature of animalization—that is, to the figure of Friday in J. M. Coetzee's novel *Foe* (a work steeped in the literary tradition) to think through some of these differences between literary and humAnimal silence.

BRUTE SILENCE

Foe is a recasting of Daniel Defoe's *Robinson Crusoe,* a novel that is associated in popular memory with the rise of the novel form in English. In Coetzee's engagement with this text, which bespeaks a literary tradition and the legacy of the *Robinsonade,* the narrator and would-be novelist Susan Barton is shipwrecked on an island "ruled" by Cruso with the mute Friday as his servant. At Cruso's death, Susan returns to England with Friday in tow, where she seeks out Daniel Foe, the famous author (who is, however, on the run from his creditors), to help her write the novel about her adventures on Cruso's island and Friday's severed tongue. What ensues is the strange episode of entering and inhabiting a differentiated silence whose spaciousness seems to take the legacy of the literary itself to task.

The first thing we notice about the novel is that it presents itself as a novel *to be* written and then as a novel that *cannot* be written. From Susan's initial summary recapitulation of her experience as a castaway on Cruso's island—"facts" that she wishes transposed into literature by one who has the "art"—the subsequent chapters are her ostensibly "artless" record and a report of living incognito in Foe's London home. In these chapters, Susan addresses herself to Foe as the potential author of her narrative. In the final two sections, when she at long last finally encounters Foe "face-to-face," the account is a straightforward first-person narrative spoken directly to the anonymous reader, while the final section dispenses with the narrative point of view altogether. We do not know who is speaking, witnessing, recording, and closing (if not ending) the novel. It is a disembodied voice. These last sections are the space of an unfolding, an acknowledgment of the impossibility or the nonrepresentability of what is at the heart of the experience—Friday's absolute alterity. In other words, from attempting to speak and say everything about Cruso's island as well as her own exile in England, Susan is led to discover the possible impossibility of literature that has up to now only seemed like the challenge of an impossible possibility. An unspeakable and intractable alterity haunts and structures every act of narrating, most of all the narration that aspires, as Susan's story does, to give a fictional account of the truth. This other can be understood as a figurative "foe" that is the secret of the eponymous *Foe*, who is both the fictional would-be author and the real has-been author of a certain inaugural novel of a literary tradition called *Robinson Crusoe*. And this "foe," through its intractable alterity, invariably deauthorizes Foe, the canonical author who tells stories. Consider the following scene, which arrives toward the end of the text when Susan begins to realize the impossibility of literature given the fact that each one of them is in some sense a "helpless captive" of the other:

> "Mr Foe" I said, "I have come to a resolution."
> But the man seated at the table was not Foe. It was Friday, with Foe's robes on his back and Foe's wig, filthy as a bird's nest, on his head. In his hand, poised over Foe's papers, he held a quill with a drop of black ink glistening at its tip. I gave a cry and sprang forward to snatch it away. But at that moment Foe spoke from the bed where he lay. "Let him be, Susan," he said in a tired voice: "he is accustoming himself to

his tools, it is part of learning to write." "He will foul your papers," I cried. "My papers are foul enough, he can make them no worse," he replied—"Come and sit with me." (Coetzee, *Foe*, 151)

In this iconic image—the languageless Friday sitting at the desk of England's first major novelist, pen poised in the air, a suspended act of nonwriting—we have something like the antithesis of the original logocentric author marked by his privileged access to the signified, to meaning, and to closure. What we have instead is the signifier, non-meaning, and repetition as beginning.

> I turned back to Friday, still busy at his writing.
> The paper before him was heavily smudged, as by a child unused to the pen, but there was writing on it, writing of a kind, rows and rows of the letter *o* tightly packed together. A second page lay at this elbow, fully written over, and it was the same.
> "Is Friday learning to write?" asked Foe.
> "He is writing, after a fashion," I said. "He is writing the letter *o*."
> "It is a beginning," said Foe. "Tomorrow you must teach him *a*."
> (Coetzee, *Foe*, 152)

It is also at this point in the text that the questions raised earlier about the difference between humAnimal silence and literary silence come into view and insist upon us with some urgency. It is tempting to resolve this image of Friday by reading it in purely figurative terms as a trope for the secret "of" and "in" literature. Friday as "foe" or otherness, then, would refer us to the necessary suspension and with-holding (what Derrida terms the meteoric nature of literature)—the secret self-forgiveness that is the condition of possibility of all fiction (i.e., fiction as betrayal). In other words, Friday's deployment of the signifier would be nothing if not writing freed of its dependence on speech as presence. The novel fully provides us with the license to read this scene as the disclosure of the priority of writing as metaphor of *différance* over speech as presence and truth. I quote the follow-ing scene in its entirety, as every line raises issues that are crucial to my concerns. It pertains to Foe's suggestion that Susan teach Friday to write:

> "All my efforts to bring Friday to speech, or to bring speech to Fri-day, have failed," I said. "He utters himself only in music and dancing,

which are to speech as cries and shouts are to words. There are times when I ask myself whether in his earlier life he had the slightest mastery of language, whether he knows what kind of thing language is."

"Have you shown him writing?" said Foe.

How can he write if he cannot speak? Letters are the mirror of words. Even when we seem to write in silence, our writing is the manifest of a speech spoken within ourselves or to ourselves.

"Nevertheless, Friday has fingers. If he has fingers he can form letters. Writing is not doomed to be the shadow of speech. Be attentive to yourself as you write and you will mark there are times when the words form themselves on the paper *de novo*, as the Romans used to say, out of the deepest inner silences. We are accustomed to believe that our world was created by God speaking the Word; but I ask, may it not rather be that he wrote it, wrote a word so long we have yet to come to the end of it? May it not be that God continually writes the world, the world and all that is in it?

"Whether writing is able to form itself out of nothing I am not competent to say," I replied. "Perhaps it will do so for authors; it will not for me. As to Friday, I ask nevertheless: How can he be taught to write if there are no words within him, in his heart, for writing to reflect, but on the contrary only a turmoil of feelings and urges? As to God's writing, my opinion is: If he writes, he employs a secret writing, which it is not given to us, who are part of that writing, to read."

"We cannot read it, I agree, that was part of my meaning, since we are that which he writes. We, or some of us: it is possible that some of us are not written, but merely are; or else (I think principally of Friday) are written by another and darker author. Nevertheless, God's writing stands as an instance of a writing without speech. Speech is but a means through which the word may be uttered, it is not the word itself. Friday has no speech, but he has fingers, and those fingers shall be his means . . . The waterskater, that is an insect and dumb, traces the name of God on the surfaces of ponds, or so the Arabians say. None is so deprived that he cannot write." (Coetzee, *Foe*, 142–44)

Foe, it seems, is inclined to entertain the notion that Friday's inscriptions may well constitute pure writing, a repetition of something like the secret kernel of all literature—the original meteorite, or sign (i.e., God's signature, which testifies to a withholding and a forgiveness). However, it is not at all clear that Friday's function in the novel can be exhausted by such a trope, and Foe seems well aware of it when he wonders if Friday may have been "written by another and darker author."

Before we attend to the aporia of Friday's tongue, it is necessary to further consider the indebtedness of Coetzee's novel to the legacy that, according to Derrida, initiates the literary tradition.

Insofar as Foe is a novel about the art of novel writing and engages in a modernist play of identity and presence that renders unstable the traditional separations of author, narrator, character, plot, form, reality, fiction, history, memory, and so on, it not only sustains the literary silence and secret but also invites reflection upon it. Susan is haunted by a sense of her own ghostliness. Her story is unable to be told and thus she writes to Foe,

> When I reflect on my story I seem to exist only as the one who came, the one who witnessed, the one who longed to be gone: a being without substance, a ghost beside the true body of Cruso. Is that the fate of all storytellers? . . . Return to me the substance I have lost, Mr Foe: that is my entreaty. For though my story gives the truth, it does not give substance of the truth (I see that clearly, we need not pretend it is otherwise). (Coetzee, *Foe*, 51)

This insubstantiality only becomes more pronounced as Susan goes in search of Foe and is doubly haunted by a girl who claims to be the daughter that she (Susan) had supposedly lost. Moreover, the girl carries the same name, Susan Barton, and invents an entire family history that renders all origins and memories fictional. Initially, Susan believes in the grounding of fiction in truth and fact as a force of reason. She hopes meaningfulness as such will civilize Friday, as well as bring them fame and fortune, and thus she writes in one of her letters to Foe, "[the] secret meaning of the word story, do you think: a storing-place for memories?" (Coetzee, *Foe*, 59). But in an allusion to Kafka and Joseph K's sense of the theatricality of life, the girl appears repeatedly throughout Susan's wanderings, subverting the very place of memory and identity, rendering everything absurd and contingent. Eventually, it appears to Susan that there is no certainty, least of all any truth, as to who is real and who is a figment of someone's imagination, or what is remembered and what is invented. And thus Foe says to her, "My sweet Susan, as to who among us is a ghost and who not I have nothing to say: it is a question we can only stare at in silence, like a bird before a snake, hoping it will not swallow us" (Coetzee, *Foe*, 134). Thus, she is abandoned to a deafening literary silence, out of which emerges something of the impossible possibility that is literature. The novel *Foe*, it seems, is one that cannot *not* fail *not* to be written.

In all the aforementioned contexts, and many others that I have not discussed here, *Foe* as a novel fully partakes of the secret of and in literature that Derrida uncovers as hailing from the Abrahamic legacy of forgiveness and betrayal. I refer to the structure wherein the repetition of God's signature of the covenant as the loquacity of literature simultaneously betrays as it preserves through disavowal the secret forgiveness at the heart of the literary. The secret of the island remains untold. This is the patrimony that Susan wishes to partake in by literally "fathering" (Coetzee, *Foe*, 140), as she calls it, her story upon Foe. Thus, it is left to Foe as the famous author to declare or disclose this ironic patrimony: "In every story there is a silence, some sight concealed, some word unspoken, I believe. Till we have spoken the unspoken we have not come to the heart of the story" (Coetzee, *Foe*, 141).

But what of Friday, seated at Foe's desk, pen in hand, with its drop of ink glistening at the tip, suspended above paper? Is the enigma of Friday the enigma of literature? How is his muteness related to the great silence that literature repeats as patrimony and tradition? As Susan says, it is then incumbent on us "to open Friday's mouth and hear what it holds: silence, perhaps, or a roar, like the roar of a seashell held to the ear" (Coetzee, *Foe*, 142). But the question here is whether Friday's silence should be distinguished from the silence that founds literature—God's writing, as both Derrida and Coetzee affirm—or whether it is altogether other?

What is, in fact, Friday's "condition"? Susan regards him as disabled, mutilated, and she wishes above all to remedy his condition by discovering the cause (in order to assign blame and responsibility), and to mitigate his suffering by teaching him language and thereby civilizing him. Cruso, on the other hand, like Foe, seems inclined to grant

Friday some kind of originary status. When Susan decries Cruso's indifference to language in general, he commands Friday to sing:

> "Sing, Friday," he said. "Sing for Mistress Barton."
> Whereupon Friday raised his face to the stars, closed his eyes, and obedient to his master, began to hum in a low voice. I listened but could make out no tune. Cruso tapped my knee, "The voice of man," he said.
> (Coetzee, *Foe*, 22)

Significantly, Friday remains completely unresponsive, "like an animal wrapt entirely in itself" (Coetzee, *Foe*, 70) and totally "insensible" (Coetzee, *Foe*, 98) to Susan and her efforts to interact with him. The question is not whether Susan or Cruso and Foe are "correct" in their view. Rather, it is Friday's function as some kind of an absolute limit that we must take into account. At one point, Susan wonders what Friday "knows" about death and later about sex (Coetzee, *Foe*, 45), and she is passionately driven to unlock his secret. Unlike Cruso and Foe, Susan, for all her faith in civilization, does not arrive at any point of comfort with Friday's muteness. If the men in the novel are too quick to interpret Friday's muteness as the silent crypt of God's covenant—the cipher of forgiveness that engenders the literary and writing—Susan's skepticism maintains the aporia of Friday, Friday as aporia denying closure to the novel.

How should Friday's literary function in the novel be understood? To speak in broad contours here, let us recall that for Derrida, literature bears a fundamental debt to the Abrahamic tradition. Its secret is nothing but the secret of a demand for singularity, a retraction or withholding of the demand and its meaning, and a forgiveness whose outcome is a covenant signed by God. The salient issue here is that of the literary as patrimony (one that is necessarily betrayed and disavowed in repetition, but a legacy nevertheless). In what sense would Friday in his silence, the nameless cannibal slave without language, whose very status as human is in question, be an heir to such a legacy? What would it mean to interpret Friday's severed tongue as the mark of forgiveness? When is the cutting or slaying of the other a kind of protowriting that heralds the covenant of the God of monotheism?

There is, without doubt, no modern philosopher who has done more to bring this question into focus than Derrida. And in *Literature in Secret,* at the point where he is discussing the secret forgiveness and its knowledge, he lets drop in passing the following:

> All of that belongs to a literary corpus that is as undecidable as the signature of son and/or father, as undecidable as the voices and acts that are exchanged in it without exchanging anything (Kafka's real father, no more than Abraham, perhaps understood nothing, received nothing, heard nothing from his son; he perhaps was more asinine [*bête*] than all the said beasts, the ass and the ram who were perhaps the only ones thinking and seeing what was going on, what was happening to them, the only ones to know in their bodies, who pays the price when men are forgiven, forgive each other, or forgive among themselves. (Derrida, *Literature in Secret*, 144–45; 191–92)

In the Abrahamic schema of the literary, Friday is not and cannot be in the place of the son—Abraham, Isaac, or for that matter Kafka. But can we be certain that he is in the place of the animal—the ram that is sacrificed to preserve the singularity of the face-to-face? As woman, Susan protests her exclusion from this patrimony, and she may well view Friday as unfairly assigned to the role of the sacrificial victim. However, we do not need to commit the fallacy of reading Friday as a nonfictional character in order to perceive that he remains extraneous to all designations and ascriptions and his secret remains sealed. It merits attention that his secret is not located at the level of the story line or the plot, its experimental or suggestive language (i.e., form or structure), and least of all in anything called characterization. All of these literary elements can be imputed to a literary intentionality called the author who signs as J. M. Coetzee.

Where, then, should the secret of Friday be located? I suggest that what the novel *Foe* testifies to is the limit that is reached in this rigorous meditation on the relation to the other. And this relation, let us say, is not a relation of suspension of sense, silence, and so on, as forgiveness, but one that suspends the very politics of forgiveness—where the paradox of the forgiveable and the unforgiveable (friend and foe) and its specular identification is nullified. If literature is that which, in however paradoxical a manner, responds to the other, and emerges in and through its responsibility to the other (even if this means betrayal and disavowal), it appears that here in this novel by one J. M. Coetzee titled

Foe, which undeniably partakes of the canonical heritage of Western literature, something else is responded to. This something is not only the theological tradition of God's demand, retraction, and forgiveness as the secret of writing and the literary, but also a nameless and terrifying possibility that the ultimate responsibility may be to a wholly other, an other that is truly, in a sense, "monstrous," for it is one that cannot enter into the Abrahamic covenant, let alone inherit it, that has no place, acknowledges not at all the divine call, remains insensible to God's silence as much as to his Word—that may well empty out and neutralize forgiveness and its sacrificial economy. It appears that Friday in the novel is the indication of an ultimate aporia that opens literature onto an ethics beyond ethics of the truly other. As Derrida says in his seminar *The Beast and the Sovereign*:

> The "unrecognizable" [*méconnaissable*], I shall say in a somewhat elliptical way, is the beginning of ethics, of the Law, and not of the human. So long as there is recognizability and fellow, ethics is dormant. It is sleeping a dogmatic slumber. So long as it remains human, among men, ethics remains dogmatic, narcissistic, and not yet thinking. Not even thinking the human that it talks so much about.
>   The "unrecognizable" is the awakening. It is what awakens, the very experience of being awake . . . what I am doing is simply an almost limitless broadening of the notion of "fellow" and that in talking about the dissimilar, the non-fellow, I am surreptitiously extending the similar, the fellow, to all forms of life, to all species. All animals qua living beings are my fellows. (Derrida, *Beast and Sovereign*, 155–56)

By locating ethics beyond the ethics of the similar, Derrida effectively also locates ethics as responsibility beyond the covenant. Read from this perspective, the secret of literature seems to contain its own secret, and that is of flirting with disinheritance, betraying even the necessary betrayal, of lingering at the limit where one can glimpse at the place beyond the politics of the covenant. But this place is only an egress where one exits the covenant—to a place where even forgiveness is no longer pertinent or, for that matter, impertinent. Derrida, I suspect, may not want to read literature as that which at its abyssal heart harbors the secret of exiting the covenant to enter into an outer space that resists and withdraws itself from the expanding limit. The limit that Derrida suggests (in the quotation at the beginning of this chapter) should be proliferated and multiplied. But is it possible that the silence of Friday comes from this outer space of the limit where ethics is not only the ethics of responsibility but also the thought of happiness that we cannot help but imagine beyond the covenant?

THREE

Law, "Life / Living," Language

The scene changes to an empty room. Rimbaud has gone to
Abyssinia to make his fortune in the slave trade. Wittgenstein,
after a period as a village schoolteacher, has chosen menial
work as a hospital orderly. Duchamp has turned to chess.
Accompanying these exemplary renunciations of vocation, each
man has declared that he regards his previous achievement in
poetry, philosophy, or art as trifling, of no importance. But the
choice of permanent silence doesn't negate their work. On the
contrary, it imparts retroactively an added power and authority
to what was broken off—disavowal of the work becoming a new
source of its validity, a certificate of unchallengeable seriousness.

—Susan Sontag, "The Aesthetics of Silence,"
A Susan Sontag Reader

To probe the secret of literary silence is to discover the
paradox of a certain iconoclastic fidelity to tradition and prestige. Modernism's commitment to the avant-garde, insofar as it thrives upon and
nurtures literary silence, is revealed as more deeply implicated in the
structure and demands of sovereignty than any other genre. Clearly,
its relevance to humAnimal silence as the potential to neutralize the
force of law and its decision to suspend itself is minimal—perhaps even
a distraction. As Susan Sontag says in reference to the great modernists, "to be a victim of the craving for silence is to be, in still a further sense, superior to everyone else. It suggests that the artist has had
the wit to ask more questions than other people and that he possesses
stronger nerves and higher standards of excellence" (Sontag, "Aesthetics of Silence," 184). Furthermore, Sontag writes, "silence exists as a
decision—in the exemplary suicide of the artist (Kleist, Lautréamont),
who thereby testifies that he has gone too far" (Sontag, "Aesthetics of
Silence," 185).

Following Derrida's *Literature in Secret*, I have argued that silence as the secret of literature has itself a secret, and that is the possibility of imagining an ethics of the dissimilar. And such an ethics, which begins from the unrecognizable, would also imply an encounter with a limit that renders redundant or "null and void" any participation in the politics of the covenant and thus the ontotheological heritage of literature. Whether one avows or betrays the covenant founded on the secrecy of the singular encounter (with God) and its auto-hetero-transactions of forgiveness, the silence of literature in this context is approachable only within the matrix of sovereignty. For the covenant is nothing if not a covenant of an indivisible sovereignty that, as Derrida shows, is in fact paradoxically shared by God.

To discern that a certain kind of silence absents itself from this scene of sharing and inheriting, thus rendering the covenant null, raises the question of the law and its so-called limits. As Derrida indicates, the ethical imperative toward justice may exceed or break the law, yet it still remains subject to it, in some relation to it, or to another law. But what about the alterity of this silence—the impossible muteness of the slave's severed tongue—and what effect does it have upon the law? Does it make sense to speak of a political or ethical existence beyond the law that voids the law while at the same time acknowledging that silence has everything to do with language? (It is no doubt banal to recall here that language itself is composed of laws and that there can be no law—natural, juridical, or moral—in its absence.)

The conundrums raised by the silence of humAnimal are numerous, but where the relation to politicotheological sovereignty and law are concerned, two issues can be privileged for inquiry: on one hand, the structure of the interrelation of juridical law and language and, on the other, the conception of the limits of the law, especially the relevance of terms such as being inside and outside the law. In other words, to follow the thought of humAnimal silence as repudiation or voiding of the force of law, it is necessary to (a) grapple with the complex topology of the law as the secret of its force and (b) apprehend the spacing between law and language. While it may appear that the former is diagnostic and the latter tactical, the two issues are not really separable, insofar as placing pressure on the link between law and language is invariably to disclose its topology and the so-called limits of law, just as to grapple with the structure of the law would be to discern how language and its potential for silence are deployed as force.

However, as soon as these issues and questions are raised, we encounter yet again the specter of the slave's severed tongue.

BETWEEN TONGUES: SECRETS AND SILENCES

There is a folkloric story told by the turn-of-the-century African American writer Charles Chesnutt entitled "The Dumb Witness." According to Werner Sollers in his "Note to the Library of America" edition of Chesnutt's works, the story, probably written around 1900, was not published during Chesnutt's lifetime;[1] it is one of his "Conjure" stories, set in North Carolina, and utilizes a layered framing device.

The tale is set during the period of Reconstruction, and the narrator is a white Northerner, John, who pieces together what he hears told to him in black dialect by Julius, an ex-slave. During a visit to what was once a very prosperous plantation, the narrator witnesses a strange interaction between an old white man seated on a grand oak armchair and a black woman who is his servant but obviously related to him in some way. The old man seems to be questioning the woman in tones alternating between desperation and violence about the whereabouts of some papers. The woman seems unable to speak, and then rails incoherently at the man in a babbling and outlandish jargon. The narrator describes her "speech" thus:

> She rose from her seat, and drawing herself up to her full height—she was a tall woman, though bowed somewhat with years—began to speak. I thought at first in some foreign tongue. But after a moment I knew that no language or dialect, at least none of European origin, could consist of such a discordant jargon, such a meaningless cacophony as that which fell from the woman's lips. And as she went on, pouring out a flood of sounds that were not words, and which yet seemed now and then vaguely to suggest words, as clouds suggest the shapes of mountains and trees and strange beasts, the old man seemed to bend like a reed before a storm. (160)

Struck by this extraordinary scene, the narrator subsequently discovers through a local ex-slave, Julius, that the woman, Viney, had been the old man Malcolm Murchison's slave housekeeper. Murchison managed the plantation and the estates for his wealthy, childless, freewheeling uncle and did so with authoritarian force, knowing full well that he stood to inherit the property at his uncle's death. However, when the avaricious Murchison contracts to marry a rich widow and threatens to evict Viney unless she submits to being displaced by the soon-to-be wife, Viney, resentful of her impending displacement, approaches the would-be mistress secretly and tells her "something." Julius does not know what this "something" is and the text keeps it a secret from us, but it effectively results in the white woman breaking off her engagement with Murchison. Murchison, who discovers Viney's betrayal, punishes her by cutting off her tongue and banishing her from the house to a shack on the grounds.

Meanwhile, Murchison receives a letter from his uncle announcing his own imminent death and affirming that Murchison as heir should retrieve the papers that include the will and other securities and mortgages that he had placed in a safe and secret place. The uncle's letter instructs Murchison to ask Viney, who is "of our blood," as she is the sole person entrusted with the secret. When Murchison approaches Viney lying in agony in her shack, he begins first with an apology. Chesnutt writes that tears roll down her face as she gestures at the pain in her mouth. Murchison, however, makes it clear that he has only one interest and that is to learn the secret hiding place of the papers. Thus ensue decades of mute recalcitrance, regret, and frustration that unfold through the Civil War and the abolition of slavery. And the master and slave remain locked in a mutual dependency. Murchison tries everything in his power to extract the secret from Viney—from threatening to pampering her as well as trying to teach her to read and write. But though she appears to want to communicate, Viney is unable to speak. Steeped in her own loss she is also unable to grasp the rudiments of reading and writing as imparted to her by another slave who has been hired for the purpose. She can only babble incoherently, nodding negatively to Murchison's barrage of questions about the place of hiding—somewhere in the house, the barn, the fields, and so on. She cannot lead him to the place, either; she seems to require words. Murchison, meanwhile, loses portions of his estate to other claimants and gradually loses his grip over the finances as well as his own mind.

When the narrator sees them, they are two old and demented combatants locked together in a decades-long lethal battle over a secret unable to be revealed. The story ends a year or so later when the narrator visits the plantation again to discover that Murchison has died and the property is now in the hands of Murchison's nephew. The door is opened to the narrator by Viney. When the narrator asks for the master of the house, Viney replies in words that are not inarticulate that he is within. The astonished narrator discovers through Julius that upon Murchison's death, Viney resumed speaking and had immediately revealed the secret hiding place to the nephew. The papers were under the massive oak armchair, grand as a throne, which old Murchison had sat upon all his life, even as he ruled the estate with violence and authority.

The interest of this folkloric tale lies not in the faithful recording of black dialect, the motivations of the characters, the plot device of power and vengeance, or the generic trick ending of the tale, but in the way the articulation of language and law is enforced as silence as much as it is menaced by silence. The tale provides an imaginary forum to which I shall return periodically for thinking through the spacing between language and law and the limits of the latter. The story also raises related questions as to what it means to be a subject "before the law" and how language and law are articulated by power as power over life. Undoubtedly, slavery is paradigmatic of a state where the law simply does not apply to certain lives by declaring them to be "slaves." A slave, by definition, then, is a human person stripped of his/her political existence, thereby reduced to a state of nature, which is to be exposed to an arbitrary and de facto law.[2] Therefore, Murchison may cut off Viney's tongue without being culpable in any way, and Viney has no recourse to a law that does not recognize her as a subject and treats her as property. As the narrator says, "there was no one to say him nay. The law made her his. It was a lonely house, and no angel of mercy stayed his hand" (Chesnutt, "The Dumb Witness," 165). While slaves in general were denied the benefits of reading and writing, thereby making it impossible for them to enter into contracts, Viney's punishment intends to go even further, to deny her language itself and to deprive her of speaking. It intends to condemn her to a living death, where she is effectively shut up inside herself, unable to communicate to another. The singularity of her intended punishment targets her in her illiteracy where her humanity is at its most vulnerable. To underline this potential of the law to target the singular spot of vulnerable humanity, for animalization, is also to discover the continuity in terms of structural violence among institutions that have vastly differing histories and economies, such as Southern slavery, the Nazi concentration camp, the Middle East crisis, and the contemporary war on terror. Thus, in order to understand how the violence of the law is exercised, it is necessary to turn to the secret of its topological structure.

Law's Secret: The State of Exception

Before we take up the structural relation between language and law in order to broach the question of whether language can be liberated from its function as the foundation of the law, let us revisit the notion of the secret. This time, however, the secret will be something other than a synecdoche for the private, Abrahamic sphere of the singular face-to-face with God. Does law—that is, the juridical apparatus by which human beings are granted the status of legal subject[3]—have a secret? If it is a secret, it is what is called an "open secret"—one that Agamben suggests has a lengthy genealogy in political thought, as lengthy as the history of sovereignty, pertaining to the "state of exception." The "secret," however, refers not so much to the sovereign's right to declare the exception as to the paradoxical topology of the law, whereby the outside of the law (anomia) is included as an exclusion within it. For Agamben, such a topology of the law enables the acknowledged and extreme right of law not only to *enforce* the rule of law, but also to *suspend* its own application, thereby rendering the inside and the outside of law absolutely undecidable. Agamben refers to Carl Schmitt's *Political Theology* as offering a theory of modern constitutional power that defines the sovereign as the only entity invested with the right to decide on a state of exception. Agamben's interpretation and redeployment of this "secret kernel" as the constitutive structure of the law marks a major intervention in the contemporary critiques of sovereignty.

Agamben's contribution, it may be said, is fundamentally a development of Benjamin's Eighth Thesis in "The Theses in the Philosophy of History," where Benjamin famously writes, "The tradition of the oppressed teaches us that the 'state of exception' in which we live is the rule. We must arrive at a concept of history that corresponds to this fact. Then we will have the production of a real state of exception as a task." In his essay "The Messiah and the Sovereign: The Problem of Law in Walter Benjamin," published three years before *Homo Sacer*, Agamben dwells not so much on Benjamin's appropriation of Schmitt's theory of the state of exception (the debate between Schmitt and Benjamin is treated in a chapter in *State of Exception*) as on the relevance of his altered reading to a concept of messianic time. Clearly, Agamben's interest in the question of the exception and the law is from the get-go to clear a space for the thought of the law's fulfillment or its paradoxical restoration to any future possibility. His genealogy of the state of exception and the political and ethical implications that attend upon its critique bear a signature that differs markedly from Derrida's. Postponing the necessary discussion here of Agamben's view of messianic time and its difference from Derrida's notion of messianicity without messianism, let us first briefly consider the concept of the exception as Agamben's doctrine of biopolitics.

The concept of the state of exception refers to a political situation that in English and American law is called a state of emergency—a state that can be summarily understood as the suspension of the law (i.e., the Constitution) or the norms of law. Agamben's works, particularly in *State of Exception*, testify to the salience of this concept within the history of political and juridical thought, as it raises central questions in relation to the very nature of political institutions, such as the nature of legality, the nature of the absolute sovereign right by which a given authority declares a state of emergency, the relation of sovereign power to law as constituted, the contingency of norms and civil rights, and so on. Debates around the state of exception, as Agamben demonstrates,[4] center necessarily on the constitutionality of suspending the Constitution. There are those who see the decision of the sovereign as entirely within the purview of the law—that is, a suspension of the Constitution in order to protect the Constitution—and those who see the suspension of the Constitution as the revolutionary moment when a constituting power comes to the fore. What is important in either case is the paradoxical location of the sovereign. This is paradoxical in the following sense: insofar as the kernel of sovereignty as the final juridical authority is this absolute right to suspend the Constitution, it is itself outside the law. In other words, as Agamben puts it in the opening pages of *Homo Sacer*, "The paradox of sovereignty consists in the fact the sovereign is, at the same time, outside and inside the juridical order." Further, he writes,

> If the sovereign is truly the one to whom the juridical order grants the power of proclaiming a state of exception and, therefore, of suspending the order's own validity, then "the sovereign stands outside the juridical order and, nevertheless, belongs to it, since it is up to him to decide if the constitution is to be suspended *in toto*" (Schmitt, *Politische Theologie*, p.13). The specification that the sovereign is "at the same time outside and inside the juridical order" (emphasis added) is not insignificant: the sovereign, having the legal power to suspend the validity of the law, legally places himself outside the law. This means that the paradox can also be formulated this way: "the law is outside itself," or: "I, the sovereign, who am outside the law, declare that there is nothing outside the law." (Agamben, *Homo Sacer*, 15; 21)

Agamben's stress on the concept of the state of exception is on its peculiar topology, whereby "there is nothing outside the law." In other words, his focus is on how power is exercised by sovereignty through its own suspension as the "sovereign ban." In fact, a characteristic of modern power, he suggests, is not the exercise of its direct punitive capacity, but rather by its capacity to create zones of lawlessness or anomie through a variety of methods, such as suspension of all legal codes (basic civil and human rights, including homicide and habeas corpus); deliberate neglect of people, abandoning and exposing them to arbitrary violence; and denationalizing citizens, as for instance in a concentration camp or internment camps for refugees. In the state of exception, the law is not in effect; it is suspended, but it is in force as de facto power. In the exception, the law's force is disclosed through and as silence. As Agamben writes in *The Time That Remains*, "It is important to remember that in the exception, what is excluded from the norm does not simply have no bearing on the law; on the contrary, the law maintains itself in relation to the exception in the form of its own self-suspension. The norm is applied, so to speak, to the exception in dis-applying itself, in withdrawing itself from it" (Agamben, *The Time That Remains*, 104–5). Everything "outside of the law" is inside the law's purview. Agamben's main point about the law is that, given the anomie at its heart, its capacity to ban or expose the very life of human beings beyond every political, social, and civil identity by utterly depoliticizing and consigning them to an absolutely minimal, animal, or inhuman state of survival or nonsurvival, discloses the secret nucleus of the law. And what is this nucleus? It is the ancient trajectory of sovereignty to not merely capture but also found itself on that aspect of a human being that is ostensibly excluded from or irrelevant to the polis—life, mere life at its most naked, animal, inhuman, biological, private, and impersonal level. (Agamben suggests the Greek term *zōe*, as distinguished from *bios*, as a genealogical term to refer to this basic sense of life.) To sketch a more graphic analogy, we can say that the law has the capacity, the potentiality, to skin or gut human beings—to separate political face (one's aspect) from one's animal or inhuman flesh. Significant to this analysis is the powerful structural analogy that Agamben notes between the sovereign and bare life or "homo sacer" who is "sacred" or set apart from the application of religious and juridical law. And that analogy is precisely the capacity of being included in the law through an exclusion from its application. In both cases, something like a "bare life" (*bête*?) in its difference, in its separation from the qualified life of the political norm (*bios*), secretly founds the force and violence of the law.

Thus, in modernity—as epitomized by the concentration camp—there is a total eclipse of life by the law or, to phrase it differently, there is a total union of life and law. Borrowing from Foucault, Agamben terms this unconditional union biopolitical. According to Agamben, the concentration camp is the paradigm of contemporary politics insofar as the law is increasingly experienced as silent and inert but in force as de facto power. The relevance of this contemporary paradigm to the political economy of Southern U.S. slavery as much as to the Nazi concentration camp is unmistakable. However, the case of Southern slavery introduces a complication that I cannot pursue here in the sense that, for the slave, the inaccessibility of the law was usually but not consistently legislated and enforced, whereas apropos the Nazi concentration camp, the law is in force by not signifying. If the camp is a site of violence as pure abandonment, where criminal impunity reigns, slavery presents a face of violence where the same impunity prevails through legal dictum and abandonment.

In all cases, the precise violence of the law includes (i.e., subjugates) through exclusion, thereby disclosing its greatest force when it maintains silence. The pungency of Chesnutt's tale arises from the narrative's disclosure of the silence of the law as force (the exception) and enforcement (punishment). In other words, the intended punishment reduces the illiterate woman to mere animal voice, and we discern something of the ways in which the structure of language as a necessary relation to silence is utilized by power. For Agamben, the fundamental political task would be to address this lethal juridicization and capture of a "bare" life stripped and isolated from its political form by the law's withdrawal or silence. (If, as Agamben writes in *Death and Language*, human language is the negation of animal voice, then Viney is effectively exiled not only from the law but also from humanness.)

To turn to that aspect of the tale whereby precisely this structure of the law as silence also provides a tactic of emptying power of its force is to raise the "big" question: that of justice or ethics, or the event.

Agamben's political ontology emerges from his analysis of the sovereign decision (capacity for silence) as the pivotal structure of the law and its potentiality to produce bare life. His commitment to what might be termed an "ethical-anarchic"[5] view of the event, of a community that remains or survives the law—in other words, his approach to thinking the structure of messianic time—differs markedly from that of deconstruction and what Derrida terms "the promise," the a-venir, the messianic(ity) without messianism, and so on, without, however, giving up on repetition and nonpresence. And in order to assess the stakes (which are far from being trivial), it will be necessary to grasp on his own terms, without reductive comparisons and false choices, where each thinker situates the ethical question and what that implies about his approach to the structural link or spacing between law and language. Thus, it behooves us to turn, if briefly, to Derrida's diagnosis and approach to the law and the decision.

Justice and Law: The Undecidable

Derrida's approach to the law and sovereignty may be characterized as being more ethicopolitical than biopolitical. One of his most
well-known discussions of these topics is his 1989 "Force of Law: The
'Mystical Foundation of Authority.'" Here, Derrida first establishes the
"differential character of force" (Derrida, "Force of Law," 929),[6] where
potentially "the greatest force and the greatest weakness strangely
enough exchange places" (Derrida, "Force of Law," 929). First of all,
the thought of force is also the problem of translation. The term *Gewalt*
in the title of Benjamin's "Critique of Violence," he specifies, is not well
served when translated merely as violence. "*Gewalt* also signifies, for
Germans, legitimate power, authority, public force" (Derrida, "Force
of Law," 927). For Derrida, the ambivalence of the term generates the
problem of distinguishing legitimate violence, itself unauthorized by
"any anterior legitimacy" (Derrida, "Force of Law," 927), and illegiti-
mate violence. Though he does not explore this difference directly, he
approaches the nonfoundation of right, or the self-legitimating power
of sovereignty to constitute law and establish the norm, by first introducing the ethical problem of justice and then pursuing the issue
through a close reading of Benjamin's "Critique of Violence."

As is well known, for Derrida, the nature of the law as self-
legitimating right exceeds the opposition between "convention and nature" and thereby opens itself to being constructed and deconstructed.
In fact, this nonfoundation of the law makes deconstruction possible.
However, he writes, "Justice in itself, if such a thing exists, outside or
beyond law, is not deconstructible. No more than deconstruction itself, if such a thing exists. Deconstruction is justice" (Derrida, "Force
of Law," 945). The implication of distinguishing law from justice, and
regarding the latter a metaphor for a procedure of disclosing the nonpresence of the law, is that justice as such cannot be. Justice is not some
utopian condition or even an ideal. To put it more prosaically, while the
ethical call to justice must be heeded, there can be no "justice in itself"
(Derrida, "Force of Law," 945). Justice is the trace that haunts the law as
self-legitimating right and the quotidian application of norms and rules.

In other words, justice, in the way that Derrida develops the
term, is not only the trace but also structurally similar to the sovereign

decision that exceeds the norm. Even though he devotes a chapter of *The Politics of Friendship* to an interrogation of Schmitt's view of the political as organized by a rigid demarcation of friend and enemy, here the parallel with Schmitt's theory of sovereignty is unmistakable. The parallel serves to introduce the problem of "decision without sovereignty" as a certain gesture toward justice. Thus, in "The Force of Law," as well as in the numerous writings on hospitality, friendship, and democracy, Derrida situates the thought of justice in a relation to singularity where the failure of the law as norm necessitates the dilemma of a decision. He writes,

> How are we to reconcile the act of justice that must always concern singularity, individuals, irreplaceable groups and lives, the other or myself *as* other, in a unique situation, with rule, norm, value or the imperative of justice which necessarily have a general form, even if this generality prescribes a singular application in each case? If I were content to apply a just rule and the example for each case, I might be protected by law (*droit*), my action corresponding to objective law, but I would not be just. (Derrida, "Force of Law," 949)

Law, then, enables the legal justice that is calculable insofar as it pertains to the application of a general rule. But justice as responsibility to the other, in its incalculability, raises the dilemma of the decision or the judgment in its encounter with the singularity of the subject before it.

We might well ask, then, what the deconstructive position is on the decision, or, rather, what or how a decision can be a decision without being sovereign? Here we have to grasp what Derrida means by the aporia of the decision. He writes,

> The undecidable, a theme often associated with deconstruction, is not merely the oscillation between two significations or two contradictory and very determinate rules, each equally imperative . . . The undecidable is not merely the oscillation or the tension between two decisions, it is the experience of that which, though heterogeneous, foreign to the order of the calculable and the rule, is still obliged—it is of obligation that we must speak—to give itself up to the impossible decision, while taking account of law and rules. A decision that didn't go through the ordeal of the undecidable would not be a free decision . . . it might be legal; it would not be just. (Derrida, "Force of Law," 963)

Further, in the second part of his essay, Derrida in a sense attends to the concept of the sovereign decision when he commences his reading of Benjamin's influential essay "Critique of Violence." I cannot here rehearse Derrida's meticulous and painstaking deconstruction of Benjamin's terms (such as constitutive and constituted power, the legality of ends and means, and divine and mythic violence), but I shall simply note that the question of justice comes to rest with Benjamin's problematization of the just decision as divine violence.

If earlier he had underlined the inevitability of the undecidable element haunting every decision, in an added complication, Derrida further specifies through his reading of Benjamin that divine violence is justice and on the side of decision, whereas mythic violence is on the side of law or norm and is on the side of indecision. This seeming reversal of attributions, whereby the undecidable is associated with mythic, sovereign, calculable law, and decision with divine, just, and incalculable obligation, does not at all imply an opposition between the two. Rather, this reversal introduces another level of undecidability or uncertainty. Derrida writes,

> To be schematic, there are two violences, two competing *Gewalten*: on one side, decision (just, historical, political and so on); justice beyond *droit* and the state, but without decidable knowledge; on the other, decidable knowledge and certainty in a realm that structurally remains that of the undecidable, of the mythic *droit* of the state. On one side the decision without decidable certainty, on the other the certainty of the undecidable but without decision. In any case, in one form or another, the undecidable is on each side, and is the violent condition of knowledge or action. But knowledge and action are always dissociated. (Derrida, "Force of Law," 1035)

The introduction of nonknowledge into the decision obliged by justice effectively renders justice as such unknowable (without presence). It is, after all, the element that haunts and dislocates the blind calculations of the law. The uncertainty that is here associated with justice is also correlated with constituted law. In his essay "Before the Law," on Kafka's parable of the same title, Derrida discusses the demand for accountability by a law that is prohibited and writes,

Here we know neither *who* nor *what* is the law, *das Gesetz*. This, perhaps, is where literature begins. A text of philosophy, science, or history, a text of knowledge or information, would not abandon a name to a state of not-knowing, or at least it would do so only by accident and not in an essential or constitutive way. Here one does not know the law, one has no cognitive rapport with it; it is neither a subject nor an object *before* which one could take a position. Nothing holds before the law. (Derrida, "Before the Law," 207)

Thus, whether it is justice or the law, which supports but fails it, not-knowing as trace is the inescapable structure of history and politics. For Derrida, such uncertainty or nonknowledge is also the necessary trace of an ethical responsibility toward the other.

Promise of Justice: The Messianic

The consequence of this deconstruction of justice and law, then, is not only *not* indecision but also *not* closure. On the contrary, every decision that goes through the ordeal of not-knowing opens the door to a coming (*avenir*) that is itself utterly and radically undecidable. The messianic opening to the future for Derrida is not only *structural*—a quintessential necessity of the infinite finitude of time, but also, and this despite all indeterminacy, *ethical,* "the *arrivant as justice*" (Derrida, *Specters of Marx,* 28; 56). On one hand, "the messianic" undoubtedly refers with uncompromising clarity to an inescapable condition of living—namely, that time passes, and the next second is always in the coming. There is no going around that condition unless one posits death as the messianic promise, which is to say that there isn't any. On the other hand, the openness to the event renders everything indeterminate—even time and the temporality of livingness. The messianic, then, is a profound confrontation with the historicity of the finite subject—the subject as effect or the *différance* of the "I am mortal," a fundamental syntagm that for Derrida refers to the impossibility of intentional auto-affection. (In fact, another name for the messianic in Derrida is *khōra*.)

In "Faith and Knowledge," Derrida writes,

First name: the *messianic,* or messianicity without messianism. This would be the opening to the future or the coming of the other as the advent of justice, but without horizon of expectation and without prophetic prefiguraton. The coming of the other can only emerge as a singular event when no anticipation sees it coming when the other and death—and radical evil—can come as a surprise at any moment. Possibilities that both open and can always interrupt history, or at least the *ordinary course* of history . . . Interrupting or tearing history itself apart, doing it by deciding, in a decision that can consist in letting the other come and that can take the apparently passive form of the other's decision: even there where it appears in itself, in me, the decision is moreover always that of the other which does not exonerate me of responsibility. The messianic exposes itself to absolute surprise and, even if it always takes the phenomenal form of peace or of justice, it ought, exposing itself so abstractly, be prepared (waiting without awaiting itself) for the best as for the worst . . . An invincible desire for justice is linked to this expectation. By definition, the latter is not and ought not to be certain of anything, either through knowledge, consciousness, conscience, forseeability or any kind of programme as such . . . This justice, which I distinguish from right, alone allows the hope, beyond all "messianisms," of a universalizable culture of singularities. (Derrida, *Faith and Knowledge*, 56; 30–31)[7]

The relation of the messianic to historical time is crucial for Derrida. Thus, when he writes of the possibility that the event may open or interrupt history as we know it, "interrupting or tearing history itself apart," it is to situate the messianic event as the *différance* between the finite and the infinite, the mortal and the immortal, life and death. Thus, it is not at all definitive that the event is "historical," strictly relegated to the logic of temporality, or that it is timeless, or transcendent of time. Distinguishing the eschatological from the teleological, Derrida speaks of the necessity in *Specters of Marx* of calling into question the ontotheological concept of history that governs Western metaphysics. However,

[it is] not in order to oppose it with an end of history or an anhistoricity, but, on the contrary to, in order to show that this onto-theo-archeo-teleology locks up, neutralizes, and finally cancels historicity. It was then a matter of thinking another historicity—not a new history or still less a "new historicism," but another opening of event-ness as historicity that permitted one not to renounce, but on the contrary to open up access to an affirmative thinking of the

messianic and emancipatory promise as promise: as *promise* and not as onto-theological or teleo-eschatological program of design. Not only must one not renounce the emancipatory desire, it is necessary to insist on it more than ever, it seems, and insist on it, moreover, as the very indestructibility of the "it is necessary." (Derrida, *Specters of Marx,* 74–75; 125–26)

It is this thinking of "another historicity," then, that is at the heart of the nonknowledge that accompanies and arrives with the decision. Insofar as history ("as we know it") is always correlated with law, the messianic event as the hope for justice will be in an undecidable relation with law—for we cannot know in advance whether or not the other historicity that the event brings about will imply another law or not. We cannot know in advance the structure of this other historicity.

The pressure placed on the concept of "promise" distinguishes Derrida's thought on the messianic. Though he speaks of the "invincibility" of this promise as justice and so on, the "promise" could not be further from any soteriology. The promise that deconstruction discloses is quintessentially and unsettlingly empty. In *Specters of Marx,* Derrida speaks of the various messianisms: those of the three monotheistic religions that have mobilized in the Middle East "all the forces of the world and whole 'world order' in the ruthless war they are waging against each other, directly, or indirectly" (Derrida, *Specters of Marx,* 58; 100–101). But there is also, "despite so many modern or post-modern denials, a messianic eschatology" (Derrida, *Specters of Marx,* 59; 102) carried within what he calls "the spirit of Marxism." Interestingly, Derrida says that the fact that Marxism and the religious traditions that it repudiates share this common ground does not imply that they must be "simply deconstructed."

> While it is common to both of them, with the exception of the content [but none of them can accept, of course, this *epokhē* of the content, whereas we hold it here to be essential to the messianic in general, as thinking of the other and of the event to come], it is also the case that its formal structure of promise exceeds them or precedes them. Well, what remains irreducible to any deconstruction, what remains as undeconstructible as the possibility of deconstruction is, perhaps, a certain experience of the emancipatory promise; it is perhaps even the formality of a structural messianism, a messianism without religion,

even a messianic without messianism, an idea of justice—which we distinguish from law or right and even from human rights—an idea of democracy—which we distinguish from its current concept and from its determined predicates today. (Derrida, *Specters of Marx*, 59; 102)

Derrida's "structural messianism" as the inseparable promise of the logic of temporal spacing delivers us to an aporia. And "aporia" in Derrida's lexicon is not merely to be without a way. Rather the aporia refers to repetition and responsibility—the necessity that, in fact, "a sort of nonpassive endurance of the aporia [is] the condition of responsibility and of decision" (*Aporias* 16; 37).

Interestingly, from Agamben's perspective, Derrida's conception of the messianic promise as ultimate aporia of justice that enjoins repetition is not sufficient to address the problem of law. Though he, too, is invested in thinking the promise as, in a sense, empty, it has an altogether different tonality from Derrida's. His point of departure to consider the messianic is not the possibility/impossibility of justice as the specter that haunts law, but rather the specter of the state of exception that anchors the norm. As is well known, Agamben decisively situates the thought of the messianic in the Letters of Paul in *The Time That Remains*. Certainly no discussion of the law, whether diagnostic as pertaining to its force or tactical as pertaining to justice or ethics, can be complete without taking this work into account. However, for the sake of clarification, it is necessary to discern the distinction between the biopolitical and deconstructive positions on the *force* of law. For Agamben, it is the interpretation of Kafka's parable "Before the Law" that provides a basis for marking some of these distinctions and their impact on the conception of the messianic as hope, promise, remnant, and so on.

AFTER THE LAW

As is well known, Derrida's essay on Kafka's parable is devoted to a deconstruction of the law (its impossible presence) through a disclosure of its contamination and mutual dependence with the literary. Here, Derrida shows that not only is the foundation and origin of the law the site of fiction but the autonomous foundation of the literary (its expansive freedom of expression) is also entirely a legal fiction. The law prohibits, but what it prohibits is the law itself—in other words, the possibility of its deconstruction. Law and literature dissimulate each other in order to present themselves as separate and discrete significations of a logocentric truth. However, this move also structurally obligates decision to be ruled by uncertainty—to let the undecidable ultimately prevail over decision. It is not certain if what Derrida intends by uncertainty, or the undecidable, is the same as what he intends by the term "indecision." However, despite the radical openness and emphasis on nonknowledge in Derrida (themes that find an echo in Agamben), it is perhaps the necessary contamination of indecision in every decision that leads Agamben to interpret Derrida as ineffectual in his political critique of sovereignty.

Agamben, too, undertakes a reading of "Before the Law," Kafka's parable from *The Trial,* but derives a markedly different consequence from it. Almost as though in response to this interpretation of the law and the event by Derrida, Agamben, in his essay "The Messiah and the Sovereign," discussing the messianic potentiality of the state of exception (as thought by Benjamin), writes,

> The success of deconstruction in our time is founded precisely on its having conceived of the whole text of tradition, the whole law, as a *Geltung ohne Bedeutung,* a being in force without significance. In Scholem's terms, we could say that contemporary thought tends to reduce the law (in the widest sense of the term, which indicates all of tradition in its regulative form) to the state of a Nothing and yet, at the same time, to maintain this Nothing as the "zero point of its content." The law thus becomes ungraspable—but, for this reason, insuperable, ineradicable ("undecidable," in the terms of deconstruction). We can compare the situation of our time to that that of a petrified or paralyzed messianism that, like all messianism, nullifies the law, but then maintains it as the Nothing of Revelation in a perpetual and interminable state of exception, "the 'state of exception' in which we live." (Agamben, *Potentialities,* 170–71; 271)

This comment is an aside in Agamben's article, which primarily examines the relation of Benjamin's concept of messianic time to the decision that declares the state of exception. If in "Before the Law," Derrida was invested in disclosing the *différance* between law and literature as a "topographical system" (Derrida, "Before the Law," 201), Agamben in this essay suggests that the question of messianic time and the exception is located at an interstice where philosophy and religion are brought into their greatest proximity in their confrontation with the law (Agamben, *Potentialities*, 163; 255). To put it simply, any sustained thought or practice that deals with the radical finitude of time would necessarily be a decisive encounter with the law. Through a detailed reading of the exchange between Scholem and Benjamin on the structure of the law before the Fall and after the event of redemption that engages the Jewish mystical tradition as well as Kafka's work, Agamben suggests that Scholem, in a sense, fails to grasp the true import of messianism. He writes that Scholem's reading of Kafka's conception of the law as "being in force without significance" and "defines not only the state of the Torah before God but also and above all our current relation to law—the state of exception, according to Benjamin's words, in which we live. Perhaps no other formula better expresses the conception of law that our age confronts and cannot master" (Agamben, *Potentialities*, 170; 264). In other words, Derrida, like Scholem, leaves the law in the inert but pernicious state where its force prevails without legality or legitimacy. The Benjaminian position, he suggests, goes further toward a more "perfect nihilism that does not let validity survive beyond its meaning but instead, as Benjamin writes of Kafka 'succeeds in finding redemption in the overturning of the Nothing'" (Agamben, *Potentialities*, 171; 266). This overturning entails thinking the figure of the Messiah as double—one that is vanquished by evil and another that triumphs over it. To adopt this perspective, Agamben suggests, is to enable an alternative reading of Kafka's parable. If other commentators have read the man from the country who stands before the law hoping to gain entrance to it as ultimately failing in his pursuit, Agamben argues the possibility of the opposite meaning:

> The interpreters seem to forget, in fact, precisely the words with which the story ends: "no one else could enter here, since this door was destined for you alone. Now I will go and close it [*ich gehe jetzt und schliesse ihn*]." If it is true that the door's very openness constituted, as we saw, the invisible power and specific "force" of the law, then it is possible to imagine that the entire behavior of the man from the country is nothing other than a complicated and patient strategy to have the door closed in

order to interrupt the law's being in force. The final sense of the legend is thus not, as Derrida writes, that of an "event that succeeds in not happening" (or that happens in not happening: "an event that happens not to happen," *un evenement qui arrive a ne pas arriver*), but rather just the opposite: the story tells how something has really happened in seeming not to happen. (Agamben, *Potentialities*, 173–74; 269–70)

The double figure of the messiah as the death of the man from the country and the closing of the door of the law, Agamben suggests, corresponds to "a real state of exception" of which Benjamin speaks in the Eighth Thesis. In this conception of the *eskhaton*, Agamben specifies, there is a certain belonging to not only the time of history and its law but also the ending of this time and the law. Rather than a situation in which the law is in force and "events indefinitely differ from themselves" (Agamben, *Potentialities*, 174; 270), we apprehend the messianic event as a "bi-unitary figure" (Agamben, *Potentialities*, 174; 270). "Only in this way can the event of the Messiah coincide with historical time yet at the same time not be identified with it, effecting in the *eskhaton* that 'small adjustment' in which, according to the rabbi's saying told by Benjamin, the messianic kingdom consists" (Agamben, *Potentialities*, 174; 270).

Agamben repeats with further elaborations this interpretation of Kafka's parable in *Homo Sacer*. There he writes,

> It is precisely concerning the sense of this being in force (and of the state of exception that it inaugurates) that our position distinguishes itself from that of deconstruction. Our age does indeed stand in front of language just as the man from the country in the parable stands in front of the door of the Law. What threatens thinking here is the possibility that thinking might find itself condemned to infinite negotiations with the doorkeeper or, even worse, that it might end by itself assuming the role of the doorkeeper who, without really blocking the entry, shelters the Nothing onto which the door opens. (Agamben, *Homo Sacer*, 54; 63)

In *State of Exception*, Agamben elaborates on the exchange between Scholem and Benjamin on the state of the law in Kafka's texts and its implications for political messianism. Benjamin's statement in his essay on Kafka that the "law which is studied but no longer practiced is the gate to justice" (Agamben, *State of Exception*, 63) figures the law "as a sort of remnant" (Agamben, *State of Exception,* 63). But inquiring after what it might mean to figure the law in this manner—that is, "what becomes of the law after its messianic fulfillment?" (Agamben, *State of Exception,* 63)—Agamben is careful to specify that it is not in any case the full presence of justice. Rather, "the decisive point here is that law—no longer practiced, but studied—is not justice, but only the gate that leads to it" (Agamben, *State of Exception,* 64). It is this opening of a passage through the closing of the gate of law that Agamben suggests is prevented by Derrida and Scholem's maintenance of the empty and spectral form of the law. Kafka's characters, on the other hand, seek not only to study the law, which means to "deactivate it, [but] to 'play' with it" (Agamben, *State of Exception,* 64).

Thus, Agamben's emphasis on the violence of the decision leads him to be politically and ethically committed to a complex image of deactivating the law. To fully understand this "image" of deactivation as study or "play" requires that we take up Agamben's book on messianic time, *The Time That Remains,* to which I shall turn momentarily. However, we cannot fail to ask what Derrida himself says about the problem of the law and whether deconstruction can countenance the possibility of deactivating it. Though one may dispute or defend Agamben's reading of Derrida's position as leading to paralysis before the law conceived as a problem, the true import of Agamben's critique undoubtedly arises from the disparity in their attitudes to the law. The point is that it is not at all clear that Derrida would agree with Agamben's diagnosis of the law.

To focus for the moment only on his last writings on the question of sovereignty (namely, his 2002–2003 seminar notes, *The Beast and the Sovereign,* volumes 1 and 2), in contradistinction to Agamben's antinomianism, Derrida in fact asserts that "we can't take on the concept of sovereignty without also threatening the value of liberty" (Derrida, *Beast and Sovereign,* 401).[8] We may, for instance, be opposed to fences and enclosures that confine beasts and the mentally ill, but "who will dare militate for a freedom of movement without limit, a liberty without limit? And this without law?" (Derrida, *Beast and Sovereign,* 301). The deconstruction of the norms of sovereignty, Derrida says, is always in a relational double bind insofar as "the choice and the decision are not between indivisible sovereignty and indivisible non-sovereignty but between several divisions, distributions economies (-nomy, nomos, nemeinmeaning . . . distribution and division), economies of a divisible sovereignty" (Derrida, *Beast and Sovereign*, 402). The task, then, is to think not a postsovereignty or the inoperativity of the law, but "unconditionality . . . without indivisible sovereignty" (Derrida, *Beast and Sovereign*, 402). The difficulty of the task lies in the fact that "sovereignty has always given itself out to be indivisible, and therefore absolute and unconditional" (Derrida, *Beast and Sovereign*, 402).

Deconstruction and Biopolitics

Derrida's problematic is clearly very differently configured from that of either Foucault or Agamben. As can be expected, it is in greater continuity with his earlier work on the animal and on the question of what is "proper" to man. Thus, his field of inquiry is the instability of the categories that refer to the sovereign and the animal, each of which carries at different times and ways the trace of a certain *bêtise*. Read alongside Agamben and Foucault, Derrida clearly approaches the concept of sovereignty not in terms of the historicity of power as epistemology, but in ontological terms, where the question of human and animal propriety is dislocated by the fable of "the right of the stronger." In other words, the political problematic here is the relation (as always with Derrida) between force on the one hand and the necessity and impossibility of an irreducible justice on the other, which he insists quintessentially resists deconstruction. In the first volume of the seminar, Derrida proceeds by positing an analogy between the sovereign and "*la bête*" or the beast (which he distinguishes from the animal) and suggests that what "sovereign and beast seem to have in common [is] their being-outside-the-law" (Derrida, *Beast and Sovereign*, 38). Further, he says,

> It is as though both of them were situated by definition at a distance from or above the laws, in nonrespect for the absolute law, the absolute law that they make or that they are but they do not have to respect. Being-outside-the-law can, no doubt, on the one hand (and this is the figure of sovereignty), take the form of being-above-the-laws, and therefore take the form of the Law itself, of the origin of laws . . . but being-outside-the-law can also, on the other hand (and this is the figure of what is most often understood by animality or bestiality) . . . situate the place where the law does not appear, or is not respected, or gets

violated . . . There is between sovereign, criminal, and beast a sort of obscure and fascinating complicity, or even a worrying mutual attraction, a worrying familiarity, an *unheimlich*, uncanny reciprocal haunting. (Derrida, *Beast and Sovereign*, 38)

Given the way in which he structures the problematic of sovereignty (norm and excess), Derrida acknowledges the state of exception and its power to depoliticize as the potentiality of sovereignty, but not necessarily as the secret kernel of the force of law. Rather than opposing sovereignty (in the name of humanitarianism or antihumanitarianism), he calls for a "slow and differentiated deconstruction" (Derrida, *Beast and Sovereign*, 113):

> It cannot be a matter, under the pretext of deconstruction, of purely and simply, frontally, opposing sovereignty. There is not SOVEREIGNTY or THE sovereign. There is not THE beast and THE sovereign. There are different and sometimes antagonistic forms of sovereignty, and it is always in the name of one that one attacks another . . .
>
> In a certain sense, there is no contrary of sovereignty, even if there are things other than sovereignty. Even in politics (and the question remains of knowing if the concept of sovereignty is political through and through)—even in politics, the choice is not between sovereignty and nonsovereignty, but among several forms of partings, partitions, divisions, conditions that come along to broach a sovereignty that is always supposed to be indivisible and unconditional. Whence the difficulty, awkwardness, aporia even, and the slowness, the always unequal development of such a deconstruction. This is less than ever the equivalent of a destruction. But recognizing that sovereignty is divisible, that it divides and partitions, even where there is any sovereignty left, is already to begin to deconstruct a pure concept of sovereignty that presupposes indivisibility. (Derrida, *Beast and Sovereign*, 114)

Clearly, there is no unified concept of THE Sovereign or THE Beast to be found in either Foucault or Agamben insofar as these concepts are always effects of regimes of truth and right generated by discourse and knowledge. More specifically, power, or the force of law, is not necessarily associated with presence or purity. And this is particularly the case with modern power, which is unlocalizable, temporal, and nonsubjective. In a sense, modern power, as that which is knowable only in its functioning, is not so much indifferent as apposite to the deconstruction of presence and thus could be viewed as "post-metaphysical." Very schematically, it can be said that it is the historicity of the metaphysics of presence and not that of power that concerns Derrida. In *Of Grammatology*, once again in his debate with Levi-Strauss, Derrida folds the *différance* of power into the logo-phono-centric critical schema. Moreover, given the privileging of technology in this critical schema, one cannot expect deconstruction to charge the law and its *dispositifs* of structural oppression. It only follows, then, that Derrida will refute some of the basic premises and even inflate the logic of some of the terms of biopolitics, especially as developed by Agamben.

Thus, Derrida refutes the notion that there can ever be any conceptual separability between a notion of biological life and political life—that is, *zōē* and *bios*—either in the Greek texts (particularly Aristotle, whom Agamben cites) or, for that matter, in the long history of metaphysics and political sovereignty. By this philological and genealogical refutation, he also implies a dismissal of the problematic of *Homo Sacer*. Obviously, it is not that Derrida wishes to claim some kind of indivisible self-identity to the concept of life, thereby refusing a difference within the signifier "life." His debate with Agamben turns around his sense that the latter "wants absolutely to define this specificity by putting his money on the concept of 'bare life,' which he identifies with zōē, in opposition to bios" (Derrida, *Beast and Sovereign*, 433).[9] And Derrida suggests that this ill-judged investment falsifies the argument of the book as a whole. What is confounding here is whether any concept of biopolitics can admit of a simple identity between bare life, which is a thoroughly political concept insofar as it is produced as an effect of power, and zōē, a term whose epistemological status is ostensibly secured by a discourse of natural science. In other words, the force of biopolitics (in Foucault or Agamben's terms) derives from its capacity to work on a powerful norm—namely, organic biological life—to bring it into a "zone of indistinction" with *bios* and thereby produce bare life (or a so-called state of nature). The key point can be stated in Derridean terms as follows: biopower depends on a contamination, the trace, the *différance* between biological (natural) life and political (human) life, in order to produce the specter of bare life. The category of the "homo sacer" or bare life is not a preexisting natural category that depends for its identity upon its opposition to political life. On the contrary, bare life is produced by sovereignty as an inverse image—an excluded inclusion or an included exclusion. As Agamben writes in *State of Exception*,

> If it is true that the articulation between life and law, between anomie and *nomos*, that is produced by the state of exception is effective though fictional, one can still not conclude from this that somewhere either beyond or before juridical apparatuses there is an immediate access to something whose fracture and impossible unification are represented by these apparatuses. There are not *first* life as a natural biological given and anomie as the state of nature, and *then* their implication in law through the state of exception. On the contrary, the very possibility of distinguishing life and law, anomie and *nomos*, coincides with their articulation in the biopolitical machine. Bare life is a product of the machine and not something that preexists it, just as law has no court in nature or in the divine mind. Life and law, anomie and *nomos auctoritas* and *potestas*, result from the fracture of something to which we have no other access than through the fiction of their articulation and the patient work that, by unmasking this fiction, separates what it had claimed to unite. But disenchantment does not restore the enchanted thing to its original state: According to the principle that purity never lies at the origin, disenchantment gives it only the possibility of reaching a new condition. (Agamben, *State of Exception*, 87–88)

Derrida may not dispute the relevance of this detail, but he probably would still oppose the premise of biopolitics: the idea that, be it Western metaphysics (Agamben) or modern epistemology (Foucault), the *différance* within life could become a *dispositif* of power. In a sense, what is implicit in Derrida's rebuttal of Agamben is that the latter's insistence that biopolitical sovereignty captures the divisibility of life and manipulates it as an ultimate exercise of power is untenable. Derrida seems to read such a view of the functioning of power and the *dispositif* as a misguided positing of watertight homogeneous categories in philosophy, if not in nature, but we cannot afford to ignore the fact that biopolitics as a form of power/knowledge has a certain historicity. However, Derrida finds it problematic that, for Agamben, the problem of power's use of life as a *dispositif* can be traced beyond contemporary modalities of knowledge to the discourse of Western metaphysics, which, given its notion of the polis, necessarily regards life in terms of certain separable (and therefore collapsible) categories.[10] It is tempting to sum up by saying that, ultimately, when the chips are down, the quarrel (if that is what it is) between the two perspectives may be salient for the history of thought but not for politics. But unfortunately, I don't think such a separation can be made.

So what in fact does Derrida say about life and its *différance*? In the sixth session of his seminar, Derrida, in the context of a discussion on the notion of "stupidity," or *la bêtise*, suggests that "at bottom what is irreducibly bête . . . is life pure and simple, which is both infinitely bête and cunning, intelligent, bête and anything but bête: it is the living in life itself which outplays the opposition between bêtise and its supposed contrary, the decidable limit between the two, both in what is called man and in what is called the animal, the living being in general that is both bête and not bête, idiotic and cunning, naïve and smart, etc." (Derrida, *Beast and Sovereign*, 240). In other words, Derrida here suggests that the *différance*, the trace of life, which is the "living in life," is *bête*, as it is a form of nonknowledge, which in its "impurity, nonrigor, essential incompleteness" (Derrida, *Beast and Sovereign*, 239) is, he says, the very inspiration for the seminar. Derrida's emphasis on the trace of living in life not only enables the deconstruction of the human and the animal through the specter of *la bêtise* but also discloses the implication of life in the metaphysics of presence through the notion of the "living present." Thus, he underlines that it is not life but the phenomenological notion of the living present that should be deconstructed. In the context of his discussion of Paul Celan's speech "The Meridian," he says,

> If I use, emphasize, the expression "living present" (*lebendige Gegenwart*: living now), an expression to which Husserl, as you know, gave a phenomenological status and a sort of letter of nobility in philosophy, it is of course in order to make a strategically essential and necessary reference to Husserlian phenomenology and the transcendental phenomenology of the time . . . But it is above all to interrogate one more time this way of naming life, or more precisely the living being: not Life, the Being or Essence or Substance of something like LIFE, but the living being, the presently living being, not the substance Life that remains in life, but the attribute "living" to qualify or determine the present, the

now, a now that is supposedly essentially living, presently living, now as living (*die lebendige Gegenwart*). (Derrida, *Beast and Sovereign*, 292)

In several places, Derrida insists that death must be inscribed into a concept of life, but not by positing a stark opposition between the two. In a footnote in *Specters of Marx*, he suggests that the "very alternative (life and/or death)," should be rethought in terms of survival "or of a return of the dead (neither life nor death) on the sole basis of which one is able to speak of 'living subjectivity' (in opposition to its death): to speak of it but also to understand that it can, itself, speak and speak itself, leave traces or legacies beyond the living present of its life" (Derrida, *Specters of Marx*, 187).[11]

How does such a perspective on life—life as haunted by an undecidable trace of living—compare to the biopolitical perspective? Once again, to put it in reductive terms, it is the shift in emphasis on power versus presence that comes to matter. For Foucault and Agamben, it is the trace of living—its very undecidability, its impure preinscription in death—that is the locus of biopower. In *Society Must Be Defended*, Foucault's genealogy also traces the shift in the way death as an event is incorporated by power from the sovereign's public death sentence, to its privatization by the regime of disciplines, and finally to its trivialization. This trajectory is also accompanied by a shift that sees death as heterogeneous to life (it comes from elsewhere like the plague) to the modern view where death is not only banal but ubiquitous and requires vigilance (like a virus that must be managed and controlled).

Also in his archaeology of the medical sciences, Foucault pinpoints the moment of what he terms as the volatilization of death in terms of the new vitalism inaugurated by Bichat in the nineteenth century. In *The Birth of the Clinic*, he traces the shift in the medical gaze of the clinic from a reading of symptoms and signs on the surface of the body to the dissecting gaze of pathological anatomy that "opens up a few corpses." The understanding of death undergoes a change as well:

> Death is therefore multiple, and dispersed in time: it is not that absolute, privileged point at which time stops and moves back; like disease itself. It has a teeming presence that analysis may divide into time and space; gradually, here and there, each of the knots breaks, until organic life ceases, at least in its major forms, since long after the death of the

individual, miniscule, partial deaths continue to dissociate the islets of life that still subsist. In natural death, the animal life is extinguished first: first sensorial extinction, then the slowing down of brain activity, the weakening of locomotion, rigidity of the muscles and diminution of their contractility, quasi-paralysis of the intestines, and finally immobilization of the heart. (Foucault, *Birth of the Clinic,* 142)

With Bichat, there are multiple deaths that are partialized into "successive envelopes" (Foucault, *Birth of the Clinic,* 143), and the study of the causes of phthisis and decomposition provides a privileged perspective on the organism. Foucault writes, "Death is the great analyst that shows the connexions by unfolding them, and bursts open the wonders of genesis in the rigour of decomposition" (Foucault, *Birth of the Clinic,* 144). Thus, we can extrapolate from Foucault's discussion that insofar as medical science ignores the difference between life and death, it opens itself to a political decision. The solution, of course, is not to fortify the differences, but to interrogate the ways in which power appropriates the trace and, as Agamben might say, to free it for another use.

In both Foucault and Agamben, but particularly in the latter, the notion of survival as the wedge that deconstructs life and death takes on a different tonality—a much less benign one—in that biopolitics is nothing if not the proliferation of such undecidable apparitions. Whether it is the neomort in Agamben's schema of the homo sacer or the suicide state that Foucault identifies as the secret of the Nazi regime, the nondead is as much a locus of the political as the living present. In other words, the biopolitical perspective requires that we distinguish between the specter of power and social control and a certain spectral remainder of power. If the former is the trace as manipulated by power, then the latter is that which silently drops out of this field of management and sometimes even voids it of force and significance. To grasp this differing sense of survival, it is necessary to turn to the question of silence within language and its effect on the law.

The question can be formulated following the premise that the discursivity of the law and its unconditionality depend upon the absolute relational structure of language. In other words, this premise refers first and foremost to the absolute juridicization of speech that refers not only to the silence of the sovereign decision but also to the legal protection of taciturnity "the right to remain silent." Thus, if both speaking and not speaking are related to the law as inclusion and exclusion, how might we conceive of a relation to (or a way to be in) language where its juridicization, which serves the separation of human and inhuman, is no longer effective or deactivated? Can silence be discerned as that which neutralizes the law? Can it function as the active force of deactivation—that is, the separation of law and language? What is the relation of such a separation to the thought of the messianic promise or of messianic time?

It is necessary, then, to take up in earnest the spacing between law and language as the site of the biopolitical (state of exception) and the time of the messianic promise. This spacing can also be conceived in terms of the relation between the structure of the political state of exception (as potentiality of law) and the alterity of silence (as potentiality of language).

SHIBBOLETH, OR SOVEREIGNTY OF LANGUAGE

First, a bare and fundamental question: what is the relation, as conceptualized within deconstruction and biopolitics, between language and the force of law?

In a sense, all of Derrida's work, particularly his deconstruction of Saussurean linguistics with its dependence on a nature/culture opposition, can be said to revolve around this question, insofar as the law always bears a relation to the instituted truth. However, where the juridical law in particular is concerned, Derrida, in "Force of Law,"[12] suggests that this relation always touches on the possibility of dispensing justice. There must be a shared language for the law to function as a legal force. Thus, he writes, "It is unjust to judge someone who does not understand the language in which the law is inscribed or the judgment pronounced, etc." (Derrida, "Force of Law," 951). The problem, then, is the impossibility of sharing the same idiom. For Derrida, it is not only that a scenario of perfect sharing of language, of having a language in every sense common, is impossible but also that the very dispensation of justice is predicated on "man as a speaking animal, in the sense that we, men, give to this world language" (Derrida, "Force of Law," 951). Such a predication of the law's function of dispensing justice, Derrida asserts, necessarily excludes the possibility of "injustice or violence toward an animal, even less toward a vegetable or a stone. An animal can be made to suffer, but we would never say, in a sense considered proper, that it is a wronged subject, the victim of a crime, of a murder, of a rape or a theft, of a perjury . . . There have been, there are still, many 'subject' among mankind who are not recognized as subjects and who receive this animal treatment" (Derrida, "Force of Law," 951). For Derrida, this inherently unjust situation in the founding of justice is a symptom of what he terms, in his interview with Jean-Luc Nancy "Eating Well: Or the Calculation of the Subject," "carno-phallogocentrism" (114), or a culture of carnivorous sacrifice that is essential to "the founding of the intentional subject" (Derrida, "Force of Law," 953). Significantly, Derrida does not correlate this primary exclusion of the improper nonhuman animal from justice (or the law) with the structure of the sovereign decision, thereby salvaging a certain justice from deconstruction and maintaining a relation to law.

Another significant instance when the force of law is mentioned directly in relation to the structure of language is when Derrida discusses the place of the secret or silence. It is, as Derrida says, "the sharing of what is not shared: we know in common that we have nothing in common" (Derrida, A Taste for the Secret, 58). Further, the secret, he suggests, is always political. Structurally, it serves as the threshold between democracy and totalitarianism. Only the secret (not a secret) separates them. In a conversation with Maurizio Ferraris, he says, "I have an impulse of fear or terror in the face of a political space, for example, a public space that makes no room for the secret. For me, the demand that everything be paraded in the public square and that there be no internal forum is a glaring sign of the totalitarianization of democracy. I can rephrase this in terms of political ethics: if a right to the secret is not maintained, we are in a totalitarian space" (Derrida, A Taste for the Secret, 59). By situating the collapse of the distinction between the private and the public in the suspension of the "right" to the secret, and by referring to that situation of indistinction as political and as absolute exposure and terror, Derrida here implicitly correlates the expropriation of the secret to a situation of political emergency when all fundamental rights guaranteed by the Constitution are suspended.

Derrida, however, implies that the ethical and political task is to ensure that the juridical apparatus preserves the right to the secret. In other words, the law is implicitly called upon here to respect the division of public and private. In fact, since Derrida speaks here of right, it is law itself that must within its jurisdiction preserve the secret, but as that which is exempted from its force. The secret here, then, bears a strong resemblance to the juridical "right to silence." From the biopolitical perspective, this view of the secret raises the question of what it might mean to require that the force of law mandate the limit of its own force—to enforce the inviolability of the secret.

In several of his works, most notably in *Homo Sacer* and *State of Exception*, Agamben raises the question of the relation between the force of law and language, sometimes formulating it as a foundation and at others as a structural analogy. In his discussion of the logic of sovereignty in *Homo Sacer*, Agamben illustrates the inside/outside topology of the sovereign exception with the help of two grammatical categories: the exception to the rule, wherein the thing in question is included or belongs to the set by virtue of being excluded from it, and the example of a rule, wherein the thing in question is excluded from the set by virtue of being included or belonging to it. In short, if the exception is an inclusive exclusion, the example is an exclusive inclusion (Agamben, *Homo Sacer*, 21; 26). Agamben then goes on to secure the analogy between the grammatical structure and the structure of sovereignty with a biblical example. Citing the famous episode of "Shibboleth" in Judges 12:6, which pertains to the slaying of the Ephraimites by the Galatians, who distinguish their victims by their distinctive pronunciation of a single word, "Shibboleth," Agamben suggests that "in the Shibboleth, example and exception become indistinguishable. 'Shibboleth' is an exemplary exception or an example that functions as an exception. (In this sense, it is not surprising that there is a predilection to resort to exemplary punishment in the state of exception.)" (Agamben, *Homo Sacer*, 23; 28). While Agamben's example here of the Shibboleth refers to the intimate alliance between the performance of language and law and the lethal effects of juridicized speech, it also underscores the central lawlessness—the anomie within this structure.

More specifically, in *State of Exception*, he indicates that the structural analogy between language and law pertains to the separation between norm and application. Insofar as both language and law in the state of exception can disclose the norm only through its suspension in concrete practice (for instance, the suspension of habeas corpus in concrete practice, which is not uncommon, always discloses the formality of the norm), they found themselves on a central emptiness, a formality that can and also cannot apply to reality. Agamben writes, "It can generally be said that not only language and law but all social institutions have been formed through a process of desemanticization and suspension of concrete praxis in its immediate reference to the real" (Agamben, *State of Exception*, 37). In other words, the coimplication of law and language is founded on the emptiness of meaning and nonreference to reality.

When the nondenotational aspect of language, its pure conventionality as grammar, is suspended as semantic foundation and is instead in force as pure form, what we have is the password. The password (shibboleth) is entirely meaningless in and of itself, but it is precisely in force as meaningless law. For Agamben, this central emptiness is decisive for our understanding of the very history of Western metaphysics. Correlating the space of pure anomie with being and the law with logos, he writes, "everything happens as if both law and *logos* needed an anomic (or alogical) zone of suspension in order to ground their reference to the world of life. Law seems able to subsist only by capturing anomie, just as language can subsist only by grasping the nonlinguistic. In both cases, the conflict seems to concern an empty space: on the one hand, anomie, juridical vacuum, and on the other, pure being, devoid of any determination or real predicate. For law, this empty space is the state of exception as its constitutive dimension" (Agamben, *State of Exception*, 60).

The implication of this capture hardly needs to be spelled out, but Agamben's words immediately prior to his discussion of the difference between authority and formal power (*auctoritas* and *potestas*) provides a simple summation that also expresses an aspect of his political ontology. He writes, "And perhaps the moment has come to try to better understand the constitutive fiction that—in binding together norm and anomie, law and state of exception—also ensures the relation between law and life" (Agamben, *State of Exception*, 73). Perhaps the task of inventing a political praxis, in Agamben's terms, may well be the rescue or the deactivation of the unpronounceable letter, the silenced "h" captured by the Ephramites, from its juridical function. This political project can be even better clarified with reference to one small moment in Derrida's discussion of the nondenotational force of language. In "Shibboleth: For Paul Celan," Derrida, reading the irruption of this Hebrew word within Celan's pluralized German, pauses to decline the word in relation to the sovereignty of language, to the possibility of the poem's very existence. For him, however, the empty password is what fundamentally gives access to the poem, to language. It permits a crossing and lets the poem be. "To inhabit a language, one must already have a Shibboleth at one's disposal" (Derrida, *Sovereignties in Question*, 26). Derrida's sense that this emptiness can be both a crossing and a barring (a limit of discrimination) emphasizes the ultimate undecidability of the emptiness. It is tragically reversible, and "sometimes overtakes the initiatives of subjects" (Derrida, *Sovereignties in Question*, 30), he writes. The subtle difference here between deconstruction and biopolitics can perhaps be said to lie in their different attitudes to this reversibility. For Derrida, the password enables the poem to be within the law, to live, to speak, "[s]o as no longer to be outside the law" (Derrida, *Sovereignties in Question*, 26). For Agamben, however, the poem can perhaps be a poem only insofar as it appropriates the password, so that the password no longer permits or denies but becomes indistinguishable from the poem. The password no longer functions, thereby letting the poem take place.

But let us return to the import of the structural analogy, which lies in its disclosure of the sovereignty of language. How should this complex syntagm—the sovereignty of language—be understood? In *The Beast and The Sovereign*, Derrida cites a passage from Agamben's *Homo Sacer* on this question. Here, Agamben writes with reference to Hegel:

> Language is the sovereign who, in a permanent state of exception, de-clares that there is nothing outside language and that language is always beyond itself. The particular structure of the law has its foundation in [the] presuppositional structure of human language. It expresses the bond of inclusive exclusion to which a thing is subject because of the fact of being in language, of being named. To speak [*dire*] is, in this sense, always to "speak the law" *ius dicere*. (Agamben, *Homo Sacer*, 21; 26)

Derrida comments that this point is true and convincing because it is wholly obvious; moreover, the notion of the presuppositional aspect of language is not only a fundamental tenet in the history of philosophy and any reflection on language but it is anterior to Hegel (Derrida, *Beast and Sovereign*, 93). However, Agamben's particular emphasis on the negativity inherent in language (the structure of the ban) pertains to the *contingency* of the law's overlay of language.

For instance, in a fragment entitled "The Idea of Language II," Agamben offers an interpretation of Kafka's wellknown fable "The Penal Colony" that seems to encapsulate the essence of his thought on the consequences of neutralizing power through severing the link between language and law. He suggests several readings of the fable's ending, wherein the commandant decides to personally demonstrate to the unconvinced visitor the virtues of his exquisite torture-writing apparatus. The phrase that the apparatus was to engrave on his flesh even as it begins to malfunction horribly is "be just." The reading that Agamben finally settles on is the following:

> "Be just" does not refer to the decree the officer has broken, but is rather the instruction that shatters the machine. And the officer is perfectly aware of this . . . he inserts the instruction into the machine in the intention of destroying it. The ultimate meaning of language—the tale now seems to say—is the injunction "Be just; and yet it is precisely the meaning of this injunction that the machine of language is absolutely incapable of getting us to understand. Or, rather, it can do it only by ceasing to perform its penal function, only by shattering into pieces and turning from punisher to murderer. In this way justice triumphs over justice, language over language. That the officer does not find in the machine what others had found is now perfectly understandable: at this point there is nothing left in language for him to understand. (Agamben, *The Idea of Prose*, 117)

Agamben implies that when the law and its penal function are extirpated from language, there is nothing left in language that requires interpretation. It appears that language stands revealed not so much as a medium for law or communication, but as pure mediality itself. The immediate enigma is no doubt how, when, and by what means language can cease to mediate the penal function of the law, thereby disclosing its ultimate potentiality for a justice beyond justice. Justice, or the injunction to "be just," Agamben implies, is a performative speech act that makes happen an event. It can free language from its captivity to the law. In other words, not only is justice a performative that unmasks the limits of law—it also discloses something of law's structural relation to language. Perhaps the stakes lie in the possibility of analyzing the true and fundamental relation between law and language (its power to penalize) and proposing and thinking through the consequences of a thorough disengagement of language from the law. This task, as Agamben conceives it, mediated through Benjamin, would be not to reactivate the law (the exquisite torture-writing machine) to restore it to its original efficacy, but to deactivate it so that it is suspended and no longer in effect. In other words, it is to seize the political state of exception as a means of bringing about a "real" state of exception when the law is rendered inoperative. He writes that "only if it is possible to think the Being of abandonment beyond every idea of law (even that of the empty form of law's being in force without significance) will we have moved out of the paradox of sovereignty toward a politics freed from every ban" (Agamben, *Homo Sacer*, 59; 68). Ultimately, the question that is confronting us here is what it might mean to think through the unconditionality, the absolute relationality of the sovereignty of language. No doubt, this question is not only impossible but appears to border on the nonrational. However, Agamben approaches this issue through a certain use of modal logic.

Language and Contingency

The notion of language's possible contingency appears in *Remnants of Auschwitz* when Agamben thinks the relation between the subject and language. Here he shows that Foucault's archaeology of knowledge, which describes the functioning of language in terms of asemantic statements, in a sense, presupposes the erasure of the subject. In all of Foucault's works, the the subject is an effect and the author a function of enunciation, so that his focus on the modalities of exclusion, focused on what is said and unsaid, that secure discursive formations is a part of his metasemantic project to describe the way statements are eventuated. They are not interested in the fate of the subject per se. Agamben's intervention at this point is to reintroduce the question of the subject as a fundamentally ethical one that can be raised *not* at the site of enunciation per se, which is located between what is said and what is unsaid (which pertains to exclusions), but between the sayable and the unsayable (i.e., pertaining to the possible and the impossible). In other words, he situates the subject at a prior moment where language itself is expressed as contingency—between enunciation and its possibility. Asking "what happens to the living individual who occupies the vacant space of the subject, when he enters into the process of enunciation" (Agamben, *Remnants of Auschwitz*, 142; 132), Agamben specifies this subject position as fundamentally one of possibility or potentiality. The subject who enters enunciation—in other words, Foucault's erased subject—is the manifestation of potentiality, of the ability to have and not have language. Defining contingency as the fundamental modal category of potentiality or possibility in that it expresses being as "to be able not to be," in other words, the subject as one who "can and also can not have language" (and can thereby enter into the plane of enunciation), he shows that the subject of desubjectification is fundamentally one who is denied this possibility. Instead of possibility and contingency ("able to be" and "able not to be"), impossibility as "not being able" penetrates reality, thereby bringing about a condition of necessity, or "not to be able not to be." To be a subject of desubjectification, then, is to be submitted to an impossible necessity or a necessary impossibility. What is important here for our purposes is the notion of the subject's relation to language as expressed through contingency, not necessity or presuppositionality. There is a way to be in language, to negotiate a relation to language, that is not always determined by the ban—the said and the unsaid. This other way is to be in language as potential—"able to be" and "able not to be." Silence, of course, is nothing if not the expression of language's contingency, of its potentiality. In short, the absolute relationality of language is not a condition of necessity, but on the contrary it is the foundation of contingency, and therefore possibility. When silence is understood as the condition of language's potentiality, its contingency, then we have a situation where the law as that which is in force though it is suspended, the empty form of the law, is neutralized and can have no effect.

The topology of this zone of silence that Agamben delineates must be reviewed if we are to grasp it as the site where the subject emerges in and as the contingency of language. Silence as the sign of the contingency of language, of its potentiality, should not be assimilated to the withholding of discourse. If Foucault identifies the archive as the asemantic plane where the modalities, the pathways of the functioning of enunciation, are studied in terms of their exclusions (the archive as a flow chart), Agamben shifts the asemantic plane of study to the existence or the fact of the possibility of enunciation. Silence, then, is not to be located between the said and the unsaid but the sayable and the unsayable—the very possibility that we have language, that there is enunciation. In *Remnants of Auschwitz*, Agamben gives the name "testimony" to this potentiality—not a flow chart but a relation more akin to that between dark and light. He writes,

> In opposition to the *archive*, which designates the system of relations between the unsaid and the said, we give the name *testimony* to the system of relations between the inside and the outside of *langue*, between the sayable and the unsayable in every language—that is, between a potentiality of speech and its existence, between a possibility and an impossibility of speech. To think a potentiality in act *as potentiality*, to think enunciation on the plane of *langue* is to inscribe a caesura in possibility, a caesura that divides it into a possibility and an impossibility, into a potentiality and an impotentiality; and it is to situate a subject in this very caesura. (Agamben, *Remnants of Auschwitz*, 145; 135)

To clarify further, perhaps we can translate Agamben's move to the realm of writing to suggest that it is not the difference between what is written and not written, but that there is writing and no writing.

The political value of silence can be appreciated only if we can approach silence as a modality of being in language that offers a way to neutralize the necessities imposed by the law of discourse. Silence can effect such a neutralization by referring the subject to his/her ability to have and not have language. Perhaps the real opposition to discourse's ability to desemanticize and dehumanize comes not from a subject's location within this law that permits and forbids, thereby questioning and challenging the law in what can only be particular and individual cases, in other words, asserting one's right to speak or remain silent, but from a subject's ability to reach from discursive control all the way back to the potentiality of language—to the fact that one can and also can not have language. This way, one challenges not particular workings of discursive exclusion, but the very law that mandates discourse based on exclusions. This is the logic behind noncooperation movements that aim not so much to challenge or reform the law as to expose and therefore nullify it.

THE WORD OF SILENCE

The discussion so far has been confined to the differences between the deconstructive and biopolitical perspectives on the force of law (the sovereign decision) and the structure of the interrelation between the law and denotative language. The notion that language can be freed from this interrelation with the law, thereby neutralizing its force, I suggested earlier, requires a shift from a diagnostic to a more tactical mode of inquiry. The concept of the messianic—as the experience of disengagement with the law—is here unavoidable. What is the experience of language that is neither in a relationship to the juridical ban nor beyond it? What is life in this space of the in-between? In what sense is this space also that of the time of the messianic?

As I suggested earlier, Derrida's discussion of the messianic without messianism is deeply implicated with his concept of the a-venir and the promise as the desire for justice. To recapitulate the main points thus far, Derrida's view of the messianic is structural in the sense that it emerges from the logic of temporality and therefore incorporates an absolute openness to a radical nonknowledge. The space of the promise arises from the deconstruction of the law's presence and dissimulation of sovereignty. For Agamben, such a view of the promise remains inadequate in terms of the problem of the law—an issue that each perspective diagnoses in differing ways. Thus, the ethical charge of messianism for each is quite different as well. For Derrida, the very existence of positive law is haunted by an impossible desire and promise of justice, thereby radically calling into question the sovereignty of right and norm but nevertheless sustaining their repetition and reproduction. (In other words, the ethical is always a figure of haunting, contamination, autoimmunity, etc.) For Agamben, the ethical emerges in the neutralization of positive law and its separation from whatever is possible—life, community, happiness, and so on. (In other words, the ethical is the operation of a countercaesura.) In this sense, the remnant that Agamben delineates as the separation and conservation of pure possibility (potentiality) does differ from the Derridean trace as inevitable survival of the other within.

To further articulate the messianic as countercaesura, one must take up in detail Agamben's *The Time That Remains: A Commentary on the Letter to the Romans*. I shall not here pretend to outline the powerful hermeneutics of the book, even though the work as a whole deals with nothing but the interrelation and possible severance between law and language as event. The specific achievement of the work is its theorization of the messianic event-word as a temporal image (in Benjamin's sense) that is thoroughly historical. Agamben cites Benjamin's fragment N3,1, where Benjamin writes that images are indices of the historical:

> In it, truth is charged to the bursting point with time. (This point of explosion, and nothing else, is the death of the *intentio*, which thus coincides with the birth of authentic historical time, the time of truth.) It is not that what is past casts its light on what is present, or what is present its light on what is past; rather, image is that wherein what has been comes together in a flash with the now to form a constellation. In other words: image is dialectics at a standstill. For while the relation of the present to the past is purely temporal, the relation of what-has-been to the now is dialectical: not temporal in nature but figural <*bildlich*>. Only dialectical images are genuinely historical—that is, not archaic—images. The image that is read—which is to say, the image in the now of its recognizability—bears to the highest degree the imprint of the perilous critical moment on which all reading is founded. (145)

The extent to which this concept of "image" directs Agamben's project in *The Time That Remains* is clarified by remarks made by Anselm Haverkamp in his "Notes on the 'Dialectical Image' (How Deconstructive Is It?)" on the understanding of this concept:

> The flash pictures the moment of evidence, a standstill explained in the next sentence. But what needs to be recognized first is the use of "image" as "constellation," a use of the word that is closer to Wittgenstein's "picture theory" than to any "imagistic" philosophy. The difference in translation, however, between "logical pictures" and "dialectical

images" is telling (*Bilder* in both cases). The stress, as Max Black underlines, "is upon the invisible logical form," not on the actuality of an ar-
chaic pattern. *Tractatus* 4 .01 offers some help by replacing "picture" in
the first sentence with "model" in the second: "A proposition [*Satz*] is a
picture [*Bild*] of reality. A proposition is a model [*Modell*] of reality as we
imagine it [*so wie wir sie uns denken*]" [36; my emphasis]. Like Wittgenstein's "picture," Benjamin's "image" is a schema of thought (*Denken*)
and "*Bild*" its most common and, at the time, fashionable denominator.
(Haverkamp, "Notes on the 'Dialectical Image,'" 72)

Furthermore, Haverkamp insists that the term "image" in Benjamin, which is often misunderstood, refers to an instance of language.
He refers to the conclusion of fragment N2a.3, where Benjamin says of
the image, "the place one happens upon them is language."

> Language is their natural place of existence; or, to put it somewhat
> more emphatically, the "state of aggregation" within which their para-
> digmatic instances are to be found. (The physical analogy with "states
> of aggregation" like water and air includes the possibility of change
> from the one to the other state, such as in "sublimation.") More precise-
> ly, and this is by no means self-evident, the paradigmatic instance of the
> dialectical image's existence in language is citation: language reused
> and reread. One might be tempted to go so far as to say that the word
> image is the metaphor-and a very suggestive one-for citation, while the
> word "dialectical" has to be taken as "reading." The expression "dialec-
> tical image" has to be translated in to and put to use as "reading cita-
> tion." (Haverkamp, "Notes on the 'Dialectical Image,'" 71)

Given that his reading of Paul is a palimpsest of "Theses on the
Philosophy of History," it is not surprising that Agamben not only ends
with a *Tornada* (a term that takes on messianic significance) on the relation between Benjamin and Paul but that the final words are also the
previous quotation from Benjamin. Nevertheless, it is important to ask
in what sense this view of messianic time as image is historical and not
in any sense transcendent of time or the logic of temporality.

Agamben clarifies that the concept of messianic time derives from
the image not as a picture or an idea, but as the historicity of a certain
recognizability. He writes, "*Das Jetzt der Lesbarkeit,* 'the now of legibility' (or of 'knowability,' *Erkennbarkeit*) defines a genuinely Benjaminian hermeneutic principle" (Agamben, *The Time That Remains,* 145). In

other words, the image is not open to infinite interpretation and deferral. Rather, "every work, every text, contains a historical index which indicates both its belonging to a determinate epoch, as well as its only coming forth to full legibility at a determinate historical moment" (Agamben, *The Time That Remains*, 145). Messianic time is the time of the now, a contraction of the past into the present—as a nesting of time. Language, as the carrier of temporality, contracts into the word. This structure of the event as image generates a philosophical imperative: it gives the book its expository form, as much as the exposition can be said to give the event form by bringing it to light. Thus, while the book as a whole deals with only the first line of Paul's Letter, each chapter treats a single word of this single sentence. This method, then, performs the thesis of messianic time as recapitulation and contraction and of the event as the performative word—a word of faith.

This concept of the word of faith as a linguistic performative unpacked from the perspective of messianic time-image is at the heart of Agamben's ethics and politics. Unlike the constative, the performative, Agamben suggests, is not in a "relation of truth between words and things, but rather, the pure form of the relation between language and world, now generating linkages and real effects. Just as, in the state of exception, law suspends its own application in order to ground its enforcement in a normal case, so too in the performative does language suspend its own denotation only in order to establish links with things" (Agamben, *The Time that Remains*, 133). Thus, if the performative is backed by authority of law and religion, something extraordinary takes place in what Agamben terms as the *"performativum fidei"* or the confession of faith. Agamben specifies that the Pauline word of faith is to be distinguished from the "sacramental performative" (of confession) and the penitential performative of sins. Associated with grace or *charis*, it effectively dissolves the link between, on the one hand, the personal loyalty that swears an oath and, on the other, *nomos,* or law. If loyalty as obligation and law were once conjoined, the word of faith as grace now discloses "a space of gratuitousness [*gratuita*]" (Agamben, *The Time that Remains*, 119). In other words, the experience of the word of faith is a particular kind of promise. It is a promise that, insofar as it is freed from the oath and confession with its accessories of contract, obligation, guarantee, credit, reciprocity, and so on, divides faith from law. Agamben writes,

> The promise exceeds any claim that could supposedly ground itself in it, just as faith surpasses any obligation whatsoever of counterservice. Grace is that excess which, while it always divides the two elements of prelaw and prevents them from coinciding, does not even allow them to completely break apart. The *charis* issuing from this fracture between faith and obligation, between religion and law [*diritto*], cannot in turn be taken as a substantial and separate sphere, for it can only maintain itself through an antagonistic relation to faith and obligation. In other words, *charis* can only maintain itself as the insistence of a messianic exigency in the two, without which law [*diritto*] and religion would, in the long run, be condemned to atrophy. (Agamben, *The Time That Remains*, 120)

The effect that Agamben claims that the messianic has on the law is, then, not simply destructive. The Greek term he underlines as disclosing the relation between the messianic and the law is *katargeō*, "a compound of *argeō*," which in turn derives from the adjective argos, meaning "inoperative, not-at-work (a-ergos), inactive. The compound therefore comes to mean "I make inoperative, I deactivate, I suspend the efficacy" (95). Thus, the real relation that the messianic performative has with the world can be measured in its revocation of all vocation. In the messianic calling (*klēsis*), the juridical terms by which relations and properties are instituted and identified are revoked and transformed. But this revocation is not programmatic resistance, confrontational or oppositional. Instead, the transformation is immanent to the vocation, relation, identity, and property in that the terms of the relation are inhabited "as not" (*hōs mē*) applying. Distinguishing the idea of living in a fictional "as if" from the messianic "as not," Agamben writes,

> In the *as not*, in a characteristic gesture, Paul pushes an almost exclusively juridical regulation to its extreme, turning it against the law. What does it actually mean to remain a slave in the form of the *as not*? Here, the juridical-factical condition invested by the messianic vocation is not negated with regard to juridical consequences that would in turn validate a different or even opposite legal effect in its place, as does the

fictio legis. Rather, in the *as not,* the juridical-factical condition is taken up again and is transposed, while remaining juridically unchanged, to a zone that is neither factual nor juridical, but is subtracted from the law and remains as a place of pure praxis, of simple "use" ("use it rather!"). Factical *klēsis,* set in relation to itself via the messianic vocation, is not replaced by something else, but rendered inoperative. (Agamben, *The Time That Remains,* 28)

The relevance of Agamben's theory of inoperativity (*katargeō*) to the power of a certain kind of silence to empty the power of law is unquestionable when we consider the following: In continuing to read Paul closely, Agamben shows that the Pauline *katargeō* is related to the Aristotelian concepts *dynamis* and *energeia,* translated as potentiality and actuality. (It is necessary to signal here that these terms are of central importance in Agamben's oeuvre, and cannot be taken up in detail here.) Philologically, it leads to a reading whereby to make inoperative "signals a taking out of energeia, a taking out of the act" (96). The consequence of discerning the relation between (in)operativity and (im)potentiality (for *dynamis* always contains its own privation as *adynamia*) is to discover a process by which "the messianic enacts an inversion" (Agamben, *The Time That Remains,* 97). Here, "potentiality passes over into actuality and meets up with its telos, not in the form of force or ergon, but in the form of astheneia, weakness." Thus, Agamben writes, "According to Paul, messianic power does not wear itself out in its ergon; rather, it remains powerful in it in the form of weakness. Messianic dynamis is, in this sense, constitutively 'weak'— but it is precisely through its weakness that it may enact its effects" (Agamben, *The Time That Remains,* 97).

The Witness

Returning to the example offered by the tale of "The Dumb Witness," the silence in the narrative is not merely a stubborn nondisclosure of the papers, but a certain secret to the silence. Here the figure of the slave woman appears to make a secret discovery of a possibility within language in its relation to law.

Insofar as Derrida's model of the place and function of the secret appears to capture and expatriate silence to the discretion of the law, it does not go far enough to explain Viney's outwitting of law and authority. Perhaps her secret is not some content but rather her secret is her silence—not a silence about something but her capability for silence, which manifests as simple persistence—where by accessing the place where she can and can not have language, she withholds herself from power. Viney is a witness not so much to a legal secret as to the secret of her silence, which Derrida equates with the notion of alterity as such. He says,

> There is in every poetic text, just as in every utterance, in every manifestation outside of literature, an inaccessible secret to which no proof will ever be adequate . . . Testimony that is given may be *false*, but one can never prove that there has been *false testimony*. Why? Because, on the other side, on the side of the witness, as on the side of the poet, there is always the recourse that consists in saying: what I said is perhaps false, I was mistaken, but I did so in *good faith* [emphasis added]. If that is so, then there is no perjury, no false testimony, and no lie . . . One will never be able to *prove*—what we call 'prove'—that someone is in bad faith. This stems from the fact that the other is secret . . . I will never be equal to the secret of otherness. The secret is the very essence of otherness. (Derrida, *Sovereignties in Question*, 164–65)

Derrida, of course, locates the secret as the unsaid in utterance itself and by invoking the problem of veracity versus proof or, more precisely, value versus fact, he locates the secret and the unsaid as not only within the context but also the orbit of the law. The lie can never be proven, thereby rendering the truth uncertain. The witness is always the site of the secret—the unspoken unsaid that will escape the arbitration of the law and therefore at some level pose a threat to its sovereignty. Here, in a departure from his earlier statement about the asemantic password, which is also a secret that permits one to be within the law—to be in a place where one can negotiate with the law—the secret of the witness is one that may potentially disrupt the law. It appears heterogeneous to the law, as the essence of alterity itself.

Again, we cannot fail but note the small and salient difference between Derrida and Agamben's positions. For Agamben, the secret of the witness is perhaps immanent to the secret of the law as the place of anomie. In the context of Chesnutt's story, it is the presupposed shared secret between Murchison and Viney and the violent excess that it gives rise to—it is this structure that is the true secret. However, if we read Viney's silence strictly within the limits of Derrida's location of the secret as alterity, heterogeneity, then the secret of her silence will displace the question from the law to whether she was in good faith or not in indicating her inability to communicate. In other words, her secret is undecidable only to the extent that it remains impossible to prove the wound to her tongue. However, if we read the secret as that which is excluded from the arbitration of the law by virtue of the law's own structure (anomie as excluded inclusion that prevails in the exception), then we can begin to interpret Viney's muteness as something more than a question of "good faith." We could say that she is neither in good faith nor in bad faith vis-à-vis the law as it functions.

How can we understand the idea that her silence was effectively a nullification of the law? If, as the narrator puts it, "the law made her his," then the law in effect suspends itself with reference to the master-slave relation or, more precisely, it invests the master with absolute sovereign authority. For Viney, he is the final law. If the force of law that accrues to Murchison is in good part owed to his wealth (his ability to own himself and others), and if this de facto power is granted de jure by inheritance laws—laws of property that render her mute as subject—then Viney effectively, through her muteness, nullifies the law's capacity to grant him this power. Through her silence, she renders the law entirely powerless and unenforceable. The law is suspended (the inheritance laws are ineffective) and also not in force, insofar as Murchison can do nothing about her. In other words, the true secret of her silence exceeds factual knowledge of the papers. Her silence should not be read as a silence about something but as her capability of silence, which manifests as a withholding. By fully inhabiting the outside of the law—that is, the law's capacity for arbitrary (exemplary and exceptional) punishment, its central lawlessness (in other words its foundational excess, which is its well-kept secret insofar as it is never legislated)—she disperses the law's anomie, its nonsignifying aspect, rendering indistinct the inside and the outside of the law. Viney is a witness not so much to a legal secret as to the secret of her silence. In a sense, Viney's discovery of her ability to be mute is effectively to grant herself a holiday from the law—to not just live outside, or at the door of the law, but to succeed in closing the door, if not permanently, then at least for a short while, to live in a pure "anomic" nonrelation to the law.

The performative silence in Chesnutt's folkloric tale illuminates the messianic word as a modality of silence. As Agamben writes,

> The word of faith manifests itself as the effective experience of a pure power [*potenza*] of saying that, as such, does not coincide with any denotative proposition, or with the performative value of a speech act. Rather, it exists as an absolute nearness of the word. One therefore understands why, for Paul, messianic power finds its *telos* in weakness. The act itself of a pure potentiality of saying, a word that always remains close to itself, cannot be a signifying word that utters true opinions on the state of things, or a judicial performative that posits itself as fact. There is no such thing as a content of faith, and to profess the word of faith does not mean formulating true propositions on God and the world . . . "Messianic and weak" is therefore that potentiality of saying, which in dwelling near the word not only exceeds all that is said, but also exceeds the act of saying itself, the performative power of language. This is the remnant of potentiality that is not consumed in the act, but is conserved in it each time and dwells there. If this remnant of potentiality is thus weak, if it cannot be accumulated in any form of knowledge or dogma, and if it cannot impose itself as a law, it does not follow that it is passive or inert. To the contrary, it acts in its own weakness, rendering the word of law inoperative, in de-creating and dismantling the states of fact or of law, making them freely available for use. (Agamben, *The Time That Remains*, 136–37)

FOUR

Between Derrida and Agamben

THE TASK OF BRINGING TOGETHER THE PROJECT OF DECONSTRUC-
tion and the perspective of biopolitics not only requires thinking power as the exhibition and deployment of the trace, but also asks to what
extent the "science" of writing delineated by Derrida as grammatology
intersects with the concept of the *dispositif*, in Agamben's sense, as the
social apparatus of disciplinary capture. But this is only one side of the
coin. The other side is to ask how the deconstruction of presence is being thought from the perspective of the analytics of power. In the following, I attempt to follow Agamben's relationship to Derrida's deconstruction of presence in order to mark relevant points of convergence
and divergence.

Puzzling through the relation between the perspectives of Derrida and Agamben appears as an unavoidable task at every stage when
following the track of nonsovereign power as spacing or trace within
institutional power. Though Derrida has hardly neglected to indicate
the political valence of the trace, a commitment particularly evident
in his later texts, perhaps it is not inaccurate to state that Agamben's
approach to the movement of *différance* leads to differing consequences
from that of Derrida. However, that this difference is open to being
characterized as a perceptible discord between their two styles has
perhaps been fueled in print by Derrida's not altogether impersonal
reading of *Homo Sacer* in volume I of his seminar *La bête et le souverain*,
translated as *The Beast and the Sovereign*. Whatever the unpublished
history may be of the relation between the two, the fact remains that
Agamben's displacement of Derrida's notion of the trace, and his approach to the overlay of language and law, is itself far from forming
a homogeneous text. His 1984 essay "The Thing Itself" is dedicated
to Derrida, and his subsequent essays on language display a complex of relations with the procedures and politics of deconstruction.
In the following, I focus for the most part on *"Pardes*: The Writing
of Potentiality," Agamben's 1990 essay on Derrida, as it clarifies one

aspect of Agamben's intervention and redeployment of the themes of deconstruction—namely, the concept of the trace. Another important and related aspect is Agamben's displacement in *Homo Sacer* and *The Time That Remains* of Derrida's readings of the relation between law and language. In this context, Agamben's shift in orientation with regard to the politics and ethics of deconstruction is evidenced in a more direct manner.

My interest in the relation between the two perspectives may not appear pertinent, given that Agamben appears to acknowledge only Benjamin and Heidegger as his major influences, while aligning his work with that of Deleuze, Foucault, and Guy Debord. However, the nature of my inquiry led me to sense a subterranean deconstructive current charging Agamben's thinking about language and potentiality. In short, I doubt it can be gainsaid that Agamben's work as a whole can only be understood as arising in the wake of deconstruction and the avowal of *différance*. In other words, the thought of the in-between place within self-reference and meaning, of nonpresence as trace or erasure, a faint but deep, discernible mark in Agamben's writing as well.

In order to take up Agamben's reading of Derrida, I briefly revisit the context in which Derrida elaborates the notion of the trace. However, this intention necessitates a disclaimer. The thought of the trace is situated at a strategic angle vis-à-vis the entire history of Western metaphysics. It not only addresses a lengthy and unmanageable genealogy of philosophical explorations ranging from Plato to Heidegger on what constitutes true knowledge and being, but is itself a momentous event in the story of what can simply be termed the human endeavor to reflect on one's relation to and being in the world. Thus, it would be impossible to "summarize" Derrida's achievement in relation to the trace, let alone do "justice" to it by isolating his works from their philosophical context. However, working within the limitations to which I and this project are necessarily subject, I turn to one of his early texts where the genesis of the trace event can be discerned in relation to Husserl's phenomenology.

To begin, then, with an assertion, Derrida's clearest and most important demonstration of the project of deconstruction is doubtless to be found in his 1967 critique of Husserl, *La voix et le phénomène*[1] (translated as *Speech and Phenomena*, which also contains his two most significant essays, "Form and Meaning: A Note on the Phenomenology of Language" and "Différance"). Of this early work, Derrida says,

> It is perhaps the essay which I like most. Doubtless I could have bound it as a long note to one or the other of the other two works. *Of Grammatology* refers to it and economizes its development. But in a classical philosophical architecture *Speech* . . . would come first: it is posed at a point which appears juridically decisive for reasons that I cannot explain here, the question of the privilege of the voice and of phonetic writing in their relationship to the entire history of the West, such as this history can be represented by the history of metaphysics, and metaphysics in its most modern, critical, and vigilant form: Husserl's transcendental phenomenology. What is "meaning," what are its historical relationships to what is purportedly identified under the rubric "voice" as a value of presence, presence of the object, presence of meaning to consciousness, self-presence in so called living speech and in self-consciousness? (Derrida, *Positions*, 5)

Setting aside the rich irony of referring to a "first" text of deconstruction, let us simply mark, following Derrida's comment, that this work counts as one of the inaugural texts of deconstruction and thus carries significant pedagogical value for those laboring by its shadow. For Derrida, given that Husserl's phenomenology constitutes, as he says, a watershed as the "most modern critical and vigilant form" manifested in the history of Western metaphysics, he here undertakes a close reading of the first volume of Husserl's first major phenomenological work of 1900–1901, *Logical Investigations*. As is well known, Derrida's engagement with Husserl can be traced back to his 1953–54 dissertation *La problème de la genèse dans la philosophie de Husserl* (published only in 1990 and translated in 2003). His essays "Genesis and Structure" and "Phenomenology" appeared in 1957 (reprinted in 1965 and 1967 and translated in 1978) and his translation of and introduction to Husserl's *Origin of Geometry* in 1962. While a thorough discussion of the project of deconstruction would require that one read the cluster of texts on Husserl alongside *Of Grammatology* and *Writing and Difference*, the concise intellectual tension of *Speech and Phenomena* is constitutive of any understanding of Derrida's powerful intervention into the history of philosophy.

Derrida states his argument apropos Husserl almost immediately as an attempt to show that the latter's "distrust of metaphysical presuppositions is already presented as the condition for an 'authentic theory of knowledge,' as if the project of a theory of knowledge, even when it has freed itself by the 'critique' of such and such speculative system, did not belong at the outset to the history of metaphysics. Is not the idea of knowledge and of the theory of knowledge in itself metaphysical?" (Derrida, *Speech and Phenomena*, 3; 5). In other words, Derrida's audacious argument pertains to the very premises of transcendental phenomenology, which for all its attempts to set aside traditional metaphysical presuppositions is nevertheless governed by the same. Derrida's analysis of phenomenology as a theory of knowledge then turns to Husserl's essential distinctions among signs. Since Husserl's phenomenology begins with an analysis of the linguistic element of intentionality or conscious (self-) presentation of an object (i.e., the consciousness of a given subject in presenting [an ideal] object to itself), Derrida's focus is necessarily on Husserl's theory of signs—particularly the distinctions he marks between expression as intentional meaning content and indication as material association of empty signifiers. In the introduction, which provides a dense and compact overview of the work, Derrida states that Husserl's delineation of the "authentic mode of ideality, to that which *is*" (Derrida, *Speech and Phenomena*, 4; 6)—in other words, the consciousness involved in self-presentation—is founded on the indefinite repetition of what is a profoundly *productive* act of transcendental intuition. And this inner sense where what *is* is presented as such (what Husserl terms expression), insofar as it is not empirical or worldly or dominated by the sensible, is sustained as what apodictically, simply "*is*" because it is open to being recalled indefinitely—in other words, repeated *ad infinitum*. What assures the unity of these infinite and purely ideal repetitions is the form of the present instant in and as life:

> In order that the possibility of this repetition may be open, *ideally* to infinity, one ideal form must assure this unity of the *indefinite* and the *ideal*: this is the present, or rather the presence of the *living present*. The ultimate form of ideality, the ideality of ideality, that in which in the last instance one may anticipate or recall all repetition is the *living present*,

the self-presence of transcendental life. [*La forme ultime de l'idéalité, celle dans laquelle en dernière instance on peut anticiper ou rappeler toute répétititon, l'idéalité de l'idéalité est le* présent vivant, *la presence à soi de la vie transcendentale.*] Presence has always been and will always, forever, be the *form* [my emphasis] in which, we can say apodictically, the infinite diversity of contents is produced. (Derrida, *Speech and Phenomena*, 4–5; 6)

Having sketched the architecture of Husserl's phenomenology in a few swift strokes, Derrida's fine scalpel then cuts into the (platonic) presuppositions clustered around the notion of form and being as presence—that is, being as self-presence, or auto-affection.[2] Focusing on Husserl's valorization of expression over indication, Derrida takes up the logic of these essential distinctions of linguistic consciousness to cumulatively show that Husserl's strict distinction between, on the one hand, expression as productive, intentional, and entirely ideal or nonreal and, on the other hand,, indication as unproductive, functional, and empirical, merely animated by intentionality is unsustainable. For Derrida, expression as ideal objectivity or truth (Derrida, *Speech and Phenomena*, 30) cannot be isolated as the pure realm of spontaneous self-proximate intention, dependent as this isolation is on filtering out any element of visibility and spatiality as gesture (Derrida, *Speech and Phenomena*, 35), of utterance and communication (Derrida, *Speech and Phenomena*, 38), the lag of time in the movement of idealization, and even "intuitive cognition which fulfills meaning" (Derrida, *Speech and Phenomena*, 100; 90). (However, let us mark that this latter reduction [of object intuition from meaning intention] is one that Derrida finds is too quickly unified [Derrida, *Speech and Phenomena*, 92] by Husserl—a point of no mean consequence and one to which I shall return momentarily.) Through a series of close and intricate analyses of Husserl's propositions, Derrida shows that the two kinds of signs— expression and indication—are always already intertwined in a variety of ways.

The crux of Derrida's critique, however, turns on the intricate reductions that Husserl effects *within* the expressive sign in order to isolate the kernel of pure ideality of meaning and truth as fundamentally an experience of indivisible self-proximity and presence. As he reasons it, expression understood this way as the presentative activity of pure solitary mental life implies and depends upon a number of untenable exclusions:

> Pure expression will be the pure active intention (spirit, *psychē*, life, will) of an act of meaning (*bedeuten*) that animates a speech whose content (*Bedeutung*) is present. It is present not in nature, since only indication takes place in nature and across space, but in consciousness. Thus it is present to an "inner" intuition or perception . . . The meaning is therefore *present to the self* in the life of a present that has not yet gone forth from itself into the world, space, or nature. All these "goings-forth" effectively exile this life of self-presence in indications. We now know that indication, which thus far includes practically the whole surface of language, is the process of death at work in signs. As soon as the other appears, indicative language—another name for the relation with death—can no longer be effaced.
>
> The relation with the other as nonpresence is thus impure expression. To reduce indication in language and reach pure expression at last, the relation with the other must perforce be suspended. I will no longer then have to pass through the mediation of the physical side, or any appresentation whatever. (Derrida, *Speech and Phenomena*, 43–44; 40)

Derrida's all-important critique of "the metaphysics of presence" then imparts two major incisions: first, on the notion of indivisible self-proximity or auto-affection, which ostensibly inheres in the solitary mental life of purely ideal meaning, and second, on the notion of indivisible simultaneity or instantaneity of sense upon which ideality depends. Derrida writes,

> Now . . . this determination of being as ideality is paradoxically one with the determination of being as presence. This occurs not only because pure ideality is always that of an ideal "ob-ject" which stands in front of, which is pre-sent before the act of repetition (*Vor-stellung* being the general form of presence as proximity to a viewing), but also because only a temporality determined on the basis of the living present as its source (the now as "source-point") can ensure the purity of ideality. That is, openness for the infinite repeatability of the same. For in fact, what is signified by phenomenology's "principle of principles"? What does the value of primordial presence to intuition as source of sense and evidence, as the *a priori of a prioris*, signify? First of all it signifies the certainty, itself ideal and absolute, that the universal form

of all experience (*Erlebnis*), and therefore of all life, has always been and will always be the *present*. The present alone is and ever will be. Being is presence or the modification of presence. (Derrida, *Speech and Phenomena*, 59–60; 53)

Into this notion of ideality as pure presence, Derrida introduces the movement of difference and the primordiality of repetition by showing that Husserl himself must necessarily make the presentations of sense dependent on re-presentations. In what could serve as a maxim for deconstruction, he writes, *"On dérive la présence-du présent de la répétition et non l'inverse"* or "the presence- of the present is derived from repetition and not the reverse" (Derrida, *Speech and Phenomena*, 58; 52). Thus, ideality, "which is but another name for the permanence of the same and the possibility of repetition . . . depends entirely on the possibility of acts of repetition" (Derrida, *Speech and Phenomena*, 58; 52). Going on to suggest that the force of this notion of ideality as presence and permanence of the same depends upon the notion of the "instant as a point," a "blink of an eye," Derrida proceeds to show that "no now can be isolated as a pure instant, a pure punctuality" (Derrida, *Speech and Phenomena*, 68; 61) if only because Husserl himself recognizes that every instant must necessarily be *spread out*. Though Husserl will refer to this spreading out as the "source point," for him (as Derrida cites), "the actual *now* is necessarily something punctual (*ein Punktuelles*) and remains so, *a form that persists through continuous change of matter (Ideas I, 81; ET, 237, modified)"* (Derrida, *Speech and Phenomena*, 69–70; 62). This "actual now" experienced in the instantaneity of the "blink of an eye (*im selben Augenblick*)," Derrida suggests, "defines the very element of philosophical thought, it is *evidence* itself, conscious thought itself, it governs every possible concept of truth and sense" (Derrida, *Speech and Phenomena*, 70; 62).[3] Thus, to interrogate this privilege, Derrida asserts, is not only to question the nucleus of consciousness but also to destabilize "every possible *security* and *ground* from discourse. In the last analysis, what is at stake is indeed the privilege of the actual present, the now" (Derrida, *Speech and Phenomena*, 70; 62–63). Derrida further clarifies that such an interrogation, though it introduces a meditation on nonpresence, does not imply a theory of unconsciousness or negative absence (Derrida, *Speech and Phenomena*, 63). For Derrida, this nonpresence within presence is manifested by the unavoidability or "irreducibility of re-presentation . . . to presentative perception, secondary and reproductive memory to retention, imagination to the primordial impression, the re-produced now to the perceived or retained actual now, etc." (Derrida, *Speech and Phenomena*, 71; 64). This irreducibility, he suggests, is to be understood as absolutely integral to perception as primary memory and expectation. (Husserl's terms are retention and protention, respectively.) In a definitive sentence that scarcely leaves the political out of consideration, Derrida writes, *"il y a une durée du clin d'oeil; et elle ferme l'oeil"* (Derrida, *Speech and Phenomena*, 73); "there is a duration to the blink, and it closes the eye. This alterity is in fact the condition for presence, presentation, and thus for *Vorstellung* in general" (Derrida, *Speech and Phenomena*, 65). It is at this crucial juncture in his exegesis that Derrida introduces the concept of the trace and of *différance* in its paradoxical primordiality. He writes,

> The possibility of re-petition in its most general form, that is, the constitution of a trace in the most universal sense—is a possibility which not only must inhabit the pure actuality of the now but must constitute it through the very movement of différance it introduces. Such a trace is—if we can employ this language without immediately contradicting it or crossing it out as we proceed—more "primordial" than what is phenomenologically primordial. For the identity of the form (*Form*) of presence itself implies that it be infinitely re-peatable, that its re-turn, as a return of the same, is necessary *ad infinitum* and is inscribed in presence itself . . . Does not the fact that this bending-back is irreducible in presence or in self-presence, that this trace or différance is always older than presence and procures for it its openness, prevent us from speaking about simple self-identity *"im selben Augenblick"*? Does this not compromise the usage Husserl wants to make of the concept of "solitary mental life," and consequently of the rigorous separation of indication from expression? (Derrida, *Speech and Phenomena*, 75–76; 67–68)

In other words, the notion of *différance* testifies to the impossibility of presence as pure auto-affection, or self-identity understood as an absolute (temporally instantaneous) simultaneity of meaning where the sign (as the *material and temporal* relation between signifier and signified) is reduced and rendered derivative, and the repetitive structure of ideality disavowed. Paradoxically, then, the trace, by introducing the temporality of repetition, marks the spreading out (a spatial metaphor) of expression; in other words, time here is shown to be as heterogeneous to consciousness as is space.

In the penultimate chapter of the work, Derrida engages in a discussion of this impossible self-identity or auto-affection in terms of Husserl's privileging of one of the most traditional concepts in philosophy: the voice and the notion of interior monologue (i.e., the experience of hearing oneself speak, which functions as a paradigm of ideality where the subject is presumed to be present to itself in an absolute immediacy without mediation or temporal gap). Derrida suggests that there is an "unfailing complicity" (Derrida, *Speech and Phenomena*, 84; 75) between idealization and the voice and that the advent of the *phōnē* is marked by "an essential tie" (Derrida, *Speech and Phenomena*, 86; 76) to expression. The reason the phoneme functions as the paradigm of ideal signs pertains to the fact that "when I speak, it belongs to the phenomenological essence of this operation that *I hear myself* [je m'entende] *at the same time* that I speak" (Derrida, *Speech and Phenomena*, 87; 77). This absolute self-proximity guarantees the pure ideality of the object, which "seems to depend on the voice and thus becomes *absolutely accessible* in it" (Derrida, *Speech and Phenomena*, 87; 78). This notion of "hearing oneself speak," Derrida suggests, is an auto-affection of a "unique kind" (Derrida, *Speech and Phenomena*, 88; 78). It is unique because unlike other forms of auto-affection, such as seeing oneself or touching oneself, the silent voice need not "pass through what is outside the sphere of 'ownness' or forgo any claim to universality" (Derrida, *Speech and Phenomena*, 88; 78). For Derrida, this claim to universality on the part of the phenomenological voice is ultimately the kernel constituting the truth of the ideal object. He suggests that the very purity of the voice as auto-affection betokens universality because it implies the "unity of sound (which is in the world) and *phōnē* (in the phenomenological sense)" (Derrida, *Speech and Phenomena*, 89; 79). In other words, this unity is privileged because it is "the sole case to escape the distinction between what is worldly and what is transcendental; by the same token it makes that distinction possible" (Derrida, *Speech and Phenomena*, 89; 79). Thus, the voice as auto-affection, Derrida shows, functions in this system as consciousness itself. This time, the scalpel that Derrida deploys is that of a metaphor. It is the metaphor of "movement" that Husserl takes recourse to in order to account for the retention of the now in another now. The root of this metaphor (and metaphors of course exemplify the "'in the place of' (*für etwas*) structure which belongs to every sign" [Derrida, *Speech and Phenomena*, 98; 88]), Derrida says, can only be primordial, and "all the concepts of metaphysics—in particular those of activity and passivity, will and nonwill, and therefore those of affection or auto-affection, purity and impurity, etc.—*cover up* the strange 'movement of difference'" (Derrida, *Speech and Phenomena*, 95; 85). In the seminal paragraph of the entire work, which could serve as a manifesto for his entire philosophical project, Derrida writes,

> The living present springs forth out of its nonidentity with itself and from the possibility of a retentional trace. It is always already a trace . . . the self of the living present is primordially a trace. The trace is not an attribute; we cannot say that the self of the living present "primordially is" it. Being-primordial must be thought on the basis of the trace, and not the reverse. This protowriting [*archi-écriture*] is at work, at the origin of sense. Sense being temporal in nature, as Husserl recognized, is never simply present; it is always already engaged in the "movement" of the trace, that is in the order of "signification." (Derrida, *Speech and Phenomena*, 95–96; 85)

Thus, in the place of the sheer immediacy of voice and speech, an immediacy without presuppositions that secures absolute subjectivity, the principle that grounds the truth of being, Derrida discloses nonphonetic writing and the asemantic play of the signifier—a mark without origin or end, with the consequence that "the thing always escapes" ("*la chose même se dérobe toujours*"; Derrida, *Speech and Phenomena*, 117; 104). This gap, this "hetero-affection" in auto-affection, is what Derrida terms in various contexts the trace, *différance*, supplement, to mark the absolute noncoincidence of the signified to the signifier, of sense or meaning to object, of intention to intuition, of speaking to language, and of the subject to itself. "Since the trace is the intimate relation of the living present with its outside, the openness upon exteriority in general, upon the sphere of what is not 'one's own,' etc., *the temporalization of sense is, from the outset, a 'spacing.'*" (Derrida, *Speech and Phenomena*, 96; 86). The thought of this temporalized spacing, which Derrida says is the "power and the limit of phenomenological reduction" (Derrida, *Speech and Phenomena*, 96; 86), is also the thought of the other because always for Derrida the "world" is primordially implied in the movement of temporalization.

Perhaps the one element of Derrida's prolific thought of the trace that appears to provide an opening for Agamben to intervene is precisely this last point about the primordiality of the trace—what Derrida terms "the supplement of the origin." His multiple undertakings with the "arche-trace" (what it means to speak of it, or how to speak of it) seem to mark some of his earliest published works, such as the 1984 essay "The Idea of Language," his 1982 work *Language and Death: The Place of Negativity* (where he discusses it briefly but pointedly), and more recent works, including *The Time That Remains*. My attempt to trace the modality of Agamben's displacement of the trace, given that the references are scattered throughout his writings, left me with a single certainty—that such a task is impossible to undertake in the space of a few pages, if only because the diverse implications that Agamben draws from such a displacement redouble themselves in multiple and sometimes paradoxical directions. Perhaps it can be said that the displacements are themselves marked by *différance,* thus making it impossible to state Agamben's relation to Derrida as consistent propositions or positions.

In *Language and Death: The Place of Negativity,* a seminar that dates to 1979–1980 and was first published in 1982, Agamben briefly critiques Derrida in the context of the work's exploration of voice and its relation to signification. Providing an overview of the seminar in the introduction, Agamben writes,

> The question that gives rise to this research must necessarily assume the form of a question interrogating the place and structure of negativity. Our attempt to respond to this question has led us—through a definition of the field of meanings of the word being and of the indicators of the utterance that constitute an integral part of it—to an examination of the problem of Voice and of its "grammar" as a fundamental metaphysical problem, and, at the same time, as an originary structure of negativity. (Agambe, *Language and Death,* xii)

Given the themes of negativity and voice, being and utterance, one is invariably led to question the relation of this work's argument to Derrida's *Of Grammatology*. No doubt, such a task demands patient scrutiny of both texts before any interpretive claims can be made. I cannot here undertake that task or even offer a précis or do justice to Agamben's argument as a whole. However, it may suffice to note that Agamben appears to question the model of phonocentrism and the repression of writing as the support of metaphysics that Derrida vouchsafes. Agamben interprets the voice not as self-affection; rather, he distinguishes the voice as sound (i.e., animal *phonē*) and voice as the taking place of language. The former (animal) voice is that "which must necessarily be removed in order for meaningful discourse to take place" (Agamben, *Language and Death*, 35). However, the silent voice, which is the site of the taking place of language, cannot be construed as presence and meaning. Rather,

> In as much as this Voice (which we now capitalize to distinguish it from the voice as mere sound) enjoys the status of a *no-longer* (voice) and of a *not-yet* (meaning), it necessarily constitutes a negative dimension. It is *ground*, but in the sense that it goes *to the ground* and disappears in order for being and language to take place. According to the tradition that dominates all Western reflection on language from the ancient grammarians' notion of *gramma* to the phoneme in modern phonology, that which articulates the human voice in language is a pure negativity.
>
> In fact, the Voice discloses the place of language, but in such a way that this place is always already captured in negativity, and above all, always already consigned to temporality. (Agamben, *Language and Death*, 35)

The superfine distinction that Agamben makes here is to a space that emerges within the voice when it has been separated from objective sound and is however not yet correlated to the signified. Referencing Augustine's *De Trinitate*, Agamben gives the example of hearing a word whose meaning is unfamiliar and yet is recognized as having the intention to signify. It is the "sense of the voice as an intention to signify and as pure indication that language is taking place" (Agamben, *Language and Death*, 34). While Agamben, for the most part, frames his analysis in this work entirely in the terms of Hegel and Heidegger, he does engage in a brief excursus on Derrida. Interestingly, Agamben cites the well-known passage from *De Interpretatione* (16a, 3–7), which Derrida had famously cited in *Of Grammatology* to demonstrate the sense of writing as derivative, but to a different purpose. It is the passage in which Aristotle says that the voice contains the symbols of mental experience and in turn the written word symbolizes what is in the voice. From this Agamben infers that

> from the beginning, Western reflections on language locate the *gramma* and not the voice in the originary place. In fact, as a sign the *gramma* presupposes both the voice and its removal, but as an element, it has the structure of a purely negative self-affection, of a trace of itself. Philosophy responds to the question, "What is in the voice?" As follows: Nothing is in the voice, the voice is the place of the negative, it is Voice—that is, pure temporality. But this negativity is *gramma*, that is, the *arthron* that articulates voice and language and thus discloses being and meaning. (Agamben, *Language and Death*, 39)

The suggestion here is of a certain anterior phono-grammatology insofar as voice is "always already captured in negativity" (Agamben, *Language and Death*, 35) in the sense that it is marked by temporality. Alternatively, the argument (which is unsurpassably recondite) is something in the order of thinking the logos (being and meaning) as founded on a certain negativity that is the nonsemantic and silent voice (purified of, and yet carrying the trace of the animal *phonē*), which is also writing. It is only by locating writing in voice as negativity that we can locate the trace as the mark of neither presence (meaning) nor absence (animal *phonē*), but something quite other, which it is not. With regard to any perceived proximity or distance to Derrida, Agamben makes certain corrections. Having located writing in the voice above, he writes,

> From this point of view it is possible to measure the acuteness of Derrida's critique of the metaphysical tradition and also the distance that remains to be covered. Although we must certainly honor Derrida as the thinker who has identified with the greatest rigor—developing Lévinas's concept of the trace and Heidegger's concept of difference—the original status of the *gramma* and of meaning in our culture, it is also true that he believed he had opened a way to surpassing metaphysics, while in truth he merely brought the fundamental problem of metaphysics to light. For metaphysics is not simply the primacy of the voice

over the *gramma*. If metaphysics is that reflection that places the voice as origin, it is also true that this voice is, from the beginning, conceived as removed, as Voice. To identify the horizon of metaphysics simply in that supremacy of the phone and then to believe in one's power to overcome this horizon through the *gramma,* is to conceive of metaphysics without its coexistent negativity. Metaphysics is always already grammatology and this is *fundamentology* in the sense that the *gramma* (or the Voice) functions as the negative ontological foundation. (Agamben, *Language and Death*, 39)

Agamben's interpretation aims to distinguish itself from Derrida's by sighting the trace in what he calls the voice as writing as "the taking place of language." However, readers of *Of Grammatology* will recall that in his critique of Saussure, Derrida himself performs a rigorous deconstruction of the *phonē* as distinguished from the signified in linguistics. In the section "The Outside Is the Inside," Derrida recalls the salience of the distinction between the "sound-image" and the "objective sound" in Saussure's system. He comments, "The sound-image is what is *heard*; not the *sound* heard but the being-heard of the sound. Being-heard is structurally phenomenal and belongs to an order radically dissimilar to that of the real sound in the world. One can only divide this subtle but absolutely decisive heterogeneity by a phenomenological reduction" (Derrida, *Of Grammatology*, 63; 93). Thus, the trace appears not as the being heard of the sound, which corresponds to Agamben's presemantic voice, but to the difference between the being heard of the sound and the sound heard. He writes in concluding that section:

The unheard difference between the appearing and the appearance [*l'apparaissant et l'appraître*] (between the "world" and "lived experience") is the condition of all other differences, of all other traces, and *it is already a trace.* This last concept is thus absolutely and by rights "anterior" to all *physiological* problematics concerning the nature of the *engramme* [the unit of engraving], or *metaphysical* problematic concerning the meaning of absolute presence whose trace is thus opened to deciphering. *The trace is in fact the absolute origin of sense in general, which amounts to saying once again that there is no absolute origin of sense in general.* (Derrida, *Of Grammatology*, 65; 95)

As is evident from this quotation, Agamben's sense that the trace should be displaced to a moment when sense is in a state of pure potentiality where it is "no longer voice and not yet meaning" is not in fact a correction; if anything, it is perhaps a repetition of Derrida's deconstruction of the phenomenological voice. But given this articulation of writing and voice, in what sense is this repetition also a displacement?

Turning then to Agamben's "The Idea of Language," and reading it in relation to Derrida's deconstruction of presence, one might be surprised to learn that the essay proposes to analyze the revealed "word." The essay begins by hailing those who have been raised as Christians and Jews and also those who have "simply lived" in an environment where these religions hold sway and their "familiarity with the word *revelation*" (Agamben, *Potentialities*, 39). Regardless of how one might self-identify, a reader might legitimately wonder if Agamben is simply restituting us to ontotheology[4] by invoking revelation and citing the famous words of the Gospel of St. John, "in the beginning was the word." But a less obtuse reading permits us to discover that the logos that Agamben is referring to is not the logos of reason with "its original and essential link to the *phonè*" and being as presence, but something like the disclosure of a truth that "concerns language itself"; in other words, it pertains to the space of "language taking place." Referring to revelation as that which cannot be known through human reason, he writes,

> The content of revelation is not a truth that can be expressed in the form of linguistic propositions about a being (even about a supreme being) but is, instead, a truth that concerns language itself, the very fact that language (and therefore knowledge) exists. . . .
>
> The proper sense of revelation is therefore that all human speech and knowledge has at its root and foundation an openness that infinitely transcends it. But at the same time, this openness concerns only language itself, its possibility of existence. (Agamben, *Potentialities*, 40–41)

This meditation on the apothegm that language exists, and that "*language is what must necessarily presuppose itself*" (Agamben, *Potentialities*, 41; original emphasis) does not, however, refer us to a "metalanguage," which Agamben claims is impossible (Agamben, *Potentialities*, 43). In a significant passage, Agamben writes,

> Philosophy considers not merely what is revealed through language, but also the revelation of language itself. A philosophical presentation is thus one that, regardless of what it speaks about, must also take into account the fact that it speaks of it; it must first of all say language itself. (Hence the essential proximity—but also the distance—between philosophy and theology, a proximity that it at least as ancient as Aristotle's definition of first philosophy as *theologikē*). (Agamben, *Potentialities*, 43)

What is the import of this assertion? To follow Agamben's injunction that we meditate on the fact that language presupposes itself is to cope with the *mise en abyme* of self-reflexive thought. He calls this "the paradox of pure philosophical intention," the fact that it must needs "speak of language, exposing its limits without making use of a metalanguage" (Agamben, *Potentialities*, 43). Having noted that any attempt to name "the taking place of language" can only appear as asemantic, Agamben, however, writes that something like a "negative theology" marks what he terms, repeatedly without mentioning authors or citing texts, "contemporary thought."

> It is legitimate to ask oneself if the recognition of the presupposition of language that characterizes contemporary thought truly exhausts the task of philosophy. It could be said that here thought believes that its task consists simply in recognizing what constituted the most proper content of faith and revelation: the dwelling of the *logos* in the beginning. What theology proclaimed to be incomprehensible to reason is now recognized by reason as its presupposition. All comprehension is grounded in the incomprehensible.
>
> But does such a thought not obscure precisely what should be the philosophical task par excellence, that is, the elimination and "absolution" of presuppositions? Was philosophy not perhaps the discourse that wanted to free itself of all presuppositions, even the most universal presupposition, which is expressed in the formula "there is language"? Is philosophy not concerned precisely with comprehending the incomprehensible? The fact that current philosophy has abandoned this task may constitute its fundamental difficulty, condemning the handmaiden to a marriage with its theological master, even as the difficulty of faith coincides with its acceptance by reason. (Agamben, *Potentialities*, 44–45)

Agamben's particular supplement to this unexpected reading of "contemporary thought," then, is to suggest that rather than forgetting and abandoning the original task of reaching the principle (*arkhe*) that is entirely free of presuppositions, our task is to wrestle anew with the *arkhe*. "The task of philosophy is therefore to be assumed exactly at the point at which contemporary thought seems to abandon it" (Agamben, *Potentialities*, 46). For Agamben, this experience of the happening of language—the immediate mediateness of language that also exposes its limits—is also the proper site for thinking ethics and community. He writes,

> Language, which for human beings mediates all things and all knowledge, is itself immediate. Nothing immediate can be reached by speaking beings—nothing, that is, except language itself, mediation itself. For human beings, such an *immediate mediation* constitutes the sole possibility of reaching a principle freed of every presupposition, including self-presupposition. Such an *immediate mediation* alone, in other words, allows human beings to reach that *arkhē anypothetos*, that "unpresupposed principle" that Plato, in the *Republic*, presents as the *telos*, fulfillment and end of the *autos ho logos*, language itself: the "thing itself" and essential matter of human beings. (Agamben, *Potentialities*, 47)

No doubt it would be an egregious and ironic mistake to interpret this experience of "the mediateness of language" as simply a conversion of *différance* itself into a new condition of presence. Therefore, if we turn to his later essay "*Pardes*: The Writing of Potentiality" from 1990, which deals directly with Derrida, such a potential misreading is averted and we can discern the consistency between the earlier essay and his current thinking.

THE ASSISTANT

In "*Pardes*," Agamben once again begins with a theological frame, but this time with a Talmudic parable whose larger relevance to the text's undertaking I cannot discuss here. However, the story offers us a clue to the structure of the essay as a whole as silently performing the theme of the essay. Everything turns around allegory, and the several allegories are made to reflect and resonate with each other in complex ways. For instance, the design of the text, which is made up of subsections, each invoking a different context for the main theme, serves as an allegory of allegory, the main one being the Talmudic parable, which is presented as an allegory for deconstruction. The figure of allegory in the story (Rabbi Aher) is an allegory for Derrida, and his act (cutting the branches) is an allegory for the project of deconstruction; thus, Agamben's project, insofar as it allegorizes, is itself avowing a filiation of sorts to the project of deconstruction as allegory (or the "in the place of" structure of signs). Also, it seems that Agamben himself seems to be aiding or assisting Aher to gather the cut branches. As I hope to show later, this seemingly facetious allegory of association, if pursued seriously, is in fact not without some efficacy in clarifying the relation between the two thinkers, but for now I simply acknowledge that the content of the Talmudic parable as allegory for deconstruction deserves a lengthy discussion that I am ill-equipped to undertake.

I shall focus here only upon Agamben's approach to Derrida. In this text, Agamben poses a question that addresses the status of Derrida's terminology. First of all, Agamben notes that the invention of a term, which is the moment when a name is bestowed, constitutes something like the poetry of thought. However, the fact is that today it is precisely this poetic moment of philosophy that has suffered a "displacement and transformation" because "their referential character can no longer be understood simply according to the traditional scheme of signification [and] now implies a different and decisive experience of language" (Agamben, *Potentialities*, 208). According to Agamben, Derrida is distinguished by the fact that he not only takes this displacement into account, but that his entire oeuvre is dedicated to the exposure of this crisis (Agamben, *Potentialities*, 208). What then does it mean to say that deconstruction "suspends the terminological character of philosophical vocabulary" (Agamben, *Potentialities*, 209)? Does this mean that once the terms have been lopped off like branches of knowledge from the tree of life, whereby the naturalized and instantaneous links between signifier, signified, and referent are severed, these terms are now consigned to an "infinite wandering and interpretation" (Agamben, *Potentialities*, 209)? Agamben is clear that there can be no worse misunderstanding than this of the project of deconstruction, for the all-important reason that Derrida in fact launches a diverse train of terms such as the trace, *différance*, and so on, but with the caveat that "the status of this terminology has [now] wholly changed, or more exactly has revealed the abyss on which it always rested" (Agamben, *Potentialities*, 209). Agamben then asks, "But what is at issue in the terms of Derrida's thought? What is named by a philosophical terminology that no longer wants to refer to something and yet, at the same time, above all experiences the fact that there are names?" (Agamben, *Potentialities*, 209). Focusing attention on Derrida's repeated insistence that *différance* is not a name, and that "the trace is produced as its own erasure," Agamben's question is a repeated abrading and beleaguering of the status of these undecidable signifiers. The fact is that these so-called terms do not refer to "something unnameable or ineffable" (Agamben, *Potentialities*, 211), to presence or absence, or for that matter even to themselves as signifiers. In other words, the liberation of the word "trace" from any reference does not mean that it now refers to the "acoustic or graphic consistency of the word" (Agamben, *Potentialities*, 212) t-r-a-c-e, which would then constitute the word itself as an object. What function, then, does it serve—this term that nevertheless signifies? For Agamben, whatever graphic or phonic thing one might deploy to mark the impossibility of presence, it cannot stand for something else. Rather, it must "above all refer to the 'standing for' itself. The aporia of Derrida's terminology is that in it, one *standing for* stands for another *standing for*, without anything like an objective referent constituting itself in its presence" (Agamben, *Potentialities*, 212). Such a signification of intentionality, Agamben suggests, dislocates signification as such. It is at this point that a subtle displacement of Derrida occurs, and one that can be understood as follows.

There is, I believe, little disagreement that for Derrida, such a "signification of intentionality" (words that I suspect Derrida himself would hesitate to use) or the status of the non-name trace would not so much constitute some kind of meta-ideality such as the "thinking that thinks itself" but rather the condition of possibility for an irrecuperable *alterity* that dislocates signification as identity and presence. Where Agamben is concerned, however, his attention seems to be turned toward the fact that there is nevertheless a philosophical intentionality of irreducible alterity. (Derrida might call it the experience of the arche-writing, while qualifying the term "experience" as itself metaphysical.)[5] The non-naming of the trace itself constitutes an intention-intuition and insofar as it is not a sign, the trace as such (if one can use such an oxymoronic construction as "the trace as such") is in some sense an objective event—an event of radical alterity. So is this, then, the moment that Derrida (see previous note) might term "ultra-transcendental," which runs the risk of resembling the "precritical" one of presence? I suggest that ultimately Agamben's displacement of Derrida here is a species of Derridean undecidability, not because the experience of arche-trace is being reassimilated to metaphysics but because it is forced to redouble itself as the trace between presence and non-presence, sameness and alterity—to disclose itself in a structure of redundancy.

Agamben's next move is to turn to the figure of Aristotle, who is characterized in the *Suda* (a Byzantine lexicon) as the "scribe of nature who dipped his pen in thought" (Agamben, *Potentialities*, 214). Agamben pursues this characterization closely as one that speaks of a "writing of thought" (Agamben, *Potentialities*, 215). Once thought is expressed as writing, all is familiarly Derridean again—expression and indication, we have learned, cannot be so neatly separated. But it is not quite so straightforward. Insofar as the writing of thought invokes Aristotle's metaphor of a writing tablet to describe *nous* as the potential intellect, Agamben translates what Husserl might term pre-expressive sense (founded on the reduction of the totality of language [Derrida, *Speech and Phenomena*, 80; 90]) into a writing of potentiality.[6] If potentiality is the potential to do and also to not do a given action (in other words, a potentiality that is not exhausted in actuality), the cosigning of thought/writing to this power delivers us to a thought/writing that is capable of not thinking/writing: "The pure potentiality of thought is potentiality that is capable of not thinking, that is capable of not passing into actuality. But this pure potentiality (the *rasum tabulae*) is itself intelligible; it can be itself thought: 'it [the intellect] is intelligible like other intelligibles' (*De Anima*, 430 a 2)." (Agamben, *Potentialities*, 215)

Such (im)potentiality, according to Agamben, signifies philosophical intentionality—the "thinking that thinks itself": "The thinking of thinking is first of all a potential to think (and *not to think*) that is turned back upon itself, *potential potentiae*. . . . Potentiality, which turns back on itself, is an absolute writing that no one writes: a potential to be written, which is written by its own potential not to be written, a *tabula rasa* that suffers its own receptivity and can therefore *not not-write itself"* (Agamben, *Potentialities*, 216).

The implication of this insistence, that the trace should be located as a transcendental intuition of itself as a writing that writes about the potentiality of thought/writing, does not lend itself to being captured in a (metaphysical) definition as sensible or intelligible. What Agamben does is to open an encounter with the *mise en abyme* of the trace as arche-writing. However, what must be remarked is the move here by Agamben to displace the trace from a discourse of heterogeneity and irreducible alterity to immanence. What is undecidable, then, is in what sense Agamben's notion of the trace as immanent writing disrupts the self-identicalness of sense. Agamben writes,

> It is in the context of this writing of the potentiality that no one writes that we must situate Derrida's concept of the trace and its aporias. The trace is nothing other than the most rigorous attempt to reconsider—against the primacy of actuality and form—the Aristotelian paradox of potentiality . . . The trace, writing "without presence or absence, without history, without cause, without *arkhē*, without *telos*," is not a form, nor is it the passage from potentiality to actuality; rather, it is potentiality that is *capable* and that experiences itself, a writing tablet that suffers not the impression of a form but the imprint of its own passivity, its own formlessness. (Agamben, *Potentialities*, 216)

Though largely consistent with Derrida, Agamben nevertheless here definitively and paradoxically returns sense/writing to auto-affection. This is the point of displacement and undecidability, for what does it mean to say *that sense as writing is auto-affection?* And how can auto-affection be anything but presence? How can there be an event such as deconstructing the already deconstructed notion of auto-affection as hetero-affection? Agamben does not hesitate to pile on the paradoxes but, as we will see, such pyramiding is not without consequence. It does ultimately lead to an ethics and a politics.

As a matter of fact, Agamben himself poses the question of the implications of his own displacement with regard to self-reference. He turns now from Aristotle to Plotinus to inquire after the notion of an experience of passivity and indetermination. Glossing Plotinus's Second Ennead Tractate 4, which uses the metaphor of the eye's experience of darkness as an affirmative metaphor to speak of the soul's indetermination, he writes,

> In the dark, the eye does not see anything but is, as it were, affected by its own incapacity to see; in the same way, perception here is not the experience of something—a formless being—but rather perception of its own formlessness, the self-affection of potentiality. Between the experience of something and the experience of nothing there lies the experience of one's own passivity. The trace (*typos, ikhnos*) is from the beginning the name of this self-affection, and what is experienced in this self-affection is the event of matter. The aporias of self-reference thus do not find their solution here; rather they are dislocated and (according to the Platonic suggestion) transformed into *euporias*. The name can be named and language can be brought to speech, because self-reference is displaced onto the level of potentiality; what is intended is neither the word as object nor the word insofar as it *actually* denotes a thing but, rather, a pure potentiality to signify (and not to signify), the writing tablet on which nothing is written. (Agamben, *Potentialities*, 217–18)

Thus, to answer the question posed earlier with regard to ideality and immanence, the auto-affection of writing as potentiality is not in any way a pure ideality, a transcendental intuition, since Agamben insists that "this is no longer meaning's self-reference, a sign's signification of itself; instead, it is the materialization of potentiality, the materialization of its own possibility. . . . The potential to think, experiencing itself and being capable of itself as potential not to think, makes itself into the *trace of its own formlessness*, a trace that no one has traced—pure matter" (Agamben, *Potentialities*, 218; emphasis added).

If, as Agamben suggests, the signification of intentionality is fundamentally an event of *matter*, then here the displacement displaces itself. The name of the non-name that is the experience of matter opens the abyssal thought of Plato's *khōra*: "Khōra is thus the perception of an imperception, the sensation of an *anaisthesis*, a pure taking-place (in which nothing takes place other than place"" (Agamben, *Potentialities*, 218). Given the salience of *khōra* in Derrida's texts, one can reasonably claim that at this point in the essay, where an absolute conceptual limit is reached and discerned, some synchrony between Derrida and Agamben can be discerned. And yet, the obscure metaparadoxes and the displacements of displacements that Agamben proliferates seem to belie any simple relation of discipleship or even friendship. How then should this relationship be grasped?

Parody of Parody

Let us here return to the context of allegory and assistance invoked earlier. My sense is that Agamben's deployment of the trace should be understood as falling strictly under the sign of what he terms parody. In his essay on parody in *Profanations*, Agamben suggests that there is a "concealed meditation on parody" in his friend Elsa Morante's novel *Arturo's Island* "that very likely makes a decisive statement about her poetics" (Agamben, *Profanations*, 37). Anyone familiar with Agamben's procedure will be immediately alert to the possibility that parody may well constitute a concealed meditation on his own poetics. Turning to the classical world, Agamben traces parody as a term that designates the original separation between song and speech—*melos* and *logos* (Agamben, *Profanations*, 39). The prose that emerges in and through this separation, then, is always in some sense in mourning for its lost connection to song. For some readers, Agamben may here seem to be intending an allegorical parallel of song with the phenomenological voice. In "serious parody" such as Morante's, Agamben suggests, this separation whereby prose is "beside the song" (i.e., the original or parodied work), this mourning is rigorously maintained as a poetic principle. In other words, "the parodist [must] renounce a direct representation of his or her object" (Agamben, *Profanations*, 41). The object itself is in fact unnarratable, even unrepresentable. "In approaching a mystery, one can offer nothing but a parody" (Agamben, *Profanations*, 41), so much so that parody becomes the "very form of mystery" (Agamben, *Profanations*, 42). In other words, parody is strictly whatever indicates nonpresence—whether substantiated as the idea of innocence, happiness, love, or the sublime, or leading up to the limit of language itself, whereby language itself is parodied by those poets to whom it reveals nothing but itself (Agamben, *Profanations*, 45). Where fiction is concerned, however, Agamben suggests that parody is, in fact, at the farthest remove. If fiction calls reality into question, where parody is concerned "the object is so intolerably real . . . that it becomes necessary to keep it at a distance. To fiction's 'as if,' parody opposes its drastic 'this is too much' (or 'as if not') . . . parody holds itself, so to speak, on the threshold of literature, stubbornly suspended between reality and fiction, between word and thing" (Agamben, *Profanations*, 48). The structure that Agamben delineates for parody is unmistakably that of a spacing between sign and voice, or more properly song as voice/phone, and meaning as sign. In fact, he suggests that it is in a supplementary relation to metaphysics:

> [P]arody is the theory—and practice—of that in language and in being which is beside itself—or, the being-beside-itself of every being and every discourse. Just as metaphysics is impossible—at least for modern thought—except as the parodic opening of a space alongside sensible experience (but a space that must remain rigorously empty), parody is a notoriously impracticable terrain . . . parody as paraontology expresses language's inability to reach the thing and the impossibility of the thing finding its own name. (Agamben, *Profanations*, 49–50)

Before we leap to a reading that would produce an identity between parody and deconstruction, and the *para* of being beside itself with the trace, let us note here the ambiguity of parody as allegory for modern thought. At no point does Agamben produce an identity between parody and the trace, or for that matter what he terms elsewhere the remnant (the life lived "as not") and *différance*. Rather, what we are faced with is, in fact, something like a "serious parody" of deconstruction insofar as the trace is "properly" unnameable and is not a name, a concept, or an idea. Thus, it is through this redoubling of parody that Agamben produces the ironies of writing as auto-affection and so on. Perhaps parody, then, is definitively Agamben's procedure in relation not only to Derrida but philosophical thought in general. And while the notion of parody as the only recourse of philosophy in the wake of the closure of metaphysics will (ironically enough) not come as a surprise, what is surprising in Agamben's parody is what he implies but never actually says about the practice of philosophy under the shadow of what he terms the negativity (voice) that makes language possible and/or the trace. The seriousness of Agamben's parody as an effective strategy is

evidenced by the simple fact that at no point does he forefront his procedure, thereby producing an unreadable and imitative postmodern text
rather than a serious parody. Parody, then, is not pedagogy, and it is not
transmitted as a philosophical procedure but is rigorously practiced and
performed at the boundaries of the discipline.

Another surprising aspect of Agamben's parody emerges from
his decision to locate an ethics and a politics of power in the parody of
parody. In other words, the paradeconstruction that Agamben engages
in results not in infinite play but in the irony of ironies—transgression
and fulfillment. Toward the end of the essay on parody, Agamben introduces the trope of parabasis as the "only resolution" (50) for the vertigi-
nous movement of parody. What does parabasis do to the representation that is parody? Interestingly, it is not crude deflation or dissolution
of representation. Rather, in parabasis, Agamben suggests, there is an
opening up of a "space between worlds" (Agamben, *Profanations,* 51).
"If parody, the split between song and speech and between language
and the world, commemorates in reality the absence of a proper place
for human speech, in parabasis this heart-wrenching atopia becomes,
for a moment, less painful and is canceled out into a homeland . . . as it
were" (Agamben, *Profanations,* 51). In utilizing the trope of "dwelling"
for trace, Agamben once again studiously parodies Derrida.

This notion of the "space between worlds" (parody, exception,
poetry) as a possible dwelling place is a recurring theme in Agamben
and is finally the move by which he aims to surpass the impasses of
deconstruction. Undoubtedly, this move is also the locus of his politics
and his ethics, and it would be impossible to discuss this issue without
a concrete reference. Thus, while I hope to draw out some of these
differences in the following chapters in other contexts, I conclude here
with a single example.

In *Remnants of Auschwitz,* Agamben invokes the question of
auto-affection in his chapter "Shame, or on the Subject," first with reference to Kant's first critique, where space-time are constitutive pre-
conditions of representation. Focusing on the inherent passivity of the
subject to itself in this thinking of time, Agamben extends the analysis
of passivity to the experience of language not only in poetry and other
situations of glossolalia but also in the act of speaking itself. He suggests that in the speaking being, insofar as he/she emerges through a

split between the "silent voice of conscience (Voice)" and the "articulated voice, *phonē enarthos*, in which language is securely joined to the living being by being inscribed in its very voice" (Agamben, *Remnants of Auschwitz*, 129; 120), there is a core of desubjectification inherent in every subjectification. The tradition of Western metaphysics, he suggests, has been generally to attempt something like an articulation between the two. He then writes,

> It is in this place of articulation that deconstruction inscribes its "trace" and its *différance*, in which voice and letter, meaning and presence are infinitely differed. The line that, in Kant, marked the only possible way to represent the auto-affection of time is now the movement of a writing on which "the look" cannot "abide" (Derrida 1973: 104). But precisely this impossibility of conjoining the living being and language, phone and logos, the inhuman and the human—far from authorizing the infinite deferral of signification—is what allows for testimony. If there is no articulation between the living being and language, if the "I" stands suspended in this disjunction, then there can be testimony. The intimacy that betrays our non-coincidence with ourselves is the place of testimony. Testimony takes place in the non-place of articulation. In the non-place of the Voice stands not writing, but the witness. (Agamben, *Remnants of Auschwitz*, 129–30; 121)

In other words, it is the liberation of the "I" from any stable reference or meaning that makes testimony possible. Once again, the proximity with Derrida is sensed. In the latter's discussion of the first-person pronoun and Husserl's attempts to unify intuition and intention despite the subjective context, Derrida suggests that in fact it is the dissociation of intention and intuition that renders the I a testament (Derrida, *Speech and Phenomena*, 96; 107). In short, Derrida agrees with Agamben. Unquestionably, both testimony and the witness are concepts that function as trace events of holocaust survival and knowledge, with the "difference" that for Agamben, instead of *différance* facilitating the movement of representation, the trace is tethered to the place (experienced here as shame) where the *thought of the impossibility* of self-affection (i.e., of the hetero-affection in self-affection) *is the self-affection* that marks subjectivity or consciousness as being "consigned to something that cannot be assumed" (Agamben, *Remnants of Auschwitz*, 128; 120).

In what sense, then, does Agamben aid Derrida, figured as Rabbi Aher, to gather the cut branches? What kind of assistance does he give? In the chapter directly preceding the one on parody in *Profanations,* entitled "The Assistants," Agamben delineates the function of the comical-grotesque good-for-nothing figures that populate the texts of Kafka (and also Collodi's *Pinocchio*). I do not at all wish to imply that Agamben shares something of the carnal-spiritual character of the assistants that he so delicately draws for us; however, perhaps there is something like an allegory that we can read into the work that the assistants do in relation to the ones they help and the displacement that Agamben enacts in relation to Derrida. Who, then, are the assistants? These are "intermediate creatures" (Agamben, *Profanations,* 33), he suggests, who "lay claim to the aspect of oblivion that resides in everything" (Agamben, *Profanations,* 33). The assistant is nothing if not our own intimate relation to the "formless chaos" (Agamben, *Profanations,* 35) of this oblivion—of all that is lost, forgotten, and ruined. He is our relation to our own "ontological waste," but he is "at home in all this" (Agamben, *Profanations,* 35). For what does the assistant in fact do? Well, first of all he has something to do with the end of time. "He spells out the text of the unforgettable and translates it into language of deaf-mutes. Hence his obstinate gesticulations coupled with his impassive mime's face. Hence, too, his irreducible ambiguity. For the unforgettable is articulated only in parody. The place of song is empty. On every side and all around us, the assistants are busy preparing the Kingdom" (Agamben, *Profanations,* 35).

II. The Exemplary Plane

The Exemplary Plane

That there is something absurd about citing historical examples of life lived in the suspension of law's relation to language is indubitable. For how can a life that is marked by the singularity of its exceptional situation pretend to exhibit anything typical in the sense of belonging to a class of which it is a part? The problem of the example and its relation to other rhetorical modes of expressing part-whole relations is taken up by Agamben in his essay "What Is a Paradigm?" Referring to his analysis of figures such as the homo sacer *and the* musselman, *Agamben says, "while these are all actual historical phenomena, I nonetheless treated them as paradigms whose role was to constitute and make intelligible a broader historical-problematic context" (9). Going on to clarify the meaning of the term "paradigm" in his work, Agamben aligns himself with Foucault to suggest that it is a definitive methodological tool in any archaeological investigation that is concerned with the politics of epistemology—that is, the shift from theoretical form to a consideration of the politics of statements and discursive regimes (14).*

In the following, I trace the outline of two historical figures that serve as examples of life lived in the neutralization of the law–language relation: the so-called "wild child" and the rigorous acrobat. While my discussion cannot pretend to the scale of an archaeological investigation, it is nevertheless characterized by one of the more crucial elements of the paradigm: its prevalence on the plane of the particular. Glossing Aristotle's Prior Analytics *(69a 13–15) Agamben says:*

> While induction proceeds from the particular to the universal and deduction from the universal to the particular, the paradigm is defined by a third and paradoxical type of movement, which goes from the particular to the particular. The example constitutes a peculiar form of knowledge that does not proceed by articulating together the universal and the particular, but seems to dwell on the plane of the latter. (19)

Where the wild child is concerned, its particular plane of existence, as we shall see, constitutes a class of all particulars that have no class. The acrobat, as well, reveals singularity, but in the mode of what is an entirely common possibility.

FIVE

The Wild Child
Politics and Ethics of the Name

Like a child's legend on the tideless sand
Which the first foam erases half, and half
Leaves legible.
　　　—Percy Bysshe Shelley, *Fragments of an Unfinished Drama*

[The] infant . . . would find himself in the condition of being
able to pay attention precisely to what has not been written, to
somatic possibilities that are arbitrary and uncodified; in his
infantile totipotency, he would be ecstatically overwhelmed,
cast out of himself, not like other living beings into a specific
adventure or environment, but for the first time into a *world*.
He would be truly listening to being. His voice still free from
any genetic prescription, and having absolutely nothing to say
or express, sole animal of his kind, he could like Adam, *name*
things in his language. In naming, man is tied to infancy, he is
for ever linked to an openness that transcends every specific
destiny and every genetic calling.
　　　—Giorgio Agamben, *The Idea of Prose*

WHEN LOOKING THROUGH THE PORTRAIT GALLERY OF ROGUES AND
outlaws ranging from criminals, the insane, bums, social dropouts,
hermits, ascetics, monks, and even gypsies and the legendary thugs
of British India, the wild child stands out as the most particular of the
particular. For what distinguishes the wild child is its relation to language. Unlike thugs and gypsies who are marked as rogues due to the
secret languages they employ, the wild child is in language insofar as it
is silent and does not speak. In other words, the wild child alone seems
to occupy a zone of indistinction between human and animal where
language is revealed in its capacity to be semantic and asemantic, to

signify and not signify. Thus, to take up the wild child, not so much in scientific or historiographical terms but as a political example of what Agamben terms "inoperativity," is to encounter crucial questions regarding the operational elements that articulate law and language. More narrowly, the wild child makes visible what is in fact the essence of this relation—the status and function of the name—by thoroughly problematizing its politics and ethics.

As an enigma of history, the wild child as a figure of scientific interest emerged during the classical period—the period of the growth of natural sciences when the question of the origin of language and identifying a human essence in its purity preoccupied the most eminent minds. The wild child, therefore, arrived as a tailor-made specimen for such inquiry and engaged naturalists such as Linnaeus, Buffon, and Rousseau and was also studied and analyzed by La Condamine, Lord Monboddo, and Blumenbach. This figure also emerges peculiarly in mid-nineteenth- and early twentieth-century colonial India, where a rash of cases is reported, recorded, and studied by colonial officers such as William Sleeman and European and Indian missionaries. Aficionados of stories about feral children can immediately name the few well-known documented cases, such as that of Peter of Hanover (found in 1724), Marie Angelique Memmie Le Blanc (found in 1731), Victor of Aveyron (sighted around 1799 and captured in 1800), and the wolf girls Kamala and Amala (found in 1920).

These isolated cases, insofar as they attracted the attention of scientific luminaries of their day, have engendered, despite the relative monotony of the archive, a seemingly disproportionate level of academic scrutiny and sympathetic commentary. Like the delinquents Foucault chronicles in "The Lives of Infamous Men,"[1] who flare up just for a moment in a given discourse and are irretrievably gone, their stories can be told in a few sentences, as the broad outlines of all of these cases are somewhat similar. The children (usually preadolescent) are glimpsed running about the woods at the outskirts of remote villages naked or in rags. They are captured by force and taken to local authorities, whereupon they are confined and attempts are made to civilize them. Their wildness or animality is typically evinced by their discomfort with clothing and cooked food (Victor abhorred meat, whereas Marie Angelique and Kamala apparently had a taste for blood and raw meat); extreme emotional passivity, except for anger; and insensitivity to sensory stimuli. Each of these children is mute, displaying little or no understanding of the need for language. And though Marie Angelique eventually did learn to speak a little and Kamala mastered fifty words, none of them was ever able to use language as anything more than a random pile of words with uncertain indexical functions—never as a mode of symbolic expression. The few biographical details about these children almost always proceed according to a predictable pattern, beginning with a haunting and ending with a forgetting. The first scenes, where the wild child appears and haunts the villagers who have sighted "it," are followed by scenes of capture, then attempted domestication (the anecdotes here providing maximum entertainment and sensation), then invariably the grand failure of the scientists to integrate them into society, and finally a willed forgetting. The children melt away into obscurity, having metamorphosed from being interesting feral creatures to simply asocial, pathetic, and abnormal adults.

Ultimately, what is interesting about them is not the so-called individual distinction of their stories of capture and domestication, the peculiarity of their survival in the wild, and so on. In fact, all of their life stories are narrated in the same monotonous discourse about the possibility or impossibility of discovering human essence when reduced to its most basic expression—a discourse accompanied by debates over perfectibility. What distinguishes these children from the discourse in which they find themselves captured is what they hold in common—the very condition of not-sharing. The singularity or particularity of these children, then, pertains not to their biographies (their ontical condition) but to the way in which each of them is in language—neither technically mute (as in speech-impaired) nor speaking—silent and beyond reach with no proper name of their own.

The fundamental inaccessibility of these children; their impenetrable immunity to social categories, including those of idiocy and delinquency; and their refusal to answer to or own the appellations that were bestowed upon them render them fundamentally exiled from human society and the law. Some basic observations can be made about this status. First, compared to other outlaws, the wild child cannot be said to belong to a grouping of any kind. The wild child is not merely homeless; it is unhomely (*unheimlich*) and always already undomesticated, feral, unhoused—unable to be housed. While other outlaws form alternate communities or enclaves mandated by laws of their own making, the wild child alone is distinguished not only by its silence but also by the singularity of its being without the law.

Second, the wild child cannot simply be said to be a nonhuman animal. If animals today are no longer subject to the law or held responsible to it as they once were in medieval Europe, they are today, nevertheless, objects of the law in the sense that they are bound in every way by the law as personal and state property, national and global heritage, and environmental responsibility. On the other hand, even those who are not recognized as autonomous juridical subjects, such as infants and children, the insane, the diseased, and so on, are ruled like the aforementioned animals, their behaviors regulated by the law. Customs, conventions, and laws govern the care and responsibility owed to them by individuals and the state. And the actions by such "minors"; their daily lives; and the permissible and nonpermissible boundaries of decision and action, be they witting or unwitting, violent or nonviolent, still elicit the force of law. None of this applies to the wild child.

Finally, insofar as to be outside the law is to be a violator and a threat to society, the wild child is the only possible outlaw that is not a threat to society, kinship, and property, and neither can it be said to be (like a slave) property in and of itself. There are no rules, customs, traditions, or laws that mandate the proper disposition of the law toward this figure. The state's care does not extend to this wild child, and this not caring, or absence of care, is not biopolitical in the sense that there is an act of deliberate sovereign neglect or abandonment of life here. The wild child is always *unexpected*, a surprise, an anomaly, a contingency for which the law is unprepared and must remain unprepared. As the absolutely unenclosed, the wild child confronts the force of law, familial as well as juridical, with an equanimity that can disclose its limits. It does so simply by not answering.

Thus, if we look closely, we begin to see that the wild child's nonrelation to the law, its absolute lack of accountability to answer to the law in any shape or form, has very much to do with the fact that it has no proper name of its own. The idea of the wild child as unspeaking and lawless serves to make visible and bring to the forefront certain salient questions of politics and ethics that arise in any consideration of the name as such.

Turning, then, to the two thinkers who have guided my questioning thus far, both Derrida and Agamben discuss the name and naming as the fundamental link between law and language. In the following, I take up their respective analyses of the relation between the proper name and law through the paradigm of the wild child in order to discover the ethical consequences of their positions. The chapter proceeds in three parts. In part I, I suggest that where Derrida is concerned, it is the impropriety of the proper name that implicates language in law, whereas for Agamben the juridicization of language finds its locus in the complex structure of the oath. In part II, the issue is the limit of the logos. This is raised by Agamben's critique of the oath and the problem of the consistency of language and links up with Plato's *Cratylus*, which deals with the correspondence of words and things. This issue then opens certain ethical questions. The discovery here of silent names appears fortuitous in light of the nameless wild child. The name here is disclosed as an ethos and an ethics. In part III, I suggest that if for Agamben ethics is related to infancy (a mode of inoperativity) and for Derrida it is the conundrum of hospitality, which is once again tied to the politics of the name, the question that then arises is one of place. What is the place of the wild child if it is indeed beyond the reach of the law?

In the Name of the Law

Derrida: Violence and the Name

To interest oneself in the problem posed by the wild child to the concept of the proper name, and the question of its access to the name in general, is invariably to interest oneself in the politics of naming as act. In a sense, we may say that such a politics has been one of Derrida's primary preoccupations from his earliest writings to the last.

In *Of Grammatology*, Derrida famously takes up the question of the properness of the proper name in his discussion of Claude Levi-Strauss's narrative in *Tristes Tropiques* of Nambikwara naming practices. Derrida's declared intention is to discover Levi-Strauss's "Rousseauism"—that is, his logocentric bias toward the purity of speech over writing with all the attendant implications that such a bias entails, such as an ethnocentric notion of what constitutes literacy, the privileging of alphabetic or phonetic writing, and the assumption of innocence in the absence of writing. Unsurprisingly, Derrida's analysis is not intended to correct the record regarding the Nambikwara, but is on the trail of the trace or the *graphein* in the "obliteration of the proper." Given his definition of writing as the "original violence of language" (Derrida, *Of Grammatology*, 106), which refers to the irreducibility of metaphor, Derrida is, of course, skeptical of Levi-Strauss's romanticized imaging of the Nambikwara as a gentle and nonviolent people *because* they have no conception of writing. As Derrida makes clear, such idealizations presuppose unsustainable oppositions between us and them, nature and culture, alphabetic and nonalphabetic signs that are ultimately expressive of Western ethnocentrism though it manifests itself as antiethnocentrism.

Derrida's criticism begins with an analysis of the anthropologist's confession about the scene of proper names, which the latter evinces as an instance of primitive innocence. Given the fact that the Nambikwara prohibit the free use of proper names, which they keep secret, and only use nicknames, Levi-Strauss relates an anecdote when he manages by a clever ruse and manipulation to extract the names of the entire village from a group of little girls. If, for Levi-Strauss, this is evidence of their fundamental innocence, shattered by Western intrusion—a violence from without—Derrida offers two salient observations. First, he reminds us of Levi-Strauss's own theory of proper names as being little more than classifications. Derrida cites the following lines from Levis Strauss's *The Savage Mind*: "one . . . never names: one classes someone else . . . [or] one classes oneself" (Derrida, *Of Grammatology*, 109). The proper name has no propriety; it is always already improper. Regarding the Nambikwara prohibition, Derrida writes,

> [T]his prohibition is necessarily derivative with regard to the constitutive erasure of the proper name in what I have called arche-writing, within, that is, the play of difference. It is because the proper names are already no longer proper names, because their production is their obliteration, because the erasure and the imposition of the letter are originary, because they do not supervene upon a proper inscription; it is because the proper name has never been, as the unique appellation

reserved for the presence of a unique being, anything but the original myth of a transparent legibility present under the obliteration; it is because the proper name was never possible except through its functioning within a classification and therefore within a system of differences, within a writing retaining the traces of difference, that the interdict was possible, could come into play, and, when the time came, as we shall see, could be transgressed; transgressed, that is to say restored to the obliteration and the non-self-sameness [*non-propriété*] at the origin. (Derrida, *Of Grammatology*, 109)

Thus, for Derrida, the fundamental structure of language is inescapably grounded in the violence of an *arche* writing. All peoples, insofar as they erase their properly proper names, are already participants in the violence of the letter and its threefold structure of foundational impropriety or the improper (*arche*-writing, the law that protects the nonfoundation, and the transgression of that law). In other words, unless one defends a very narrow definition of writing, there is no question that the Nambikwara are far from being an innocent people without writing who suffer violence from without. The very prohibition against the use of the proper name, according to Derrida, presupposes and serves to prove the contrary.

In short, Derrida's argument serves to bring the Nambikwara to a full membership with all other human communities. They, too, are marked by the erasure of the proper name and, despite Levi-Strauss's presumption, are as implicated in writing as any other human community. Even at the most simple manifestation, such as Nambikwara society, man seems to be characterized by his capacity for language and thus the obliteration of the proper name. In fact, Derrida writes that Levi-Strauss's descriptions of the Nambikwara "give them *of course* a rightful place within humankind, so-called human society and the 'state of culture.' They speak and prohibit incest" (Derrida, *Of Grammatology*, 108; emphasis added). Despite the "of course," it is not the case that Derrida is in doubt regarding their humanness; however, denying humans as such their propriety, Derrida makes it clear that "so-called human society" is distinguished by the capacity for language and barred sexuality. What is the relevance of this assertion for our understanding of the wild child?

If the economy, institutions, and technologies of the Nambik-wara can be said to manifest humanness at its most simple and basic level, there is a clear analogy with the wild child, who can be said to share in a similar simplicity. In the least, they share in similar appur-tenances of what can be said to constitute simplicity: they are for the most part naked, practice no art forms, and have no stories to tell about the world or their origin, and during their nomadic period, they spend the entire day foraging for food. But such a hasty assimilation of legend to anthropological fact would overlook the obvious: the wild child has no community and therefore is bereft of even the semblance of institu-tions (such as marriage and family) and, even more importantly, the wild child is mute. He or she, as a "so-called human being," cannot speak, write, or signify and, having no conception of kinship, cannot have a notion of incest. In fact, the two bare elements of being human "of course" that Derrida identifies—speech and barred sexuality—are irrelevant to our understanding of the wild child. A gulf yawns between the Nambikwara and the wild child, and it could not be wider. Where, then, does this leave us in the consideration of the proper name of the wild child?

Where the act of naming is concerned, both Foucault and Derri-da implicitly agree that proper names are only classifications that func-tion within a system of differences. Obviously, without this classifying functionality, the interrogation of the proper name (the very value of identity papers) would not be of relevance in the scene of hospitality. Proper names, Derrida suggests, bear a fundamental relation to the foundational violence of language: "There was in fact a first violence to be named. To name, to give names that it will on occasion be forbid-den to pronounce, such is the originary violence of language which consists in inscribing within a difference, in classifying, in suspend-ing the vocative absolute" (Derrida, *Of Grammatology*, 112). However, with wild children, these propositions reach their limit insofar as the naming of the wild child indicates nothing if not this suspension of the proper. It is not only that each of their names is a classification unto itself, but that their classification is their only name.

Let us consider the tenth edition of Linneaus's *Systema Naturae*: under the order of primates, Linneaus, who incidentally called himself the new Adam, lists the genera of *Homo—nosce te ipsum, Simia*, Lemur, and Vepertilio (bat). The genus of *Homo* is characterized by its ability for self-recognition (*nosce te ipsum*, or know thyself), but lest we believe that "man" is a lone species, Linneaus corrects that presumption by adding troglodytes as also "self-knowing." Next comes the level of varieties, and we discover that the species sapiens boasts six varieties—the four racial types (red, white, yellow, and black); monsters; and, of course, *ferus*. While each of the varieties is described by their group characteristics, the table of *ferus* alone is made up of appellatives, if not proper names. Linneaus translates the appellative of each and every known case of wild children into Latin—*Juvenis Ursinus Lithaenus* 1661 (the bear child of Lithuania), *Juvenis Lupinus Hessensis* 1344 (the wolf child of Hesse), *Juvenis Hannoveranus* 1724 (the youth of Hanover), and so on—and lists them as classifications (classes with necessarily single members). While even the monsters (Alpini, Hottentots, and Patagonians, etc.) are merely types or varieties of *Homo*, wild children appear as singular creatures, each a subvariety unto itself. This anomaly is rarely remarked upon, and yet it reveals a fault significant to the consistency and logic of the discipline of classification and naming. This moment of historical singularity in the classification discloses the appellation of the wild child as both class and name without the latter suspending or concealing the function of the former. Insofar as it is always already improper, the proper name in general (as appellation) carries the trace of classification, and the classification carries the trace of the name; however, the appellation/class of the wild child refers to nothing if not to the trace of the proper name itself. It is as if the wild child and the trace referred to each other in a space that is eminently readable. Each of the names of feral children in Linneaus's list is poised between the proper name and the common noun, between the unique individual and membership in a group. Referring, then, only to its own self-erasure, its own effacement, the proper name of the wild child may well be "no man"—the name of an unnaming or a no-name that, as Ulysses the exemplary man demonstrates, enables an escape from imprisonment.

However, this discussion, though it deals with Derrida's deconstruction of the proper name, does not address what it is about the structure of the name that implicates it in the law. It also does not address the specific manner in which the wild child troubles the signifying function of the name, which invariably brings the political significance of the act of naming into sharp relief. In other words, how do the name and the act of naming coimplicate language and law?

Agamben: Trust in the Name

In *The Sacrament of Language: The Archaeology of the Oath,* Agamben proffers the pendant to the fundamental premise of his argument in *Homo Sacer* regarding the structure of the powerful analogy between law and language. In the earlier work, this analogy was discussed in terms of the state of exception as the suspension of law's signifying function. In the more recent work, Agamben turns more directly to language to analyze the mode of its entry into the realm of law by locating it in the structure of the oath. In the opening pages, he suggests that what is at stake in the oath is the very identity of the human being as political animal and goes on to offer the following definition: "The oath does not concern the statement as such but the guarantee of its efficacy" (Agamben, *Sacrament of Language,* 4). Insofar as it serves mainly to secure a certain promise, the oath is related to the question of trust and faith in the expression and giving of one's word. Agamben suggests that a constitutive element of the oath, its trust-securing function, is its recourse to the name of God. In uttering the name of God, there is an accomplishment of the guarantee. "The testimony that is in question in the oath must therefore be understood in a sense that has little to do with much of what we normally understand by this term. *It concerns not the verification of a fact or an event but the very signifying power of language*" (Agamben, *Sacrament of Language,* 33; emphasis added). In other words, to swear in the name of God, or even one's own, is a performative speech act that relates words to actions. But what does it mean to call on God as a witness? Agamben clarifies that it is never by God that one swears, but always in the name of God, for God's logos is pure oath—accomplishment. The name of God, then, performs something like a practical function and "has a double valence" (Agamben, *Sacrament of Language,* 38)—that is, of guaranteeing the truth and guarding against perjury by referring respectively to the force and weakness of language (Agamben, *Sacrament of Language,* 36). In the invocation of the name of God, there occur simultaneously an utterance of faith in words and also a curse in the event of violation of this faith. What the curse attests to, in other words, is the separation of the correspondence between words and things. And as a political speech act, the curse as *sacratio* engenders the law. Agamben suggests that what distinguishes Judeo-Christian metaphysics is something like a transformation of the necessary faith in the word into the faith of the word. In other words, "*God's* name [*il nome di Dio*] names language itself . . . the divinization of the *logos* as such, to the name of God as archi-event of language that takes place in names. Language is the word of God, and the word of God is, in the words of Philo, an oath" (Agamben, *Sacrament of Language*, 49). Thus, the name of God "expresses the status of the logos" (Agamben, *Sacrament of Language*, 53) as oath or a perfect performative speech act. Insofar as the performative and the denotative are, however, "co-originary" in the logos, perjury is always already "inscribed in the very act of speaking" (Agamben, *Sacrament of Language*, 56). In this context, any strategy of safeguarding against perjury, whether it is the curse or penal law, becomes a "sacramental" (i.e., political) one—a "sacrament of power" (Agamben, *Sacrament of Language*, 59). For Agamben, given the split within the logos between performative and the denotative, it is ultimately to secure the consistency of the word that religion and law arise. He writes,

> Religion and law do not preexist the performative experience of language that is in question in the oath, but rather they were invented to guarantee the truth and trustworthiness of the *logos* through a series of apparatuses, among which the technicalization of the oath into a specific "sacrament"—the "sacrament of power"—occupies a central place. (Agamben, *Sacrament of Language*, 59)

Thus, force as such issues from language's capacity for effective speech. In short, the force of speech founds the force of law (Agamben, *Sacrament of Language*, 62–63). What is being argued here is the capture by the law of a certain germinal experience of language—that is, the experience of *fides* (trust)—which can be evident in the word of personal loyalty or faithfulness that entails the necessary "correspondence between language and actions" (Agamben, *Sacrament of Language*, 23). What is significant here is the notion that insofar as language is performative and denotative, law as power isolates and separates the two in order to exercise and maintain its force.

He writes,

> The "force of law" that supports human societies, the idea of linguistic enunciations that stably obligate living beings, that can be observed and transgressed, derive from this attempt to nail down the originary performative force of the anthropogenic experience, and are, in this sense, an epiphenomenon of the oath. (Agamben, *Sacrament of Language*, 70)

For Agamben, this insight into the structure of the oath as the juridicization of trust in the relation between words and actions raises the question of anthropogenesis or humanness. To be in language as a speaking being, suggests Agamben, is to confront the problem of the "efficacy and truthfulness" of one's words (Agamben, *Sacrament of Language*, 68). However, Agamben says that, today, the privilege of the oath is in decline, that there is a rapid and ongoing collapse of its structure, and that its eclipse enjoins a radical rethinking of the very place of language (or speech). This is an argument whose logic is analogous to contemporary sovereignty's separation and collapse of human beings' bare life and political existence, which renders the state of exception the norm. The consequences he draws from this observation are laid out in the last two pages of his book. Here he suggests that "[i]t is perhaps time to call into question the prestige that language has enjoyed and continues to enjoy in our culture, as a tool of incomparable potency, efficacy, and beauty" (Agamben, *Sacrament of Language*, 71). However, given the particular virtue of human language, which entails that the speaker place his/her very being at stake in words by assuming the place of the first-person pronoun, it also implicates the human being in an ethical situation as determined by the politics of the oath (swearing or cursing, truth-telling or perjuring). Agamben writes,

> Philosophy begins in the moment in which the speaker, against the *religio* of the formula, resolutely puts in question the primacy of names, when Heraclitus opposes logos to *epea*, discourse to the uncertain and contradictory words that constitute it, or when Plato, in the *Cratylus*, renounces the idea of an exact correspondence between the name and the thing named and, at the same time, draws together onomastics and legislation, an experience of the *logos* and politics. Philosophy is, in this

sense, constitutively a critique of the oath: that is, it puts in question the sacramental bond that links the human being to language, without for that reason simply speaking haphazardly, falling into the vanity of speech. In a moment when all the European languages seem condemned to swear in vain and when politics can only assume the form of an *oikonomia*, that is, of a governance of empty speech over bare life, it is once more from philosophy that there can come . . . the indication of a line of resistance and of change. (Agamben, *Sacrament of Language*, 72)

Agamben's gesture of positioning philosophy as the critique of the privilege of the name and of the oath opens a small door for the wild child to reenter the scene. As an essentially nameless being unrelated to the violence of the name, the wild child, insofar as he/she cannot take the oath, tell the truth, or lie, poses a powerful challenge to the sovereignty of the name and the oath. The "line of resistance and change," however, should not be mistaken as an opposition to language. Rather, if we take up the ethics that its silence opens and "promises," we may well be led to discern that it holds in reserve the meaning of the name itself.

What the Name Is

Knowledge and the Name

Let us approach the proper name once again—the concept as well as the act of naming—this time in reference to the theme of knowing and knowledge, which is related to both Derrida's notion of the improper name as well as Agamben's problem of faith. While the *Cratylus* would be the logical text to turn to, perhaps the relevant entry into that difficult dialogue can be provided by another text by Derrida (this time a late one): "The Animal That Therefore I Am (More to Follow)," where he discusses what he calls the "scene of name-calling" in Genesis. In the version of creation where Adam is created before Eve (the second narrative), it is man alone without woman who gives the names to the creatures that precede him. Derrida quotes from the Chouraqui translation: "He has them come toward the husbandman *in order to see* what he will call out to them" (Derrida, *Animal That Therefore*, 17). Underlining the phrase "*in order to see*," Derrida suggests that it marks *at the same time* the infinite right of inspection of an all-powerful God *and* the finitude of a god who doesn't know what is going to happen to him with language. And with names. In short, God doesn't yet know what he really wants: this is the finitude of a God who doesn't know what he really wants with respect to the animal, that is to say, with respect to the life of the living as such, a God who sees something coming without seeing it coming, a god who will say *"I am that I am"* without knowing what he is going to see when a poet enters the scene to give his name to living things. This powerful yet deprived "in order to see" that is God's the first stroke of time, before time, God's exposure to surprise, to the event of what is going to occur between man and animal, this time before time has always made me dizzy. (Derrida, *Animal That Therefore*, 17)

Derrida makes it clear that here, in the second narrative, the act of naming is a quintessentially human and poetic task (a "making") that opens an abyss that discloses God's limits. Rather than revealing knowledge of things as they are by discovering the correct names of the creatures of God, the act of naming discloses the limits of being itself. The name comes from nowhere; it surprises even God. Derrida asks us to consider the implications of God's exposure to surprise, his curiosity as to how or what naked man will call the creatures he has created, and what or how he might call him the creator: "Is he going to call me, is he going to address me? What name is he going to call me by, this naked man, before I give him woman . . . ?" (Derrida, *Animal That Therefore*, 18). For Derrida, the politicization of this moment by the Greek and the Abrahamic traditions is to be critiqued. He discerns here an "imperturbable logic" that posits man as having a primal lack so that "from within the pit of that lack, an eminent lack, a quite different lack from that he assigns to the animal, man installs or claims in a single stroke *his property* (the peculiarity [*le propre*] of a man whose property it even is not to have anything that is proper to him), and his *superiority* over what is called animal life" (Derrida, *Animal That Therefore*, 20). Derrida suggests that this is a profoundly postlapsarian perspective that evolves within the framework of redemption, whereas he prefers to situate himself in the time frame before the fall, "before evil," to ask how we can approach the animal.

Where do we situate the wild child in this scene of pre- or post-lapsarian naming? Though a child of nature, the feral child is fundamentally not a creature of God, if only because it does not participate in creation. Therefore, it certainly can have no place in the pageant of animals waiting to be named. By naming, man assumes domination over the animals, in that he proposes to know them through his prerogative of saying who they are; the wild child nevertheless escapes this scenario by not being a part of creation—neither animal nor man, named or name-giver. If man's act of naming opens an abyss because the name comes from somewhere beyond God's knowledge, beyond the foundation, the wild child opens yet another abyss insofar as the categories of human language fall short of saying who or what the child is. In a sense, though it can obviously be indicated and referred to, it does not possess a name, or rather, its name cannot be known. Thus, it opens the well-known wedge within naming itself between the name and knowledge of things. In other words, we travel from the lack of foundation of our knowledge of things to the limits of logos itself, or from discerning the nonfoundation of epistemology to discerning the limits of our discernment.

This latter limit of language can perhaps be said to encapsulate the theme of Plato's *Cratylus,* a dialogue in which Socrates occupies himself with the correctness of names in relation to the act of naming and the knowledge they may be said to deliver. The dialogue begins with Socrates trying to mediate the debate between Cratylus and Hermogenes, who hold radically opposite views about names. While the former believes that names have an essential correctness in that they belong to their referents by nature, the latter holds that names are merely social conventions. He even cites the arbitrary naming of slaves (384d) to demonstrate that names are correct merely through usage. Socrates brings Hermogenes to recognize the contradictions in his position after ensuring that he believes in the essential identity or truth of things and actions. It follows, then, that insofar as speaking and naming participate in the "things that are," they too have an essence that makes them true or false. Naming is an action that teaches how to distinguish and discern, and the name is a tool to accomplish that goal. If it must succeed in this endeavor, then the tool or the name must be well made and accord with its true or natural function (386a–388c).

At this point, Socrates suggests that just as tools are made by specialist craftsmen, so names, too, are made by a specialist name-maker—who can only be a *nomothetês* (388e)—a name that the translator says in a footnote is "usually a legislator or lawgiver, but here someone who establishes the rules of usage that give significance to names" (11). On the other hand, in his magisterial commentary on the dialogue in *Being and Logos*, John Sallis refers to *nomothetês* simply as "lawgiver" and suggests that "not every man is capable of naming but only he who possesses the relevant art . . . which, consequently, accomplishes the proper end of such activity" (Sallis, *Being and Logos*, 209). We can perhaps understand the lawgiver as the one who possesses the art of separating and dividing the "things that are." Simply put, he is the one who can name "body" by differentiating it from "soul," or "human" from "animal" or "plant," and so on. Socrates then goes on to say that the lawgiver uses the bare elements of language to embody the proper name as such by looking not to existing names, but to the original form (*eidos*) of the name. And the person who judges the value and accuracy of the name or the name-maker's work is, Socrates suggests, none other than a philosopher—for it is he alone who can look to the forms by which the lawgiver made names. Socrates proceeds to examine the etymology of various names, beginning with the names of gods and then proceeding to even more primary names such those of the sun and moon; the elements; abstract nouns; the virtues, such as wisdom, understanding, justice, and so on; and common nouns, such as man and woman, until he gets to the name "name" itself: "Well, *onoma* (name) seems to be a compressed statement which says, 'this is a being for which there is a search,'" or, as Sallis translates it, "'being of which the search is'" (421b; Sallis, *Being and Logos*, 262). All of the names investigated, Socrates suggests, indicate motion, as though the "things that are" are constantly coming into being (411c).

Before he engages the hitherto silent Cratylus in an even more profound investigation, Socrates brings Hermogenes round to see that primary names, or names as such, imitate in sound "the being or essence that each thing is" (423e) and thus should not be mistaken for crude imitation of sounds in nature. John Sallis writes, "Socrates has drawn the entire problematic together in the problem of naming only to transpose this positing of names into the remote sphere of a primal lawgiver. The problem of mediating between Cratylus and Hermogenes has been recast into the task of mediating between the primal giver of names and the user of names" (Sallis, *Being and Logos*, 210). Having noted the "primary" distinction drawn by Socrates, Sallis goes on to remark,

> Socrates has succeeded in mediating between Cratylus and Hermogenes only at the cost of opening a gulf between the natural names and the properly human names . . . Cratylus, on the other hand, continues to maintain utter silence, thus aptly portraying that side of the gulf corresponding to his position—the side of those natural names which are inherently unsounded and which must be put into sounds by an artisan of names.
>
> But what are these natural names which, like the *logos* in the world-soul (*Timaeus* 37b), are prior to any sounding and which subsequently are put into sounds and syllables by the artisan of names? (Sallis, *Being and Logos*, 214)

Is it, then, the case that the name as such is necessarily silent because the search for the name is what the name is?

Turning to Cratylus, who professes to have been in total agreement, Socrates engages him in the most significant debate of the dialogue. Cratylus claims, "The simple truth is that anyone who knows a thing's name also knows the thing" (435d). For Cratylus, names are names insofar as they are correct, and they are correct because they disclose things themselves. Shifting focus now from the act of naming to the name itself, Socrates brings discourse itself to its limit. He demonstrates the circularity of Cratylus's logic by arguing that "if things cannot be learned except from their names, how can we possibly claim that the name-givers or rule-setters had knowledge before any names had been given for them to know?" (438b) Socrates brings Cratylus to agreement that things can be known without names; he then continues challenging Cratylus on the infallibility of names. As an acolyte of Heraclitus's doctrine that the things that are are always in motion, Cratylus has approved Socrates's philological exercise with Hermogenes where the etymology of proper names and nouns revealed eternal movement. But now, Socrates uses his own etymological work to prove the fallibility of names. Quite simply, if being doesn't stay the same, it cannot be named: "indeed, it isn't even reasonable to say there is such a thing as knowledge, Cratylus, if all things are passing on and none remain" (440a). Disagreeing with Heraclitus on the nature of being and demonstrating Cratylus's contradictory stance in believing in the infallibility of names despite the movement of being, Socrates concludes with a comic flourish, saying,

> Surely no one with any understanding will commit himself or the cultivation of his soul to names, or trust them and their givers to the point of firmly stating that he knows something, nor will he condemn both himself and the things that are as totally unsound and all flowing like leaky pots, or believe that things are exactly like people with runny noses, or that all things are afflicted with colds and drip over everything. It's certainly possible things that that way, Cratylus, but it is also possible that they are not. (440d)

Having recast the terms of the debate itself, Socrates sends the two men on their way. But what are we left with at the end of the dialogue? John Sallis suggests that though Socrates will freely acknowledge that man is bound to logos,

> yet the names and the *logos* to which he is bound do not guarantee what they institute. As we are told in the *Seventh Letter*, where names and *logos* form, respectively, the first and second of those things which are necessary means by which to bring about knowledge, names are not stable . . . Names cannot be guaranteed by an appeal to their origin nor by an appeal to other names . . . the only appeal is an appeal to that which names and *logos* serve to let be manifest. (Sallis, *Being and Logos*, 310)

Sallis's reading shows that the *Cratylus* is occupied with "the problem of the limit of logos . . . and the way in which the limiting is accomplished [as its proper end] . . . what is made manifest by the *Cratylus* has to do with the virtue (*arête*) of logos" (Sallis, *Being and Logos*, 184). With this astonishing interpretation of the dialogue, we find ourselves once more confronting the improper of the proper name, but this time as its virtue, its proper end. If we locate silence (the nameless) as this impropriety at the limit of the logos, we cannot fail to perceive that it opens the door to an ethics that revolves around the status of the name.

Ethics and the Name

One of the richest interpretations of the relation between the concept of the (im)proper name and ethics (ethics construed as responsibility) is offered by Derrida in his discussion of hospitality. On the other hand, Agamben's ethics, insofar as it evokes "happiness" rather than the law of responsibility, aims to disclose it in potentiality or inoperativity. Another modality in which he thinks this concept is infancy, which is very germane to the example of the wild child.

The Language of Hospitality

The initial context that Derrida establishes for this discussion is the political import of language in the transaction between the host and the stranger. To raise the question of hospitality in relation to the stranger is not simply to raise one particular question. Insofar as the stranger as such is in question, Derrida asks that we acknowledge the basal nature of the question: it is the condition of possibility for questioning itself. "As though the foreigner [*l'étranger*] were being-in-question, the very question of being-in-question, the question-being or being-in question of the question" (Derrida, *Of Hospitality*, 3). In what sense, however, is the question of the stranger fundamental? It is not simply that the stranger arrives *as* a question and thereby "puts me in question" (Derrida, *Of Hospitality*, 3). By invoking the word "parricide" uttered by the Eleatic stranger in *The Sophist* as well as Socrates's address to the Athenian judges in *The Apology*, Derrida indicates that the question of the "stranger-question" is a site conditioned by law—the familial law of the father and the juridical law of the polis. And this conditioning by law of "being in question" is above all a *question of language*—the language in which the questioning can happen below and beneath who or what is questioned. The stranger, Derrida writes, is he

> who, inept at speaking the language, always risks being without defense before the law of the country that welcomes or expels him; the foreigner is first of all foreign to the legal language in which the duty of hospitality is formulated, the right to asylum, its limits, norms, policing, etc. He has to ask for hospitality in a language which by definition is not his own, the one imposed on him by the master of the house, the host, the king, the lord, the authorities, the nation, the State, the

father, etc. This personage imposes on him translation into their own language, and that's the first act of violence. *That is where the question of hospitality begins.* (Derrida, *Of Hospitality*, 15; emphasis added)

The question begins with the possibility of hospitality as that which is predicated on translation, or the imposition of translation upon the other, but the muteness of the wild child would bring this very imposition (by the law) to a crisis by refusing even this predication of hospitality upon translation. This refusal is not a counterquestion. In a sense, the question of hospitality neither begins nor ends here; rather, it loses its form, its shape and threatens to become incoherent. In other words, the experiment of thinking hospitality in relation to the wild child implies a confrontation with an extreme radicalization of every facet of this terrain of questioning. Extending the spatial metaphor of terrain, we can perhaps say that Derrida, insofar as he measures the boundaries of this space in terms of the predication of hospitality on translation, marks the polar regions of this site as law and right on one end, ethics at the other (as antinomy, not opposition, as he insists), with language as the equator between the two. Language, then, is not only the foreign language of the law in which the stranger must ask for hospitality but also the language of ethics (lying, truth-telling, promising) in which the alterity of the stranger is in play. In a series of complex moves, Derrida will disclose the space between hospitality and law, but he will also show the space between ethical hospitality and a "certain ethics," thereby rendering hospitality indeterminate, undecidable, aporetic.

What does the introduction of the limit figure of the silent wild child into this terrain do to the (ultimately ethical) notion of hospitality as undecidable? Can we discern a place of welcome made possible by the wild child that is beyond any (in)decision? We can, in a sense, say that Derrida situates hospitality not at the door but on a fence. He differentiates between "the laws" of hospitality, which are the legal and social conventions of a society, and the singular "law" of hospitality that implies an inevitable transgression of the laws' constraints. However, insofar as the former implies right and the latter justice, they are invariably contaminated by each other. Thus, Derrida's topography of hospitality, insofar as it is circumscribed by legalities and their transgression, necessarily entails either the assertion or execution of the laws or delay of the *decision* of "the law," which is the kernel of the *force* of that law. However, because of the tension between the two poles, and because pure hospitality as such is impossible, decision flips into indecision without ever losing its reference to the laws/law. What, then, is a hospitality that occurs in the neutralization of this reference, where decision and indecision, assertion and delay, play no part in the scene of welcome?

Let us examine Derrida's map of hospitality by first taking up the two poles: Derrida begins by describing and analyzing the laws of hospitality, governed as they are by rights, duties, and obligations, and directed always toward the legitimate foreigner. (Here the foreigner [*xenos*] is not an absolute other, "a barbarian"; rather, he or she is one with whom a pact [*xenia*] is made.) At the other pole, Derrida maintains, is the singular law of hospitality. The former laws (in the plural) refer to traditional hospitality, which invariably colludes with power, "which is to say the necessity, for the host, for the one who receives, of choosing, electing, filtering, selecting their invitees, visitors, or guests, those to whom they decide to grant asylum, the right of visiting, or hospitality. . . . Injustice, a certain injustice, and even a certain perjury, begins right away, from the very threshold of the right to hospitality" (Derrida, *Of Hospitality*, 55). On the other hand, the latter singular law of hospitality (which, let us be clear, must not be mistaken for hospitality *as such*, or hospitality *proper*) demands the transgression of the laws of hospitality and does not discriminate between the legitimate foreigner and the absolute other—the one with whom we have no pact and can have no pact, the one who is beyond rights. "It is as though hospitality were the impossible: as though the law of hospitality defined this very impossibility" (Derrida, *Of Hospitality*, 75), thereby enjoining upon us a transgression of the multiple laws of hospitality that determine the rights and legal entry of the foreigner. Derrida does not wait to acknowledge that this latter singular law of "absolute, unconditional, hyperbolical hospitality" (Derrida, *Of Hospitality*, 75) has a privilege (this privilege is dogma and is not, perhaps cannot, be reasoned) over the multiple juridicosocial laws. "*The* law is above the laws. It is thus illegal, transgressive, outside the law, like a lawless law, *nomos anomos,* law above the laws and law outside the law *anomos*, we remember, that's for instance how Oedipus . . . is characterized" (Derrida, *Of Hospitality*, 79). (Oedipus, of course, invokes parricide again. But parricide here is not deployed, apropos the Eleatic stranger; rather, parricide here refers to an ultimate transgression of the laws that opens onto the space of questioning and therefore of unconditional hospitality.) And Derrida simply says:

> Let us say yes *to who or what turns up,* before any determination, before any anticipation, before any *identification,* whether or not it has to do with a foreigner, an immigrant, an invited guest, or an unexpected visitor, whether or not the new arrival is the citizen of another country, a human, animal, or divine creature, a living or dead thing, male or female. (Derrida, *Of Hospitality*, 77)

Given the privilege of the law of hospitality over the laws (which thereby makes hospitality coextensive with ethics), the question is not whether or not to say "yes" to the wild child. Rather, the question remains at the equator where language joins and separates the laws and the law. No doubt, the wild child demands an absolute hospitality if only because it has been abandoned by every law, is expelled from every city, and manifests a life against which no crime can be recognized as crime. But how can hospitality be expressed to one who has somehow persisted, stayed alive as an exile from the law, who has been abandoned by the law, for whom no law speaks, to whom no law is addressed? In what terms can the "yes" be expressed and indicated, given that the other has no language? How, under what rubric, must we say "yes"? The problem of translation, it seems, will not simply go away, and in fact arises beyond the law courts and the border patrol as an even more urgent question in the scene of the unconditional welcome.

We must set aside the persistence of translation for now and follow Derrida's thinking between the two poles on language and domicile. Derrida acknowledges that for displaced peoples, determined as they are by the prospect of dying in a foreign land (he cites the example of Oedipus again), the mother tongue is claimed as a mobile home. It is thought to be the ultimate homeland. Derrida brings up Hannah Arendt's well-known comment in an interview that what remains of Germany for her after the war is language or the mother tongue. Derrida terms this notion of language belonging, of language as the mobile home, as "the most unbreakable of fantasies" (Derrida, *Of Hospitality*, 91). It is a fantasy, primarily of an auto-affection, the simultaneity of hearing oneself speak, of hearing ourselves speaking to each other, and so on. In other words, Derrida calls into question the very notion of a "so-called mother tongue," which is always already "the other's language" (Derrida, *Of Hospitality*, 89), as part and parcel of the metaphysics of presence, an auto-nomy, an auto-mobility that is invariably haunted by the trace of difference.[2] Derrida asks, "is there hospitality without at least the fantasy of this auto-nomy? Of this auto-mobile auto-affection of which language's hearing-oneself-speak is the privileged figure?" (Derrida, *Of Hospitality*, 137).

What is the import of this classic deconstructionist move to the terrain of questioning that is hospitality? (In this peregrinating text, where the discourse seems to wander from one theme to another, one example to another without a resting place that would constitute a thesis, several doors open and close inviting us to enter, interpret, and exit.) Insofar as the mother tongue as one's personal domicile is the basis of hospitality, any interrogation of our ownership of language also invokes the impossibility of hospitality—impossibility not as the unachievable, but as that which can never be properly offered or accepted insofar as it has already happened. If the mother tongue is always already the other's language—if the language we dwell in, the language in which we invite and are invited, is not our own—then not only can there be no proper hospitality, but language itself is always already an opening, a fundamental hospitality. Therefore, Derrida cites Levinas saying "language *is* hospitality" (Derrida, *Of Hospitality*, 135). It follows, then, that where unconditional hospitality is concerned, language seems to fall silent. He writes,

> Nevertheless, we have come to wonder whether absolute hyperbolical, unconditional hospitality doesn't consist in suspending language, a particular determinate language, and even the address to the other. Shouldn't we also submit to a sort of holding back of the temptation to ask the other who he is, what his name is, where he comes from, etc.? Shouldn't we abstain from asking another these questions, which herald so many required conditions, and thus limits, to a hospitality thereby constrained and thereby confined into a law and a duty? . . . It is true that this abstention ("come, enter, stop at my place, I don't ask your

name, nor even to be responsible, nor where you come from or where you are going") seems more worthy of the absolute hospitality that offers the gift without reservations; and some might also recognize there a possibility of language. Keeping silent is already a modality of possible speaking. (Derrida, *Of Hospitality*, 135)

It is not clear whether Derrida's invocation of silence is a direct answer to the question (cited earlier) that he asks himself a little later—that is, whether there is a possibility of hospitality without a fantasy of language's auto-affection—but its pertinence to the question is unmistakable. Though silence as such can be exemplary of language's auto-affection,[3] and is the very figure of metaphysical presence, the silence that Derrida is speaking of here is not that of transcendental self-presence or totality; rather, it is a silence that expresses and indicates the dispossession of one's own language, one's impossible ownership or domicile in language, which always entails conditions. In other words, Derrida can be said to be alluding to a complex silence that testifies to the interval within the signifier, to the trace. Thus, all questions, especially those that pertain to identity and proper belonging, such as "What is your name?," "Where do you come from?," and so on, serve to erase and occlude this interval in the interest of linguistic property.[4] It is as if the very act of identification—asking and saying who one is—presupposes possession of self and language and, needless to say, possession "as such" is precisely what the wild child can never be said to have. Thus, to say "yes" to the strange, the unknown, the absolute, and mute other with whom we have no pact, can have no pact, is to imagine a form of hospitality beyond the "fantasy of language's auto-affection," beyond the proper of propriety and property. To imagine such an event of welcome in the interval that informs ownership in language and therefore exceeds the law brings one to confront what is meant by the question posed at every door: "who is there?" To put it more starkly, the phenomenon that appears at the door discloses a gap or an interval between the appearing and an identity. Thus, identity in terms of how what appears can be expressed, indicated, or be repeated reaches a radical point of crisis. Derrida's point is that unconditional hospitality emerges in relation to this interval between phenomenon and identity.

Consider, then, the moment of unconditional hospitality, the host's apprehension of the appearance of the so-called wild child in its indefinite delay in self-identification, lacking not only a name but a mother tongue. As that which surprises the law, the wild child appears in between sense and understanding, expression and indication, inside and outside. In other words, given its legendary status, the so-called wild child is neither with nor without language; rather, it discloses the *différance*, the play of difference that engenders language as signification. And yet, if at the same time it is inside and outside language, it also paradoxically cannot be said to be subject to the play of difference that is signification, or what Derrida terms "writing."

This exemplary disclosure by the appearance of the so-called wild child of language's happening is perhaps best grasped in relation to the function, place, and possibilities discerned in the concept of the proper name, if only because the proper name, too, is considered to be not subjected to "writing." Thus, in order to elaborate this scenario of unconditional hospitality as it emerges in the gap between appearance and identity, I shall here take up the most important aspect of this confrontation: the scenario of the proper name, which is usually regarded as the element of language that escapes the play of difference as the fundamental badge of proper belonging, ownness, self-identity, and auto-affection.

Hospitality and the Name

Hospitality, be it in accordance with the laws or the law, implies calling the guest by name. Conventional, conditional hospitality, Derrida underlines, is founded on the recognition of the legal name functioning as an identity badge of the rightful foreigner. "Because hospitality, in this situation, is not offered to an anonymous new arrival and someone who has neither name, nor patronym, nor family, nor social status, and who is therefore treated not as a foreigner but as another barbarian. . . . [T]he difference, one of the subtle and sometimes ungraspable differences between the foreigner and the absolute other is that the latter cannot have a name or a family name" (Derrida, *Of Hospitality*, 23). The fundamental function of the name is ultimately to hold the named accountable to the law. Borders and thresholds may not be crossed without proper identification. Unconditional hospitality, therefore, would break with the logic and rationale of recognition. It mandates an openness toward an absolute alterity, to the "unknown, anonymous other, and that I *give place* to them, that I let them come, that I let them arrive, and take place in the place I offer them, without asking of them either reciprocity (entering into a pact) or even their names" (Derrida, *Of Hospitality*, 25). But in keeping with the inevitable undecidability of hospitality, Derrida acknowledges a dilemma here—to ask the stranger his/her name, to want to call the other and to call the other as the other would wish to be called: "is it more just and more loving to question or not to question? to call by the name or without the name? to give or to learn a name already given? Does one give hospitality to a subject? to an identifiable subject? to a subject identifiable by name? to a legal subject? Or is hospitality rendered, is it given to the other before they are identified, even before they are (posited as or supposed to be) a subject, legal subject and subject nameable by their family name, etc.?" (Derrida, *Of Hospitality*, 29).

Where the wild child is concerned, the question of the name exceeds the "to ask or not ask" question, and even the scenario of recognition and refusal. It is not simply that the wild child seems to lack a name or cannot say its own name, that it is given a name outside the family bond, or that the ability of the wild child to respond to the name as its own (rather than a signifier that summons him or her like a bell) is doubtful. Rather, the question of the name in relation to the mute wild child raises an ontological question: when the wild child is introduced into the scene of hospitality, the act of naming as the Adamic function and quintessential prerogative of man, the very concept of the proper name, the status of the vocative, and the name's privilege within language move to center stage and can no longer be presupposed. The ethical questions of hospitality and community that this figure raises for us by testing the limits of norms and laws center ultimately and crucially on the ethics and politics of naming—not only what we call this figure, how it is named and designated, and what we presuppose about its response but, even more importantly, on the ancient metaphysical question of the name as such. In other words, we cannot ignore questions pertaining to our presuppositions about the proper name—what it is and how it functions, its proper place in language, its intimacy, and finally the possibility that what the name has in common with the wild child may well be an internal silence.

Once again, we perceive that the wild child tests the limits of hospitality, conditional and unconditional, by troubling even the question of the question that attends the stranger as such simply by its uncertain relation to the name—not only its name, but the very human prerogative to name, the function of the name in establishing identity, and the name as the fundamental and zero point of language (the name proper).

As alluded to previously, the scenario of unconditional hospitality, Derrida says, is one where questions as such reach their limit. To invite the stranger in without interrogations pertaining to identity (who?), causality (how?), or destination (where?), to simply say "yes" to whoever or whatever, is no doubt recognizable as a principle of the hyperbolic welcome, but as Derrida himself recognizes, what gives us pause here is the element of indifference that attends upon such altruism. Derrida ponders whether it is "more just and more loving to question or not to question? To call by the name or without the name?" (Derrida, *Of Hospitality*, 29), thereby aligning the ethical law of hospitality with love and aligning love with the discerning use of the name.

To have one's name pronounced correctly, to hear it used with ease, can seem (for those with so-called difficult names) an extraordinary gift of welcome. Each time someone refuses to know, learn, or pronounce the ostensibly "difficult" name, there is enacted a violence that consigns the de jure foreigner to a de facto barbarian. In other words, it is not only that the name as such holds the subject accountable to authority, but that refusing the legal name can be a worse dispossession in that it dismisses and diminishes the subjectivity bequeathed by convention. From this point of view, the onomastic violence toward African slaves who were called ridiculous nicknames by their masters or were bequeathed the cognomen of their masters as labels of property belonging to an estate is not derivative violence. Rather, it is undoubtedly the foundation of a violence that sustains slavery as such. In *Roll Jordan Roll*, Eugene Genovese cites the Supreme Court of Louisiana's 1827 declaration that "slaves being men are to be identified by their proper names" (Genovese, *Roll Jordan Roll*, 444). Later in the same chapter he suggests, "the idea that black people's names today are 'slave names' is true but distressingly twisted, for it overlooks the formidable black initiative in their creation" (Genovese, *Roll Jordan Roll*, 447). In other words, Genovese proposes that slaves and ex-slaves took on the names of white plantation owners or local patrons as a way of establishing a real history (Genovese, *Roll Jordan Roll*, 446) and testifying to a family experience. However, as Saidiya Hartman argues in *Scenes of Subjection*, for ex-slaves the so-called self-fashioning into autonomous free subjects meant a "burdened individuality" that "effectively conscripted the freed as indebted and dutiful worker and incited forms of coercion, discipline, and regulation that profoundly complicated the meaning of freedom" (Harman, *Scenes of Subjection*, 121–22). Is the function of the name fundamentally to establish accountability and thereby make subjectivity juridical? Consequently, is the name (as the history of slavery reminds us) the site of autonomy and dignity of the subject? To raise the question whether the concept of the proper name can have a different status within language, one that could potentially neutralize the violence that couples language and law, we should, of course, turn to Agamben.

THE LEVEL OF NAME: INFANCY

In "The Thing Itself," an essay published in 1984 that Agamben in fact dedicated to Jacques Derrida, Agamben, in the context of analyzing Plato's Epistle VII, marks the significance of two categories of language—the level of discourse (*logos*) and the level of names (*onoma*). However, it is in the earlier essay on Benjamin that the concept of *onoma* is taken up as the linguistic element with the potential to both engender and cancel history.

To elaborate, names, Agamben suggests, are quintessentially historical in the sense that they are always given, received, and transmitted. "Every act of speech presupposes the level of names, which can be reached only historically, through a 'thus it is said' that is in fact a 'thus it was said'" (Agamben, *Potentialities*, 50). In other words, names are iterative devices that derive their function and authority from citation and transmission. Thus, insofar as names are always handed down, their "origin" is as such lost in the shadows and is impossible to grasp through reason. Alluding, then (but not in so many words), to

the origin of language, Agamben establishes with Derrida the fundamental historicity of the letter and suggests that "language thus always
anticipates the original place of speaking beings" (Agamben, *Potentialities*, 50). This "anticipation of the origin" is history itself. Further,
he writes, "history is the cipher of the shadow that denies human beings direct access to the level of names: *history is the place of names.*
The transparency of language—the ungroundedness of every act of
speech—founds both theology and history. As long as human beings
cannot reach the origin of language, there will be the transmission of
names. And as long as there is the transmission of names, there will be
history and destiny" (Agamben, *Potentialities*, 50–51). Thus far, we are
of course still within the Derridean problematic in *Of Grammatology*,
but now Agamben takes a step further with Benjamin as his guide.

A hairline fracture is introduced between history and language.
Quoting and commenting on Benjamin's writings on language, Agamben suggests that for Benjamin, "the cohesion of language and history
is not total. It coincides, indeed, with a fracture in language itself, that
is, with the fall of language (*Wort*) from the 'pure life of feeling' (*reines
Gefühlsleben*), in which it is 'the pure sound of feeling,' into the domain
of meaning (*Bedeutung*)" (Agamben, *Potentialities*, 51). Significantly, the
"prehistoric" condition of language, in which it was the pure sound of
feeling, was nonsemantic, without meaning. In his "On Language as
Such and the Language of Men," Benjamin asserts that this prehistoric
condition is pure language marked by names that have no logos whatsoever. Agamben comments that "the status of this Adamic language
is therefore that of speech that does not communicate anything other
than itself and in which spiritual essence and linguistic essence thus
coincide. Such a language does not have a content and does not communicate objects through meanings; instead, it is perfectly transparent
to itself" (Agamben, *Potentialities*, 52).

One implication of this transparency of language as nonmean-
ing is its absolute extirpation of any notion of the unsayable. The unsayable in language, Agamben explains, relies on the concealment of
communication. Revealed language, on the other hand, is fully sayable
and transparent. Thus, if the fall of language into meaning and signifying communication degrades language to a tool or a means, the
invariable outcome for Benjamin is the Babel of tongues. Agamben

suggests that for Benjamin, the redemption of language and its messianic fulfillment is precisely the project that is assigned to the translator as task. What connects all historical languages is the fact that they all aim at pure language. Or, as Agamben phrases it, *"all languages mean to say the word that does not mean anything"* (Agamben, *Potentialities*, 53). Agamben suggests that the "expressionless word" of pure language, which is the level of the language of names, as the binding aim of all languages, remains unsayable in the language of communication, and in fact "sustains the signifying tension of languages." (To multiply the paradoxes, we could also say that what remains unsayable or incommunicable in everyday language is precisely the sayability of language itself—language communicating itself as pure communicability. To recall the *Cratylus*, insofar as "name" is the name of the being for which the search is, it is the name of the name that is ultimately unsayable.) For Benjamin, redeemed humankind necessarily entails a universal language that will overcome the Babel of tongues and bring about the fulfillment of language and history. Agamben goes on to make the point that according to the doctrine of the Kabala as interpreted by Benjamin's friend Gershom Scholem, "the foundation of every human language is the name of God," and that this name is constituted by pure letters. This notion of "the supremacy of the letter or *gramma* (as the originary negative foundation of language)," Agamben argues, is found in its secularized version in Derrida and other French thought.

The departure, then, from Derrida and negative theology is inaugurated by Benjamin's view that, as Agamben puts it, "the language of redeemed humanity has 'burst the chains of writing' and is a language that 'is not written but festively celebrated.'" (Agamben, *Potentialities*, 57–58). Agamben insists that this conception of fulfillment is not to be understood as an infinite task that serves merely to perpetuate the historical and linguistic process. Rather, Agamben writes, "Benjamin criticized this conception without reservation when he wrote that the past must be saved not so much from oblivion or scorn as from 'a determinate mode of its transmission,'" and that "the way in which it is valued as 'heritage' is more insidious than its disappearance could ever be" (Agamben, *Potentialities*, 60). The pure language of names is not written in any sense and therefore cannot be transmitted as heritage. In other words, with the concept of pure language, Benjamin envisions not a covert means to perpetuate and reproduce history and language as communication, but to end it, to bring it to fulfillment. I shall return to this point momentarily, but here let us simply note Agamben's description of this space of universal history/language. He writes,

> Here the language disappears as an autonomous category; it is possible neither to make any distinct image of it nor to imprison it in any writing. Human beings no longer write their language, they celebrate it as a holiday without rites, and they understand each other "just as those born on Sunday understand the language of birds." (Agamben, *Potentialities*, 60–61)

Freed from writing and therefore the diachronic time in which communication and signification occurs, language as name reveals itself as pure contemporaneity. And if, as Agamben argues in "Playland," the realm of diachrony is history whereas that of synchrony is that of ritual and play, then language at the level of names (onomatopoeia) or synchrony is also language as play.

It is now time to rethink the question of the wild child and its access to language at the level of names, the *onoma* as meaningless, desemanticized words, the zone of pure language as synchrony and play. Agamben's citation of the biblical legend serves to affirm that there can be no doubt that every wild child is born on a Sunday. We can even say that the onomatopoeic wild child is perhaps the only human being who truly dwells in language at the level of name. Agamben has a term for such dwelling: he terms it "infancy," a condition in which the originary is also the most contemporary. In *The Idea of Prose*, Agamben offers a meditation on infancy, and it could well serve as a fit description for the wild child:

> The neotenic infant . . . would find himself in the condition of being able to pay attention precisely to what has not been written, to somatic possibilities that are arbitrary and uncodified; in his infantile totipotency, he would be ecstatically overwhelmed, cast out of himself, not like other living beings into a specific adventure or environment, but for the first time into a *world*. He would be truly listening to being. His voice still free from any genetic prescription, and having absolutely nothing to say or express, sole animal of his kind, he could like Adam, *name* things in his language. In naming, man is tied to infancy, he is for

ever linked to an openness that transcends every specific destiny and every genetic calling. (Agamben, *The Idea of Prose*, 96–97)

The wild child, then, is the human being in the state of infancy—a state that is neither of the past nor the future but is radically contemporary to the structure of time and language. It is the condition in which language constitutes an experience rather than a tool, a means to an end. In his essay *Infancy and History*, Agamben explores this space between mythos and logos, past and future, fact and fiction in terms of an experience of language. It is important to state at the outset that by infancy, Agamben is not a referencing a chronologically prior experience or state of being that precedes speech. He writes, "It is not a paradise which, at a certain moment, we leave for ever in order to speak; rather it coexists in its origins with language—indeed, is itself constituted through the appropriation of it by language in each instance to produce the individual as subject" (Agamben, *Infancy and History*, 48). It is also not a limit of language that is outside language. It is not the "vulgarly ineffable. The ineffable, the un-said, are in fact categories which belong exclusively to human language" (Agamben, *Infancy and History*, 4) and are merely that which language must presuppose in order to signify. "In terms of human infancy, experience is the simple difference between the human and the linguistic. The individual as not already speaking, as having been and still being an infant—this is experience" (Agamben, *Infancy and History*, 50).

It is necessary to clarify that for Agamben, infancy as experience is "freed from the subject's conditioning" (Agamben, *Infancy and History*, 49)—that is, it is unconditioned by any notion of a so-called individual subject. It is the experience of a lag between the subject and language as sign that thereby installs a nonsubject at the heart of subjectification. "It sets up in language that split between language and discourse which exclusively and fundamentally characterizes human language. For the fact that there is a difference between language (langue) and speech (parole), and that it is possible to pass from one to the other, and that each speaking individual is the site of this difference of this passage . . . is the central phenomenon of human language" (Agamben, *Infancy and History*, 51). It is an indication of the split within language between the semiotic and the semantic, langue and parole that "first opens a space for history" (Agamben, *Infancy and History*, 52). Situating infancy as a space or an interval between human being and language, a place between having and not having language, as that which gives place to the very possibility of the repetition of signs, Agamben speaks of an experience of language that is in potential. In that sense, it is to enter into a purely empty dimension, where experience is necessarily mute. In the experience that is infancy, neither language nor the not-yet subject is free or determining of the other; rather, both are caught up in a circle of reciprocity where each exceeds the other. Man is therefore neither simply determined by language nor wholly free, but is subject to a language that is split at the origin.

Infancy is the experience of language as *arche*, the moat between langue and parole. It is this split within language that registers the specificity of the human being in relation to language, whereas animals, Agamben says, are not exiled from language, but, rather, are always already one with their language. He writes,

> It is not language in general that marks out the human from other living beings—according to the Western metaphysical tradition that sees man as *zōon lógon échon* (an animal endowed with speech)—but the split between language and speech, between semiotic and semantic (in Benveniste's sense), between sign system and discourse. Animals are not in fact denied language; on the contrary, they are always and totally language. In them *la voix sacrée de la terre ingénue* (the sacred voice of the unknowing earth)—which Mallarmé, hearing the chirp of cricket, sets against the human voice as *une* and *non-decomposée* (one and indivisible)—knows no breaks or interruptions. Animals do not enter language, they are already inside it. Man, instead, by having an infancy, by preceding speech, splits this single language and, in order to speak, has to constitute himself as the subject of language—he has to say *I*.
> (Agamben, *Infancy and History*, 51–52)

What distinguishes the human being, then, is his/her temporal noncoincidence with language. Insofar as human beings experience this lag (have an experience of infancy where language is in potential), they are given a possibility for muteness and silence that testifies to nothing if not to the potentiality of language itself. The wild child undoubtedly appears in this space of silence, in the interval between langue and parole. As a human child abandoned and isolated, he or she is in a relation to language that is at the tip of the tongue. In a sense, then, the wild child is not so much "deprived" of language so much as it is on the other side of the "moat" between langue and parole. Human relation to language is inescapably disjunctive—an absolute simultaneity of language as meaning is denied to our speech. If the speaking person finds him/herself on the side of signification yet haunted by the trace, the wild child dwells in the trace and is hunted if not haunted by the sign. Agamben, of course, does not address the exceptional instance of the wild child, but he says the following:

> In the human individual, exposure to language is indispensable for the acquisition of language. It is a fact whose importance can never be over-emphasized in understanding the structure of human language that if a child is not exposed to speech between the ages of two and twelve, his or her potential for language acquisition is definitively jeopardized. Contrary to ancient traditional beliefs, from this point of view man is not the 'animal possessing language', but instead the animal deprived of language and obliged, therefore, to receive it from outside himself. (Agamben, *Infancy and History*, 56–57)

In not speaking, the wild child demonstrates its radical humanity—for only humans have the potential to be mute, in the space between having and not having language, between *logos* and *onoma*. The wild child is the experience of the human being at its most original and contemporary condition.

Infancy and Hospitality

Having plotted, if in a cursory way, the wild child's relation to the name as the onomatopoeic level of language distinguished from meaningful communication, we can now return to our original problematic of hospitality as set out by Derrida: How does one render hospitality to that "no-man" which appears in this place of infancy and at this place where quite clearly the undecidable oscillation between the legal laws and the hyperbolic law of hospitality is itself stopped? How does one give place to this indeterminate place, this nonplace?

But first, we must ask with Derrida, in his essay *Khōra*, "what is place?" (Derrida, *On the Name*, 111). This is a question that Derrida poses at its most radical level in his essay on the discourse of *khōra* in Plato's *Timaeus*. While it may seem a non sequitur to situate a discussion of infancy, or the in-between place of the wild child, within a context as originary as *khōra*, it bears recalling that the discourse on the wild child is also always a problem of thinking the *arche*—the *arche* of man and language—if not of the world and the cosmos.[5] Without making a detour into the dialogue itself and Derrida's careful textual analysis of the appearance of the word *khōra* therein, and his magisterial deconstruction of Platonism through that reading, I shall merely signal here the stepping stones in Derrida's essay that bring together hospitality and infancy.

A key linking point between Derrida's reading of the discourse on *khōra* and the theme of the wild child's place (infancy) is the "legendary" aspect of both. "*Khōra* reaches us, and as the name" (Derrida, *On the Name*, 89), writes Derrida in the opening sentence of the essay. But lest we are led by our habits of thought to imagine that this at last is a "proper" name, or the only proper name, Derrida hastens to dispel the misunderstanding. "We would never claim to propose the exact word, the *mot juste*, for *khōra*, nor to name it, *itself*, over and above all the turns and detours of rhetoric, nor finally to approach it, itself, for what it will have been, outside of any point of view, outside of any anachronic perspective" (Derrida, *On the Name*, 93). For *khōra* defies not only the "opposition of *logos* and *mythos*" (Derrida, *On the Name*, 90) but all other oppositions as well, such as those between the intelligible and the sensible, speech and writing, fact and fiction, and so on. Referring to the terms or names of these oppositions, the name *khōra* can be said to designate not a something beyond, but indeed the very slippage from one set of terms to another, the metonymic movement when "names are displaced from types [*genres*] of being to types [*genres*] of discourse" (Derrida, *On the Name*, 91). Thus, Derrida specifies, *khōra* cannot be referred to as "the *khōra*," for "the definite article presupposes the existence of a thing, the existent *khōra* to which, via a common name . . . it would be easy to refer. But what is said about *khōra* is that this name does not designate any of the known or recognized or, if you like, received types of existent, *received* by philosophical discourse . . . what *there is*, there, is not . . . which, by the way, gives nothing in giving place" (Derrida, *On the Name*, 96). Derrida insists on the paradox that the name *khōra* cannot refer to a determinate existent—it is always already effaced; however it "lets itself be called or causes itself to be named without answering, without giving itself to be seen, conceived, determined. Deprived of a real referent, that which in fact resembles a proper name finds itself also called an X which has as its property (as its *physis* and as its *dynamis*, Plato's text will say) that it has nothing as its own and that it remains unformed, formless (*amorphon*). This very singular impropriety, which precisely is nothing, is just what *khōra* must, if you like, *keep*" (Derrida, *On the Name*, 97). In other words, rather than the name "proper," *khōra* designates the impropriety of name, to the nonfoundation that enables and challenges the boundaries of whatever appears phenomenologically.

As preorigin, *khōra* would refer to the enigma of the trace, of what Derrida calls the "primordially repetitive structure of signs in general" (Derrida, *Speech and Phenomena*, 51) and later "such a trace is—if we can employ this language without immediately contradicting it or crossing it out as we proceed—more 'primordial' than what is phenomenologically primordial" (Derrida, *Speech and Phenomena*, 67). *Khōra,* then, is the place where primordiality takes shape—it engenders forms *schemata* that are "of it without belonging to it" (Derrida, *On the Name*, 95). So how, then, must we conceive of this self-effacing place that leaves a trace on the forms of being and forms of discourse?

Khōra cannot be anthropomorphized; nevertheless, "she" can only be thought as receptacle that receives the following:

> *Khōra* receives, so as to give place to them, all the determinations, but she/it does not possess any of them as her/its own. She possesses them, she has them, since she receives them, but she does not possess them as properties, she does not possess anything as her own. She "is" nothing other than the sum or the process of what has just been inscribed "on" her, on the subject of her, on her subject, right up against her subject, but she is not the *subject* or the *present support* of all these interpretations, even though nevertheless, she is not reducible to them. Simply this excess is nothing, nothing that may be and be said ontologically. This absence of support, which cannot be translated into absent support or into absence as support, provokes *and* resists any binary or dialectical determination, any inspection of a philosophical *type*, or let us say more rigorously, of an *ontological* type . . . *if there is place*, or, according to our idiom, *place given*, to give place here does not come to the

same thing as to make a present of a place. The expression *to give place* does not refer to the gesture of a donor-subject, the support or origin of something which would come to be given to someone. (Derrida, *On the Name*, 99–100)

Here, Derrida clarifies that *Khōra* should not be mistaken for being either in terms of the meaning of being or the truth of being, for it is beyond even presence and absence. Moreover, if it/she receives, it/she does not do so actively for it/she receives no marks or impressions (Derrida, *On the Name*, 94). As a "third genus," it/she can never become "the object of any tale, whether true or fabled" (Derrida, *On the Name*, 117), as it/she is the receptacle of all narrative receptacles. The enigma of *khōra* pertains to the point that "it/she gives place to all stories, ontologic or mythic" (Derrida, *On the Name*, 117). As *pandekhēs*, it/she receives as in "to welcome, to gather, or even to expect, for example, the gift of hospitality . . . it is a matter of returning (*antapodidōmi*) the gift of the hospitality of (the) discourses. And in the dialogue, it/she gives place above all to Socrates, who himself who 'is disposed to receive everything he is offered'" (Derrida, *On the Name*, 110). Derrida writes,

> Socrates is not *khōra*, but he would look a lot like it/her if it/she were someone or something. In any case, he puts himself in its/her place, which is not just a place among others, but perhaps place itself, the irreplaceable place. Irreplaceable and unplaceable place from which he receives the words(s) of those before whom he effaces himself but who receive them from him, for it is he who makes them talk like this. And us, too, implacably.
>
> Socrates does not occupy this undiscoverable place, but it is the one from which, in the *Timaeus* and elsewhere, *he answers to his name*. (Derrida, *On the Name*, 111)

Is Socrates, then, a proper name? Not quite. Derrida indicates that the pertinent question is rather "what takes place under these names?" (i.e., *khōra* or Socrates). Derrida himself suggests that what takes place is "the gift of hospitality"—a hospitality of discourses, a mutual giving and receiving of words that is, however, enabled by effacement or silence of *khōra*/Socrates rather than by loquacity. This gift of hospitality in its passivity and effacement cannot even be said to take place as an event in time—for it is not even "unconditional" in the sense that it transgresses or suspends the conditions of hospitality. Indeed, the hospitality of *khōra* is beyond all decision. Its time, then, is not that of a happening but can be likened to the open sky of a temporal paradox where the oldest or the originary as that which is in the beginning bridges the youngest or infancy as also a beginning; as Derrida says, *khōra* can be understood as both achronic and anachronic.

Thus, we have here an unexpected constellation between place as hospitality and childhood—two themes whose interrelation may be clarified with the help of the wild child who is always at the door of every thought of hospitality.

Let us turn briefly to the moments in Derrida's essay when he introduces the theme of what Agamben terms "infancy." Referring to the framing narrative of the dialogue, Derrida invokes two themes, both pertaining to the spacing between or beyond the oppositions. The first pits the orality of the Greeks against the writing of the Egyptians. The latter write Greek history in lieu of the Greeks' "childish myths." Second, this myth of origin as *writing* is itself recalled as an *oral* tale by the young Critias. A paradox is contained in the fact that this memory of the myth of Greek history (Egyptian writing) is preserved mentally by young Critias because he "heard" it in his childhood. Memory in childhood is like the virgin wax that receives durable impressions. Derrida then expatiates on the "virgin wax" of childhood to suggest that it too receives, letting everything take form in it just like *khōra*. So Derrida shows that the discourse on *khōra* interweaves infancy and primal preorigin, writing and orality, memory as writing/logos and forgetting as myth. (He also reminds us that myth derives from play and will not be taken seriously, and yet, one cannot do without myth when there is no stable logos to avail oneself of [Derrida, *On the Name*, 112].) In other words, we have a truly strange atemporal moment when the originary and primal *Khōra* is also "the younger, infant even, achronic and anachronic" (116). *Khōra*, then, is both very old—older than the oldest and younger than the youngest as well.

However, *khōra* should not be understood as simultaneously possessing the attributes of youth and age. In the concluding pages of the essay, Derrida writes, "*Khōra* marks a place apart, the spacing which keeps a dissymmetrical relation to all that which, 'in herself,' beside or in addition to herself, seems to make a couple with her" (Derrida,

On the Name, 124). As spacing, or the interval between this and that, *khōra* is like a palimpsest, tabula rasa, virginal, an infant, unmarked, and therefore cannot even properly be considered an origin (Derrida, *On the Name,* 124). Thus, this eternally unmarked space of infancy is also "a strange mother who gives place without engendering" (Derrida, *On the Name,* 124). For lack of another term, one that avoids attributes, *khōra,* let us say, constellates infancy and hospitality, infancy as hospitality. If *khōra* and infancy are metonymically associated, we can say that Agamben approaches infancy as an *experience of the potentiality of language* and trace, and not only as the structural default of signification.

We thus once again find ourselves with the language of receiving and hospitality. Human beings must receive language, but it is of course language that receives them, giving them a place to say "I" by effacing itself. And if the wild child dwells in that effacement of language, is he or she not the one who receives and welcomes? Is it not that it is the human being on the side of speech who receives hospitality from the child on the side of silence, from infancy? Like Socrates then, the wild child "answers to his name" from *khōra* by effacing himself and prompting by his silence the discourse of others. He thereby engenders a great "gift of hospitality" that is neither conditional nor unconditional but gives place to a hospitality that is beyond any auto-affection and beyond any decision.

SIX

The Wild Child and Scientific Names

THE WILD CHILD IS MORE THAN A CONCEPT. INSOFAR AS HE OR SHE is a product of the historical discipline of scientific naturalism, which Foucault suggests is a discipline of naming, this incorrigible figure appears within its annals as a problem. In attempting to name the wild child, the discipline faces a unique problem that troubles its very epistemic and discursive foundations.

SCIENCE AND THE DISCIPLINE OF NAME

Let us first take up the politics of the name of the wild child as it appears in the works of the naturalists of the classical era on what might be termed the epistemology of life. Deprived entirely of filial relations, the wild child is marked not only by its lack of a patronym but also by its own proper name, a name by which it belongs to itself. In the classical era, when the great inventories of life were undertaken, the wild child had no proper place within the newly evolved biological schemata. The designation of this mute and humanlike creature and its placement in the taxonomy of natural history invariably impinged upon the untiring question of what can be said to be proper to humans—that is, what is essential to the constitution of the human being.

To open this literature is first of all to encounter the grand schemata of zoological and botanical life as it began to be mapped systematically in the eighteenth century. Invariably, the first name one encounters is that of the great Swedish botanist and natural historian Carol Von Linné or Carolus Linnaeus (1707–78) and his invention of a new classification system of species, first put forward in his *Systema Naturae* (first edition 1735). Linnaeus's great contribution to what was to become physical anthropology was the naming of humans as *Homo sapiens* (in 1758) and the placement of humans in the first edition among the *Anthropomorpha,* or humanlike animals. Later, in the tenth edition of 1758, the order *Anthropomorpha* is revised to Primates. As the first naturalist to produce a coherent taxonomy and naming practice for the species, Linnaeus introduced a new binomial system of classification for all species, which continues to be used.[1] In the first edition, the order *Anthropomorpha* is subdivided into the genera *Homo*, *Simia* (ape), and *Bradypus* (sloth). *Homo* is then categorized as a species (*nosce te ipsum* or know thyself) and given varieties, thereby marking one of the first subdivisions of humankind into separate and distinct races: the *europaeus albese*, *americanus rubens*, *asiatic sulcus*, and *africanus niger*.[2] Interestingly, in the 1758 edition (the tenth), Linnaeus diversified the genus *Homo* into two species, *Homo diurnus* and *Homo nocturnus*, or troglodytes. *Homo diurnus*, or day man, was subdivided into the six varieties of *Homo sapiens*. To the aforementioned four races, now given attributes of characteristic humors, temperament, and clothing,[3] are added two races distinguished by the language of their attributes: ferus (wild man) and monstrosus (including Hottentots, alpine dwarves, and Patagonian giants). Ferus, though a variety of *Homo sapiens*, is particularized with a brief list of six known cases of wild children, including Peter of Hanover (*Juvenis Hannoveranus*) and Marie Le Blanc (*Pueri Pyrenaici*), and is characterized as *tetrapus, mutus,* and *hirsutus*. Night man, or *Homo nocturnus*, is divided into *Homo sylvestris* or orang outangs.

According to most scholars of the period, Linnaeus's taxonomy and his binomial system in general generated criticism, his most famous detractor being Comte de Buffon (1707–88), who protested the placement of humans in the same species as apes.[4] According to Gunnar Broberg, there were others, such as J. G. Wallerius, who wrote a dissertation in 1741 attacking Linnaeus; Theodor Klein, a leading contemporary authority on zoology; Linnaeus's own sponsor, Johann Frederick Gronovius; and his friends Albrecht von Haller, Samuel Odmann, and others, who all recommended a separate order for the genus of humans.[5] However, if we attend only to the traditional humanist question of human dignity, and the apparent scandal of Linnaeus's decision to group humans along with the humanlike creatures (i.e., wild children and monsters) and the primates, we will miss what is truly salient about this moment: the silent consensus on the modality of ordering and separating—in other words, the creative act of naming as a way of knowing beings. It is important to remember that Linnaeus was far from proposing anything remotely like the modern evolutionary schema of creatures and neither was he prompting a revolution in the self-definition of humans. As Julia Douthwaite (citing H. W. Janson) notes in passing, "Linnaeus and other early modern naturalists were not working in a proto-evolutionary mode; rather, they relied on habits of thought inherited from philology, with its emphasis on nomenclature" (Douthwaite, *The Wild Girl*, 17).[6] In other words, what is significant is the new though *unremarked* relation between, on the one hand, the ancient Adamic function of language as humans' exclusive power to name (or language as the mark of the human being) and, on the other, that of naming as the classifying and spatial arrangement of creation as the new modality of knowledge. This new relation between the function of language (naming and classifying) and being human is a change that is to be located at the very foundations of the episteme that made naming as classification possible.

So it is not just that for the first time humans' relation to animals, which had always been conceived in terms of an intimate continuity, is now conceived as a problem demanding rigorous examination and debate, or that for the first time a systematic understanding of the concept of species and a grounding for the principle of humankind would seem to be indispensable to the project of the Enlightenment itself. Rather, what is salient to an understanding of the place of *Homo ferus* is the underlying and more general epistemological shift that Foucault enjoins upon us, from the early modern attention to the interpretation of signs and similitudes to the table of representations, the mathesis and taxinomia of the Enlightenment. And, above all, it is the wild child that serves not, as one might expect, as the pivot around which debates about human nature congregate, but as the wild card that invalidates and brings to a crisis, in fact overturns, the table of knowledge and every argument mounted upon it by proving to be the most intractable and ultimate exception.

Let us take up in some detail the Linnaean moment of the emergence of the wild child and its implication in the language of taxonomy. As the father of natural history, Linnaeus is well known for being the first to classify humans as primates, thereby underscoring the animality of humans. However, the significance of his achievement lay in the relation he established between naming or classification and knowledge. In other words, to Linnaeus we attribute the full disclosure of the function of language as representation (even more than the notion of language as the distinctive attribute of the properly human) and its capacity to produce categories and map the ontogenesis of a life form in its very name. One of the concerns of Foucault's archaeology of epistemic shifts in *The Order of Things* is to show how language during the classical era shifts from the production of general similitudes, including that between human and beast, to what Foucault terms taxinomia and mathesis. The fundamental relevance of language at this moment is not merely its capacity for meaningful content; rather, for Foucault it is its transformation from opacity to transparency.

To elaborate, in *The Order of Things*, Foucault argues that there is a significant shift in epistemes in the seventeenth century from knowledges that are founded on the discovery of resemblances to knowledges as representation. Up to the sixteenth century, the ruling episteme emphasized similitudes and signs, whereas in the following two centuries it shifts to one governed by taxonomy and mathesis. In his view, the knowledge forms of early modern Europe are characterized by a theory of language that assumes two levels to a given text: a hidden enigmatic content and a "secondary language" (Foucault, *The Order of Things*, 79) of commentary and exegesis that must unearth the meaning and make the text speak. Knowledge here proceeds fundamentally through a semiological process that identifies signs and marks and the laws that link them and a hermeneutic process of reading these signs and making them speak (Foucault, *The Order of Things*, 29). There is a kinship here between knowledge and divination (Foucault, *The Order of Things*, 32; 59), and it is the establishing of resemblances that guides interpretation of texts. This episteme, Foucault argues, gives way in the seventeenth and eighteenth centuries to a new one based on language as the function of representation. Knowledge now is established not through analogy but analysis, and textual commentary is replaced by criticism. The solidity of language itself "as a thing inscribed in the fabric of the world" is dissolved, and "all language [has] value only as discourse" (Foucault, *The Order of Things*, 43). In other words, what we have is language as representation—a transparent "analysis of thought: not a simple patterning but a profound establishment of order in space" (Foucault, *The Order of Things*, 83).

Foucault clarifies that this new function of language as the transparent ordering of reality is not to be reduced to popular conceptions of so-called Cartesian mechanization or mathematicization of nature. The new epistemes of mathesis and taxinomia are to be understood thus: knowledge is

> a link with a mathesis which, until the end of the eighteenth century, remains constant and unaltered. This link has two essential characteristics. The first is that relations between beings are indeed to be conceived in the form of order and measurement, but with this fundamental imbalance, that it is always possible to reduce problems of measurement to problems of order . . . The relation to Order is as essential to the Classical age as the relation to Interpretation was to the Renaissance . . . the ordering of things by means of signs constitutes all empirical forms of knowledge as knowledge based [not on resemblances but upon] identity and difference. (Foucault, *The Order of Things*, 57)

In other words, what prevails as the dominant modality of knowledge is a system of signs—signs as "tools of analysis, marks of identity and difference, principles whereby things can be reduced to order, keys for a taxonomy . . . [a] general theory of signs, divisions, and classifications" (Foucault, *The Order of Things*, 58). Consequently, the characteristic knowledge forms of this era, whose profound interrelation at the epistemic level Foucault delineates, are general grammar, natural history, and the theory of value and exchange. Foucault offers a richly detailed analysis of each of these modalities that would be impossible and perhaps unnecessary to summarize here. However, among the four aspects of general grammar that he elaborates are language as proposition, articulation, designation, and derivation. The function of naming, which he attributes to language/representation in its articulatory mode, is intimately related to natural history.

Naming, Foucault suggests, is the way that the whole content of representation is articulated, part by part (Foucault, *The Order of Things*, 96). Names or nouns function not only to designate but to differentiate and group "together individuals that have certain identities in common and separating those that are different; such an articulation then forms a sequential generalization of groups growing gradually larger and larger . . . from the individual to the species, then from the species to the genus and on to the class, language is articulated precisely upon the dimension of increasing generalities; this taxonomic function is manifested in language by the substantives: we say an animal, a quadruped, a dog, a spaniel" (Foucault, *The Order of Things*, 97). This horizontal axis of naming is combined with a vertical one that names qualities through adjectives. Thus was a "grid of knowledge" (Foucault, *The Order of Things*, 128) established that aimed above all at a "solidity, without gaps, of a network of species and genera" (Foucault, *The Order of Things*, 150), where the role of time is not progressive or evolutionary, as may be misconstrued in hindsight, but is merely that which in the real world explains the series of events that confused and mingled the essentially spatial order of beings. Foucault's point is that natural history and the episteme of order in the eighteenth century are fundamentally a spatialized mapping and naming of life that can permit no gaps or discontinuities. From this point of view, the supposed opposition between proto-evolutionism and fixity of the species, he suggests, is superficial.

Foucault's discussion of the distinction between the epistemes of similitude and that of order and difference clarifies the stakes and brings into perspective the figure of the humanlike not-quite-human and not-quite-animal that haunts both modalities. The feral child is of course intimate kin to the concept of the humanlike, but if (thanks to the "unstable status of *Homo*") he/she was easily absorbed into studies of what H. W. Janson terms *similitudo hominis,* it is only in the eighteenth century, in the era of difference and order (i.e., natural history), that this figure's anomalous qualities begin to take shape.[7]

Now, perhaps for the first time, the specter of the not-quite-human is raised as not so much the medieval missing link that will fill the gap between human and beast and thereby secure the divine chain of being, but as an exception to the ontological ambition of the language of taxonomy. It is worth noting the difference here between the medieval notion of the ape as *naturae degenerantis homo,* where it is a horrific imitation, an imperfect resemblance, and poor relation of humans, and this modified notion of a human who is less than fully human. The conflation and confusion of human and ape in the figure of the pygmie, the humAnimal ambiguity of this hybrid figure, calls for clearer, more systematic differentiation. It is perhaps this task that, in a sense,

Linnaeus set himself in 1735, when in his *Systema Naturae* he distinguished the various genera of Anthropomorpha: *Homo* (*nosce te ipsum* or *Homo sapiens*, including the four racial varieties); *Simia*; and *Bradypus*. The Linnaean moment is best understood as the moment when a greater, more nuanced, mapping of the human was undertaken (rather than one when a new anxiety about evolutionism was mobilized), thereby solidifying the claims of natural history to show forth nature. And in this very attempt to make nature speak, to disclose its clear and rational continuum, to capture every molecule of life and give it a name, we see the necessity for the races, the *simiae*, the *monstra*, the *bruta*, and so on. But even as the grid of nature becomes increasingly finer, with *Homo sapiens* itself being distinguished within from *Homo ferus* (1758 edition), and as every effort is made to capture, name, and order all of humanity, the class of *Homo ferus* remains logically resistant to this effort.

Let us note what is obvious but entirely disregarded by commentators with regard to the way in which the wild child is classified by Linnaeus. One is arrested by the fact that this completely exceptional figure—exceptional in every sense of the term—is classified as a separate variety of *Homo sapiens*, *Homo ferus*, distinguished from the varieties mentioned in 1735 (the races of humans, such as the European, the Asian, and the African). This naming of *Homo ferus* as a specific variety aims to attribute to this creature of radical isolation and abandonment the possibility of society, even its origins. The wild child is presented in the natural history as though he/she were not singular, as though he/she were not alone, as though he/she had kin, as though he/she had a place. But the feral child is of course not the precultural savage imagined by theorists of the social contract, but is a taxonomic anomaly that fundamentally resists grouping. In fact, as a figure of abandonment, the feral child is the one who has been exiled from groups as such—human or animal. He or she has been cast out and exists in a space that is neither fully human nor animal. What is interesting, then, in this eighteenth-century attempt to group all feral children into a variety is that *we have a group of children who constitute a group on the basis that they have no group*. *Homo ferus* as the antigroup group, where the identifying characteristic is that no one of its members has a group, is profoundly anomalous.

One may argue that this is, however, consistent with the spatial will to continuity and totality that is endemic to this episteme. As Foucault points out, this will to continuity (which is really understood as preceding time) requires monsters as part of the total schema of life (Foucault, *The Order of Things*, 155). "On the basis of the power of the continuum held by nature, the monster ensures the emergence of difference" (Foucault, *The Order of Things*, 156). One may, therefore, conclude that between the will to render the abandoned child as belonging to a species and the pathos of his or her utter nonbelonging to anything or anyone, its absolute isolation, arises the idea and the class of monstrosity—inhuman, beastly—neither wholly human nor utterly animal. But, in fact, the matter is not so simple. In the first edition of his *Systema Naturae*, Linnaeus included a category of *Paradoxa* and Hybrids to class the creatures of fable, such as satyrs and centaurs. There had to be a place in the great continuum of nature for even those creatures that populate the imagination, such as werewolves and cynocephali, or dog people. And in the tenth edition, Linnaeus more clearly distinguishes the *Homo ferus* from the *Homo monstrosus,* a group that includes Patagonians, Hottentots, and the Macrocephali. The fact is that between the tenth and the twelfth editions (1766) of *Systema Naturae,* Linnaeus lists at least nine cases of *Homines feri.* Each child is named in Latin by his or her place and year of capture, thus opening the possibility of an absurdly infinite list, completely unlike the other closed classes. Because each name refers to an individual case rather than to a variety, the wild child, the status of the proper name, is here fully disclosed as nothing but classification. In other words, the proper name of the wild child is fundamentally a class of one. Moreover, being recognizably human but mute, this figure in effect threatens the fundamental aspect of humanness—the capacity for speech, as well as language's capacity to represent. Topographically speaking, the list perforates the taxonomy, opening an abyss within the language of order. In this taxonomy, then, it is humans' precariousness in the schema of life, about their place and meaning in that natural order, that comes to light. How ironic that the agent of this enlightenment should be none other than the feral child.

This raises the question as to why the enlightened episteme requires a classification for those children cast out of human society.

Why are they named as a group? In *The Open: Between Man and Animal,* Agamben writes,

> At the time when the sciences of man began to delineate the contours of his *facies,* the *enfants sauvages,* who appear more and more often on the edges of the villages of Europe, are the messengers of man's inhumanity, the witnesses to his fragile identity and his lack of a face of his own. And when confronted with these uncertain and mute beings, the passion with which these men of the Ancien Regime try to recognize themselves in them and to "humanize" them shows how aware they are of the precariousness of the human. (Agamben, *The Open,* 30)

In other words, by giving the *enfants sauvages* a distinct place in the schemata of nature as a separate variety of *Homo*—neither a contemporary ancestor nor simply a relic of a passing species, neither a missing link in the great chain of being between human and animal nor belonging to a race—enlightened humans, armed with the tools of taxonomy in seeking to discover their own place in nature, came face-to-face with their own "lack of a face."

Further in *The Open,* Agamben describes the operations of what he terms the "anthropological machine." This machine is fundamentally a discursive apparatus that works through the ceaseless separation of human and animal within the human in order to collapse that separation and render it indistinct as a function of power, as, for example, the Jew (human rendered animal) or the simian (animal made human). No doubt, the feral child constitutes a true dilemma, perhaps even a stopping of that machine. For what he/she exhibits is the abyss of humanness—that humans have no nature of their own, no face of their own—and when this not having is acknowledged, classification and its deconstruction become null and void. If we examine some of the well-known cases, we invariably perceive that humans can be wild without nature. And it is this reflection not of the animal in the human, but of the central muteness, a silence or emptiness, that threatens classification, or power as the act of naming.

Science and the Name: Some Legends

Detailed reports of wild children, appropriately enough, begin in the seventeenth century. Sir Kenelm Digby (1603–65), an English courtier and scientist who is known for his *Two treatises in the one of which the nature of bodies, in the other, the nature of mans soule is looked into in way of discovery of the immortality of reasonable soules* (Paris: Gilles Blaizot, 1644), narrates the story of John of Lige. In Chapter XVII of his treatise on the body, he discusses the senses of touch, taste, and smell and concludes that the sense of smell is not as well developed among humans as it is in beasts. John's story is simple. Wars and fear of pillaging soldiers send the child and his parents to hide in the forests. John, however, ran deeper into the forest, was lost to his parents, and was not recovered for several years. Meanwhile, he had subsisted on roots and wild meat, and his sense of smell became as sharp as a beast. When he was caught, it was soon "perceived that he was a man; though he had quite forgotten the use of all language" (Digby, *Two Treatises*, 248).

In *The History of Poland* (1698), Bernard Connor (1666–98), an Irish doctor, cites several cases of wild children whom he has witnessed going about on all fours and marked by their complete lack of language. The children brought up by bears seem to imitate bear sounds and behavior.[8] The next most well-documented case is that of Peter of Hanover, or Wild Peter, a boy of around twelve or thirteen discovered in 1724 near Hamelin in Hanover. His uncivilized and unconscious behavior was the delight of the Hanoverian court (of King George I, who maintained a home in his native land) as well as in London, where in 1726 he became a great curiosity among the courtiers who surrounded Caroline, Princess of Wales. John Arbuthnot, Swift's great friend, took charge of Peter and apparently baptized him and tried to teach him language. There were the usual slew of pamphlets and satirical plays about Peter, but of all the various accounts of this pathetic figure, Daniel Defoe's "Mere Nature Delineated" on Peter remains the most interesting and substantive account.[9]

The other famous eighteenth-century case is that of Marie Angelique Memmie LeBlanc, who was discovered in 1731 near Songi in southern France. This child was apparently about nine or ten years old but unlike the other cases, she was fierce, armed with a club and wearing a ragged dress. Her case, after Victor of Aveyron's (1798), is perhaps the best studied. La Condamine wrote a biography of Marie Angelique under the pseudonym of Madame Hecquet, and Lord Monboddo, the eccentric Scottish judge and amateur naturalist, wrote a lengthy account of her, and she served as a principal specimen in advancing his theories about the relation between men and animals. Perhaps the most famous and thoroughly discussed case is that of Victor of Aveyron, discovered at the very close of the eighteenth century in 1798 and captured in 1800. He was under the care of Jean Marc Gaspard Itard, a physician who was famous in his own day for his work with deaf-mutes. Itard wrote two reports on Victor in 1801 and in 1806, and there are several documents about Victor prior to his experience with Itard. Victor, by all accounts, was reasonable, gentle, and apparently sane, but with entirely undeveloped senses, and despite the most attentive tutoring, he remained completely incapable of grasping language and articulating speech.

Much of this detail is readily available elsewhere, so I will not repeat it here. We discover consistently that these children could not be used successfully for the purpose of drawing clear demarcations and definitions of what or who could be named as properly human and what was properly animal, let alone aiding theories about the origin of humanness. Despite the varying destinies that these children eventually faced after their capture, one element remains consistent in all of their accounts: their evident sanity; their normal vocal organs; and their complete inability to speak, grasp language, or function as linguistic beings. They were confoundingly normal and abnormal simultaneously. And despite the very different attitudes of the numerous first-hand accounts of these children, what remains consistent is the repeated acknowledgement that these children exhibited not a core of human essence, or even properly a substratum of animal intelligence or natural instincts, but an infinite malleability. Just like John of Lige, who learned to use his sense of smell in imitation of the beasts, or the Lithuanian bear children who walked like their foster-parents, or Marie Angelique, who had become a ferocious predator, or Peter and Victor, who in their isolation drew blanks, they showed that they had no nature of their own. There was nothing by which a so-called human being in a state of nature could be distinguished and thus the name of "human" could not lay claim to anything properly its own, such as a natural ability, propensity, or property. In short, the astonished observers repeatedly arrive at the realization that there is no such thing as human nature or human instinct—a set of behavior patterns that humans instinctively exhibit in the absence of language, community, and history. This was, of course, a consequential discovery in the eighteenth century, when the origins of human society and language were being debated as a way of arriving at foundational principles for government and justice. As Itard, writing about Victor in 1801, concluded:

> That man is inferior to a large number of animals in the pure state of nature, a state of nullity and barbarism that has been falsely painted in the most seductive colors; a state in which the individual, deprived of the characteristic faculties of his kind, drags on without intelligence or without feeling, a precarious life reduced to bare animal functions. (Itard, *The Wild Boy of Aveyron*, 49–50)

Itard's point, which he makes repeatedly in his two reports, is that humans reduced to "bare animal functions" are in fact less than animal and lack the intelligence and feeling of even a common dog. However, this central emptiness of humans generated two related discussions. Could one say that this malleability, the capacity to imitate, was the core faculty of humans and therefore a sign of his perfectibility? (This was Rousseau's argument in the *Discourse on Inequality*.) Or does this mean that human beings were entirely determined by their environment, therefore rendering freedom problematic? (This was the argument of the empiricists, Condillac, and others.) In any case, the identification of what is proper to humans encountered a road block, so that it was ultimately their self-recognition as humans (calling oneself human) that determined the name *Homo sapiens*.

Science, Races, and Names

To conclude this section on the politics of naming and classification, let us turn briefly to the question of how racial classification as naming impacts the wild child. As previously mentioned, Linnaeus had excluded the *Homines feri* from the four racial categories and placed them as individuals in a category of their own while terming them *tetrapus, mutus, hirsutus*. However, it appears that when *mutus* gives way to speech (a very rare occurrence), naming the child's proper racial category becomes paramount. In other words, it seems that the discourses of race and the capacity for language converge in the *Homo sapiens*, as evidenced in the case of one feral child who did acquire language and some speech.

Briefly, Marie Angelique, the fierce little girl who was found in southern France, not as naked or seemingly isolated and bewildered as the rest but ferocious and defensive of humans, eventually progressed from uttering sharp cries to grasping French and gradually speaking the language to a point of fluency in her later years. In the biography authored by La Condamine under the pseudonym of Madame Hecquet, she reports memories of her former life, of being captured and enslaved, of escaping with an African girl, and of their subsisting on their own in the wild.

These details are relevant for one reason only: the way in which it engendered feverish speculation about Marie Angelique's race. The questions asked by her interlocutors were not aimed at establishing the veracity of her memories, whether they had been suggested to her by others or whether they had been invented, and so on. Though her commentators report that the child had no language whatsoever when she first arrived on the scene, was inhuman, and merely made animal cries, her learned commentators were, however, not interested in how she could have once had language and now lost it, and what that forgetting implies about language itself. Rather, they were interested in only one thing: how to classify her racially. The assumption was that to discover her race would be to solve the enigma of her life. Both La Condamine and Lord Monboddo, her chief champions, were much exercised over this question and they put forth theories of her being an Eskimo or a Huron Indian. Though she appeared by all reports to possess Caucasian features and was declared to have white skin, there was no question of her fitness for the category of white European (*europeaus albese*). The presumption was that she belonged to a savage nation, probably somewhere in the north.

However, this overwhelming need to certify Marie Angelique's race is unique to her story. In the other cases, the feral children are merely outside the raced categories of *Homo sapiens* as *Homo ferus*, exactly in the way Linnaeus categorized them. No doubt, this child's racialization arises from the fact that she acquired speech and was now more recognizably human.[10] We have a clear instance here of the way the epistemology of taxonomy intersects with the biopolitics of race. In other words, in the imperative that humans be classified by race is also the assumption that race is the marker of the human. In other words, the child that falls into or is perceived as emerging from a state of nature effectively has either lost or has no race to speak of. Perhaps this equation of humanness with racial identity is exactly parallel to the way in which subjectivity and citizenship come to be conflated in the eighteenth century as well. However, the depositing of humanness in racial identity is also very fraught with and subject to volatile eviscerations. For the inferior races are, of course, over-embodied in their race, and are therefore always teetering on that edge of "nature" where humanness and race can be disarticulated and separated. In this event, they are invariably rendered wholly exterminable. What, then, is the difference between the biopolitics that jettisons inferior races into a state of nature by separating them from their humanity and the *Homines feri* who have no race? Clearly, it is that with the former, the inferior races are left with the husk of their identity and an empty account of humanness, whereas the wild child is assumed to be human, or is arguably human, but only *arguably* because he or she has no race—that is, the child lacks race inasmuch as it lacks speech and language. Whereas the former races lose their humanness even as their speech falls into unintelligibility, the latter lacks (or is freed from) race due to its silence.

SEVEN

HumAnimal Acts
Potentiality or Movement as Rest

The body cannot determine the mind to think, nor can the
mind determine the body to motion or rest, or to anything else
(if there is anything else).

However, nobody as yet has determined the limits of the
body's capabilities: that is, nobody as yet has learned from
experience what the body can and cannot do, without being
determined by mind, solely from the laws of its nature in so
far as it is considered corporeal. For nobody as yet knows
the structure of the body so accurately as to explain all its
functions, not to mention that in the animal world we find
much that far surpasses human sagacity, and that sleepwalkers
do many things in their sleep that they would not dare when
awake—clear evidence that the body, solely from the laws of its
own nature, can do many things at which its mind is amazed.

—Baruch Spinoza, *The Ethics*

Immense happiness!

—Philippe Petit, *Man on Wire*

AMONG THE BETTER-KNOWN BOOKS BY THE SWISS WRITER MAX
Picard is a small volume of fragmentary notes and observations first
published in 1948 entitled *The World of Silence*. For the most part, Picard
associates silence with the fullness of the ineffable—a theological experience particular to man; however, in one of his extended pastoral
visions he conjures the peasant's life as one imbued with silence but in
the material terms of an original "vocation":

> The life of the peasant is a life in silence. Words have wandered back
> into the silent movements of man. The movements of the peasant

are like a long stretched-out word that has lost its sound on a long journey.

The peasant repeats the same motions every time he mows and sows and milks, in every kind of work. The motions he performs are as concrete an image as the house he lives in and as the trees on the field. All the noise of work is absorbed into the constant pattern of the same repeated movements, and the peasant's work is surrounded with silence. In no other vocation is the pattern of daily work so clearly visible and concrete as in that of the peasant. (Picard, *World of Silence*, 125)

What interests me about this concrete image is the discerning of silence in relation to the *body* of the peasant not as an object in space, a Cartesian *res extensa* in opposition to and directed by a *res cogitans*, or a corporeal carapace that undertakes determined actions, but as a being in movement into which "words have wandered back." The body's silence is not soundless, but is rather rhythmic—action/repetition—the seamless gestures of mowing, sowing, and milking. And these movements disclose something about the body's vocation in relation to space. Picard writes,

Sometimes when a peasant moves with the plough and the oxen over the broad surface of the field, approaching ever nearer to the edge of the horizon where the sky touches the earth, it is as if the vault of the sky might the next moment, take up into itself the peasant, the plough, and the oxen, so that he might plough the soil of heaven as one of the constellations. (Picard, *World of Silence*, 126–27)

Here the peasant, his plough, his ox, and his field are together in a stillness that moves forward slowly—where the shared movement does not happen in space but instead makes space, by seeming to extend the field into the sky.

The question I pursue in the following pertains to the silence of the body—not the body that has been mutilated and rendered mute, thereby serving as a "brute" index of subjugation, but the power of the body to show itself in its humAnimal possibility—in other words, the so-called animal body as a *means* that is *capable* of silence insofar as it is essentially shared as *life*. And such humAnimal power, I suggest, can be discerned only if we approach the body in its dynamism, in time, when silence (or rest) shows itself *as* the very heart of all that is in movement. The wonder of any-body is movement (that it moves by itself); where the human being is concerned, however, such wonder is often remembered and recalled in exceptional and agile movement. In acrobatic movement, but also in movement that has been lost and recovered, the body moves in ways that defy expectations; thus, it appears to shed the limitations of its identity and shows itself as a gift of power. Though disabled bodies are more wondrous when they display such gifted movement, I here seek to avoid thinking of the body as an inert entity that is capable of moving. Rather, I approach the (able or disabled) body *as* movement—as life that is always already movement. This "fact of life," I suggest, is most apparent in the flash of agility. In agile movement, when the body is in aerial flight and appears more bird than human, or at the trapeze when it claims kinship with a squirrel, a spider monkey, the body reveals its mutability, its fundamentally protean character.[1]

In an interview with the *Irish Cinema Times* (published 31 July 2008), Philippe Petit, the tightrope walker who has pulled off several clandestine ropewalks (the most notorious being the one in 1974 between what were the Twin Towers in New York), says he enters

> the world of peacefulness, birds and clouds on the high wire . . . [in] a kind of intuitive, child-like way. If you see me getting ready before a performance . . . becoming the artist, half man, half bird, you will notice that my demeanor can be compared to that of people doing yoga, people meditating, it involves intense concentration . . . If you study Japanese martial arts you will understand that to concentrate and to meditate doesn't mean that you are totally cut off. It would be a poor state if you were completely locked into your own world. It could be dangerous, especially for the man on the wire. So what I do is create this intense concentration and lock myself in this world where I have lots of doors and windows ajar. Then if there is a little noise in the rigging, which indicates that something is wrong, I will hear that little noise. If there's humidity in the air that indicates rain, I will feel it on my skin and in my nostrils. So I am a very open, completely concentrated person.[2]

Here Philippe Petit makes it quite clear that the body's agility is founded at some level on its liminality. It is when the body appropriates itself as the *limen* or threshold, hyper-aware of its interconnectedness, that it displays its exuberance and its power—its potentiality. However, let us not mistake the threshold for the tightrope, a place that is physically entered. The threshold here is not a demarcated place into which the autonomous body enters, and in which it has a determinable experience. Rather, *the threshold is itself what the body can be.* As such, the threshold is an indeterminate zone between two spheres; it is an interval or a hiatus, that n/either separates n/or combines, thereby troubling the borders of the two spheres where the end of "this" flows into the beginning of "that." As threshold, then, the body would necessarily defy the relation between ground and figure and thus the very *temporal* notion of having a form that is one's own so as to be an identifiable or knowable being. As in the wonderful action photography of Herbert Matter, Thomas Eakins, or the contemporary photographer Howard Schatz, the body as temporality cannot be separated from space—it does not move in space, but moves or makes space. It is in a sense a body as threshold—a liminal body that moves between the just now and the not yet.

"Threshold" is one of Agamben's technical terms, for it appears as a seam between the beginnings and ends of chapters and sections in many of Agamben's works, including *Homo Sacer*. This term alludes to the liminal structure of the inside and the outside that Agamben discerns in every phenomenon—sovereignty, state of exception, language, and singularity. In general, the threshold as concept necessarily denotes a space that invites questioning—the questioning of pairs such as origin and terminus, means and ends, foundation and structure, form and content, presence and representation. Where Agamben is concerned, the term has the additional reference of indicating the entirety of his thought as not only a philosophy *of* the threshold (as is true also of Derrida) but a philosophy that is *at* the threshold—the opening of a door between prose and poetry, critique and vision, theoretical analysis and practice, and finally between the loquacity of Western metaphysics and a silence (perhaps mediated through Heidegger) that resonates with aspects of Asian thought.

The body's liminality is perceptible when it guides energy in a new way, as Petit says, for instance, in martial arts or yoga and, no doubt, also in gymnastic and acrobatic performance. Liminality composes matter, temporality, and space into the precisely guided direction of energy as in the practice of *Kung Fu, Tai Chi,* or *Aikido,* or in the performance of an aerial leap, a back flip, a cartwheel, or an impossible bodily fold as in *haṭha yoga*. Furthermore, insofar as it surprises, and rearranges space or repurposes objects, exceptional movement can disclose the body's liminality even through the dextrous manipulation of objects against common sense and meaning, such as juggling half a dozen teacups, folding a discarded square of paper into a graceful bird or a flower, working a sleight of hand with playing cards, or tying and untying knots of great intricacy.

Fundamentally, at the threshold anything is possible, for all laws—laws of physics, common sense, and reason; juridical laws; or the strictures of tradition—are suspended or interrupted. The threshold is an opening of space-time where "anything is possible," but this is not to be mistaken for a place or time where "one can do anything," which implies the redistribution of sovereignty rather than its interruption. As a syntagm that refers to the spacing of the threshold, "anything is possible" includes and implies the *im*possible. A threshold is always on the verge, it is an edge, a doorway. It is the infinitesimal split between "what was" and "what is just about to happen," and therefore it is always pure potentiality, what Agamben terms as a the potentiality or capability that cannot be exhausted in the act. As Philippe Petit is reported to have said after his first trespass to take a measure of the World Trade Center: "Impossible, yes, so let's get to work" (Petit, *Man on Wire,* 17).

Before turning to the zany performances of tightrope walkers, *yogis,* trapeze and martial artists, tumblers, jugglers, balancers, and contortionists, and their disclosure of the body's silence as potential, I ask, "in what sense can agile or acrobatic movement serve to clarify an understanding of Agamben's political ontology that opens onto an ethics?" It is well known that Agamben stresses the factor of impotentiality in his discussion of potentiality, and his valorization of Bartleby's famous "I prefer not to" has been elevated into a slogan of his politics of so-called radical passivity. However, I suggest that for Agamben, such so-called passivity is thinkable only within the context of movement understood ontologically as production. In other words, there is a strong, essential, but perhaps insufficiently discussed relation between the term movement and the concept of potentiality—a relation that Agamben alludes to and even presupposes but that has been overlooked in popular discussions of his work. And examining this relation is preliminary for any understanding of Agamben's political ontology. Such an excursus can also serve to clarify the "fundamental passivity" that is usually associated with Agamben's theory of potentiality as essentially a way of being moved—a movement that is not opposed to but essentially cobelongs with nonmovement—a perspective derived from Aristotle (and no doubt inspired by Heidegger) that he then politicizes as nonproductivity, or a form of inoperativity. In order to decipher the paradox of ontological movement (*kinēsis*) as simultaneously nonwork or nonproductivity, it is to the implications of his theory of potentiality that we must turn.

Eventually, I follow a single thread (which is itself a skein of concepts) of the larger tapestry: the theory of "pure means" as play and profanation and its relation to potentiality—concepts that have received an original elaboration in Agamben's complex and multidimensional work.

POTENTIALITY AS POLITICAL ONTOLOGY

It can be said without hyperbole that the theory of potentiality is the fulcrum that balances the complex elements of Agamben's terse philosophical investigations. Simply to trace the manner in which potentiality appears in the variety of contexts that are analyzed by Agamben, such as the realm of art and the critique of aesthetics, language and poetry, sovereignty and the state of exception, economic theology, witnessing and testimony, community and singularity, inoperativity, and so on, would require a separate monograph. However, a brief segue into how he interprets and situates the concept would be useful at this point in order to appreciate the body as the event of singularity, the body in exceptional movement.

What distinguishes Agamben's appropriation of Aristotle's conceptualization of ontological movement or *kinēsis* as *dunamis, energeia,* and *entelecheia* in *Physics* and *Metaphysics* from other discussions, namely that of Heidegger, is the extrapolation and emphasis on the *political* import of these concepts. In fact, insofar as Agamben's reading of Aristotle privileges *dunamis,* which he consistently renders as *la potenza* (power or possibility), his theory cannot be given its due unless it is received as an utterly original development that serves more as a political critique than as ontological inquiry. Nevertheless, it must be acknowledged that Agamben appears to intend his reading to be thoroughly political and ontological simultaneously. This is evident in *Homo Sacer* in the chapter entitled "Potentiality and Law," where he says, "Potentiality and actuality are, for Aristotle, first of all categories of being, two ways 'in which Being is said'" (Agamben, *Homo Sacer*, 48; 55). However, rather than attending to the context of Aristotle's inquiry, which deals with the essence of beings in nature as being-moved, this statement is preceded by a discussion of the relation between potentiality and sovereignty in terms of a structural homology. He suggests that the law's capacity to suspend itself in the sovereign ban "corresponds to the structure of potentiality (*dunamis*), which maintains itself in relation to actuality (*energeia*) precisely through its ability not to be. Potentiality (in its double appearance as potentiality to and as potentiality not to) is that through which Being founds itself sovereignly, which is to say, without anything preceding or determining it (*superiorem non recognoscens*) other than its own ability not to be" (Agamben, *Homo Sacer*, 46; 54). We cannot fail to remark that this is perhaps the most original moment in Agamben's work, in the sense that by extracting a single term *dunamis,* or potentiality, from Aristotle's ontological inquiry, Agamben makes it function as a political paradigm—a paradigm that holds up the entire career of his thought. Thus, for Agamben, the discovery of this structural homology between the law and being enjoins the ethical task

> to think both a constitution of potentiality entirely freed from the principle of sovereignty and a constituting power that has definitively broken the ban binding it to constituted power . . . One must think the existence of potentiality without any relation to Being in the form of actuality—not even in the extreme form of the ban and the potentiality not to be, and of actuality as the fulfillment and manifestation of potentiality—and think the existence of potentiality even without any relation to being in the form of the gift of the self and of letting be. This however, implies nothing less than thinking ontology and politics beyond every figure of relation, beyond even the limit relation that is the sovereign ban. (Agamben, *Homo Sacer*, 47; 54–55)

This passage raises the questions of what a power is that is freed from the iteration of the norm (constituted power) and of what potentiality is that is no longer the ontological foundation of beings. In other words, it is a task to think power beyond the ontological difference between being and beings. Here we cannot fail to note Agamben's unmistakable proximity to Derrida. Derrida's thought of *différance* is, of course, nothing if not the priority of the trace to (what Heidegger terms as) the onticoontological difference. In *Of Grammatology*, Derrida offers a powerful clarification of Heidegger's terminology by underscoring the fact that, for Heidegger, "being" is not simply a signified but is nevertheless produced only within the logos, thus pointing to a "strange nondifference" between signifier and signified (Derrida, *Of Grammatology*, 23; 37). Further, he writes,

> To come to recognize, not within but on the horizon of the Heideggerian paths, and yet in them, that the sense of being is not a transcendental or trans-epochal signified . . . but already, in a truly *unheard of* sense, a determined signifying trace . . . [E]ntity and being, ontic and ontological, "ontico-ontological," are, in an original style *derivative* with regard to difference; and with respect to what I shall later call *différance*, an economic concept designating the production of differing/deferring. The ontico-ontological difference and its ground (*Grund*) in the "transcendence of Dasein" (*Vom Wesen des Grundes*) are not absolutely originary. Differance by itself would be more "originary," but one would no longer be able to call it "origin" or "ground," those notions belonging essentially to the history of onto-theology, the system functioning as the effacing of difference. (Derrida, *Of Grammatology*, 23; 38)

Nevertheless, what sets Agamben's indication of a prior potentiality that is not the signified of sovereign being apart from Derrida's thought of the "originary" trace is the emphasis on power that appears in the suspension of the suspension (the sovereign ban) and an attempt to designate this instance as ethos (dwelling). Thus, for Agamben, this entails thinking life as it may be lived within the potentiality of the logos—silence, play, inoperativity, and so on. Given this shift in emphasis, it is then legitimate to raise the question of what the body can be (an issue that preoccupies Agamben as well in his more recent writings). This entails connecting the dots from his theory of potentiality to that of gesture, profanation, and inoperativity—or doing as nondoing.

In order to fully grasp the implications of his use of this term (potentiality), I suggest that the so-called fundamental passivity that is registered under the heading of potentiality as a cobelonging with *impotentiality* is best parsed not as quiescence or inertia but in the original sense of the fundamental capacity to be moved. In fact, one of the more interesting insights that Agamben's sense of potentiality generates is a paradoxical view of movement as a form of activity that is workless. In other words, I suggest that by situating his theory of potentiality within its ontological context, Agamben leads us to recover an original sense of movement as *kinēsis*—one that allows us to perceive human potentiality to act or do as fundamentally a form of worklessness. My sense is that such a reworking of movement can be fruitfully undertaken and grasped with the help of physical movement in agile play. Therefore, my project here is to offer an interpretation of Agamben's political ontology and its relation to ethical praxis with reference to exceptional movement. To put the argument succinctly, I suggest that when a certain kind of agile and exceptional movement (playful yet rigorous, exuberant yet ascetic, let us call it studious mischief) is actually practiced, it is invariably effected as a nuanced "profanation"—an ethicopolitical challenge to the dominance of the economy and its means-end logic.

Agamben discusses his interpretation of Aristotle's doctrine of *dunamis* and *energeia*, which he translates into Italian as *la potenza* and *l'atto* in several places, but perhaps nowhere as clearly as in his 1987 essay "La Potenza del Pensiero," translated in an abbreviated form as "On Potentiality" in *Potentialities*. Before we turn to that essay, it is necessary to address Agamben's terminology and the use of the Latin-derived terms "potentiality" and "actuality."

With regard to the Latin terms as interchangeable with the Greek, it is well known that the refutation of Latin terms for the original Greek formed a core element of Heidegger's interpretation of Aristotle and his critique of the metaphysical tradition. As Walter Brogan points out in the opening pages of his definitive study *Heidegger and Aristotle: The TwoFoldness of Being*,

> indeed, much of the vocabulary and central concepts of philosophy, for instance, substance and accident, essence, potentiality and actuality, matter and form, and so on are inherited from a Latinized version of Aristotle. Thus Heidegger's new "translations" of these terms

and concepts often challenge presuppositions about Aristotle, rooted in "metaphysical" interpretations of his terminology. Through these translation/commentaries on key passages in the central texts of Aristotle, Heidegger opens up a way of understanding the entire corpus of Aristotle's work that demands a radical rethinking of our traditional assumptions of this "father" of Western thought. (Brogan, *Heidegger and Aristotle*, 5)

Given that Agamben is as famous for his philological rectitude as he is for his allegiance to Heidegger, the fact that his terms *"la potenza"* and *"l'atto"* have been rendered in English as potentiality and actuality, which correspond to the Latin terms *potentia* and *actus,* is consequential and open to debate. (The complete Italian version has been available since 2005 but has only now in 2011 been translated into French, and the only available translation of this essay thus far has been the abbreviated one in English.) We can simply note here that Agamben never uses the terms *"potenzialità"* and *"attualità"* and that *potenza* corresponds to French *puissance*—it is a form of power, while *atto* is simply act. However, given that the terms potentiality and actuality have, for good or ill, settled into the vocabulary, it is best to set aside the debates over translation and turn to the essay itself.

In "On Potentiality,"[3] Agamben follows Aristotle to say that the experience of potentiality is fundamentally the exigency of saying at a certain moment, "I can." And this "I can," he writes, "does not mean anything" (Agamben, *Potentialities*, 178; 274) but it refers to the idea of having a faculty—a faculty, a capability, a possibility, potentiality for something. Potentiality is not simply a universal capability such that anyone can do or become anything (Agamben, *Potentialities*, 179; 276), as when we say that any child given the right circumstances and socioeconomic advantages has the potential to become anything he/she wants—a painter, an astronaut, a homemaker. Rather than this generic potentiality, Agamben develops the potentiality that alludes to a condition of "being able" with reference to a "knowledge or ability," such as being able to play an instrument, work a theorem, or cure a malady, insofar as "being able to" is situated at the *verge*, as the very figure of imminence, at the limit or the threshold of something about to be or not be, or about to occur or not occur. Thus, potentiality refers to the notion of, for example, a pianist who *can* (but is also able to not) play the piano. Thus, whatever is in potential cannot be said to be coterminous with actuality (*energeia*) as existence. As William J. Richardson, S. J. (referring mostly to Heidegger's lectures on Nietzsche, vol. 2), writes,

> When Aristotle's ενεργεια [energeia]is translated into the Latin *actus* or *actualitas*, there is a transformation in the meaning of it as well. Whereas Aristotle understood the εργον [ergon] (whose Being-structure is ενεργεια) as that which shines-forth and offers its visage to be seen, the Latins conceive it as something which is produced by work, as the term of a doing, as the result of activity . . . The Being of beings, then, becomes conceived as their actuality, and a being can be genuinely a being only insofar as it is actual. Correlative notions, v.g. potentiality (in fact even the notion of necessity), would have to be understood in terms of actuality. At this point, it is easy—even natural—to conceive actuality as *esse actu* (existence), and to distinguish it from *esse potentia understood in the sense of essence*. [W]hereas for Aristotle, according to Heidegger, essence and existence had been two different manners in which the Being-process (ενεργεια) comes-to-pass in beings, now, with the transformation of ενεργεια into *actus*, the Being-process comes to be interpreted in terms simply of existence alone. (Richardson, *Heidegger*, 318)

This is a crucial distinction for Agamben as well, who cites Aristotle's rebuttal in *The Metaphysics* of the argument proposed by the Megarins who insist that potentiality exists only in the act.[4] He writes,

> Aristotle responds, in the *Metaphysics* to the thesis of the Megarins, who affirmed . . . that potentiality exists only in the act (*energē monon dynasthai, hotan de mē energē ou dynasthai, 1046b 29–30*). If this were true, objects Aristotle, we could not consider the architect an architect also when he is not building, nor a physician a physician in the moment when he is not exercising his skill. In question is, namely, the mode of being of potentiality, which *exists* in the form of *hexis,* of lordship over [or that prevails over] a privation. It is a form, a presence of that which is not in the act, a this presence of privation is potentiality. As Aristotle affirms without reserve in an extraordinary passage in the *Physics*: "*Sterēsis*, privation, is like a form [*eidos ti*, a kind of face: *eidos* from *eidenai*, 'to see']" (193 b 19–20). (Agamben, *La Potenza*, 277)[5]

In other words, to translate potentiality into existence and only existence is to exhaust the former in the latter, whereas Agamben is interested in thinking through potentiality as a threshold of doing or being—a threshold that is not left behind but is conserved even in the occurrence or actualization of determinate being or doing.

Agamben proceeds in his analysis of Aristotle's *Metaphysics* by making two salient observations. First, he writes, "The living being that exists in the mode of potentiality is capable of its own impotentiality, and only in this way possesses its own potentiality. He can be and do, because he maintains a relation with his own nonbeing and nondoing" (Agamben, *La Potenza*, 281).[6]

Agamben's second observation is as follows. Here he once again quotes from Aristotle's text (1050b 10–12):

> That which is potential [to dynaton] can [endechetai] be not-act [mē energein]. That which is potential to be can be as much being as non being. The same is, in fact, potential, being and nonbeing [to auto ara dynaton kai einai kai mē einai]" Dechomai means "to welcome, to receive, to admit." Potentiality is that which welcomes and lets happen non being and this welcoming of nonbeing defines potentiality as fundamental passivity and passion." (Agamben, *La Potenza*, 281)[7]

It bears recalling here Derrida's reference to *khōra* as *pandekhes*—the spacing that is also the site of a fundamental hospitality and also passivity. These propositions, Agamben insists, should not be mistaken for the "choice" to do or not do, but if we imagine the pianist or the mathematician who is not playing or calculating, who perhaps listens or is at rest or contemplates, he or she is always in a relation to the unwritten work, the empty canvas—this relation of "not doing but can do" (the gathering of power and the holding of it in reserve) is potentiality that is always also (insofar as it is always gathered and reserved) *impotentiality*. This brings us to the crux of Agamben's interpretation of the concept of potentiality, which lies in the stress he places on the relation between im-potentiality and actuality. The question that Agamben pursues through Aristotle can be roughly paraphrased as follows: When potentiality passes into actuality, how is the impotential aspect of potentiality manifested? What happens to impotentiality when it passes into actuality? As answer, Agamben writes, *"If a potentiality to not be belongs originally to every potentiality, there truly will be potentiality only when at the moment of the passage to the act, it does not simply annul its own impotentiality, neither leaving it behind with respect to the act but to let it pass integrally as such carrying not-not passing to the act."* (Agamben, *La Potenza,* 285).[8] In other words, when actualized, whatever is impotential is preserved through a double negative as a not not doing, or nonimpotentiality. What we have, in effect, is a doubled impropriety of potentiality and impotentiality—a *mise en abyme* of the action and inaction, activity and passivity, possible and impossible.

For Agamben, this capacious understanding of potentiality as "potential and impotential" is also a locus for the thought of freedom. He writes, "the root of freedom is to be found in the abyss of potentiality. To be free is not simply to have the power to do this or that thing, nor is it simply to have the power to refuse to do this or that thing. To be free is, in the sense we have seen, *to be capable of one's own impotentiality* to be in relation to one's own privation" (Agamben, *Potentialities,* 182–83; 282).[9] Thus, it is necessary to distinguish potentiality from the will, an issue that Agamben addresses in his essay "Bartleby, or On Contingency." He writes,

> our ethical tradition has often sought to avoid the problem of potentiality by reducing it to terms of will and necessity. Not what you *can* do, but what you *want* to do or *must* do is its dominant theme . . . But potentiality is not will, and impotentiality is not necessity . . . To believe that will has power over potentiality, that the passage to actuality is the result of a decision that puts an end to the ambiguity of potentiality (which is always potentiality to do and not to do)—this is the perpetual illusion of morality. (Agamben, *Potentialities,* 254)

Will is posited as dominant in order to guard against the radical freedom of potentiality by regulating and tethering it to practical reason. This enables the belief that the freedom of potentiality is always curtailed by will, which is of course characterized by desire that is in conformity with the law.[10] Agamben implies that once potentiality is released from its domination by law-abiding free will, we are left with a completely renewed question of ethics. Is ethics even conceivable outside the framework of the so-called free willing subject who makes a conscious decision, a choice to be (or do) one thing rather than another? Thus, we must perforce ask, "What is human action that is freed from the decision and what kind of an ethics does this appropriation of potentiality entail? What is the ethic of potentiality?

This question can be approached only if we consider some of the conundrums that invariably arise in Agamben's interpretation of Aristotle. For instance, it is possible that the emphasis Agamben places on ability may at first appear contradictory in terms of being and nonbeing. For many who have had access only to the abbreviated version of the essay (where the discussion of *hexis* is absent), the problem turns around his seeming inattention to the difference between being and doing. On one hand, Agamben speaks of potentiality as an ontological category having to do with being, and yet he also insists that potentiality is ability that is possessed. This appears to raise the fundamental distinction between being and having. It is customary to assume that there is an ontological distinction between being and having in terms of substance and property. Usually, a being or substance is changeless and permanent, whereas property pertains to what the being has as attributes, which are not essential but incidental. In other words, the distinction between being and having refers to the split between essence and existence. Within this framework, it is also customary to view substance (what a being is) as eternal and unchanging, whereas property (what a being has) admits becoming, action, and movement. The fact that Agamben does not raise or address this issue in relation to potentiality is already an indication that he is not thinking within the parameters of the common understanding of Aristotle popularized by the scholastics that underscore and presume the dualities of substance and property, being and having, essence and existence. Thus, it is important to grasp not only how Agamben thinks potentiality as fundamentally a way of being that is also a having—the "I can" of a skilled artisan—but also how he figures potentiality as *ontological movement,* which is the ethos of a life unrelated to sovereignty.

My sense is that the originality and scope of Agamben's reading of potentiality, which rests in his elaboration of power as the *hexis* of *sterēsis,* is better discerned by referring to Heidegger's long-standing engagement with Aristotle, particularly his work on the very same Aristotle material in his 1931 lecture course on *Aristotle's Metaphysics* Θ1–3: On the Essence and Actuality of Force, first published in 1980 (English translation 1995).[11] If the apparent lacunae in Agamben's handling of potentiality can be bridged only with the help of Heidegger's reading of Aristotle, Agamben himself shows the way to do so in his 1988 essay on Heidegger "The Passion of Facticity." Here, with reference to the emphasis on how or the *way* Dasein is in the world, he writes,

Dasein must be its way of Being, its manner, its "guise," we could say, using a word that corresponds etymologically and semantically to the German *Weise.* We must reflect on this paradoxical formulation, which for Heidegger marks the original experience of Being, without which both the repetition of the "question of Being" (*Seinsfrage*) and the relation between essence and existence sketched in §9 of *Being and Time* remain absolutely unintelligible. Here the two fundamental determinations of classical ontology—*existentia* and *essentia*, *quod est* and *quid est*, *Daßein* and *Wassein*—are abbreviated into a constellation charged with tension. For Dasein (insofar as it is and must be its own "there"), existence and essence, "Being" and "Being such," *on* and *poion* are as inseparable as they are for the soul in Plato's Seventh Letter (343 b-c). (Agamben, *Potentialities*, 194; 302–03)

He then goes on to cite Heidegger's famous assertion from *Being and Time,* "The essence of Dasein lies in its existence" (Agamben, *Potentialities*, 194; 303). If, for Agamben, the traditional dualism between essence and existence is resolved with reference to the facticity of factual existence, being one's own way of being, he is interested less in the fundamental *kinēsis* that marks this *way* of being than he is in a certain ability, capability, possibility that being has (Agamben, *Potentialities*, 199). But it would not be accurate to say that Agamben ignores the link between facticity and *kinēsis.* He writes, "Heidegger likens facticity, insofar as it expresses the fundamental structure of life, to Aristotle's concept of *kinēsis*" (Agamben, *Potentialities*, 191; 298). In a footnote, he says, "If one recalls the fundamental role that *kinesis,* according to Heidegger, played in Aristotle's thought (in his seminar at Le Thor, Heidegger still spoke of *kinesis* as the fundamental experience of Aristotle's thought), one can also evaluate the central place of facticity in the thought of the early Heidegger." (Agamben, *Potentialities*, 296; 298–99). However, this is not a theme that he develops here or for that matter anywhere in his work. In other words, while the two-foldedness of being as essence and existence is mentioned in relation to facticity, it is not brought sufficiently to bear on the concept of potentiality. This also means that *kinēsis* as the context for the original understanding of potentiality or *dunamis,* which I suggest could found a theory of the body, is left unelaborated.[12]

Movement

To indicate briefly (in a very bare-bones fashion) what in Heidegger's interpretation is relevant to Agamben's theory of potentiality, there is first the context. Walter Brogan, in his monumental study *Heidegger and Aristotle: The Twofoldness of Being,* writes that "for Heidegger, the fundamental horizon of Aristotle's philosophical questioning is the problem of movement, and it is in the *Physics* that Aristotle most explicitly addresses this issue . . . Heidegger reads the *Metaphysics* in such a way as to highlight the centricity of the concepts of *dunamis* and *energeia* as ontological notions that take up the problem of movement at the heart of Aristotle's notion of *ousia* and his understanding of being" (Brogan, *Heidegger and Aristotle*, 21). Returning, then, to the issue of being and existence, the apparent dilemma of referring to potentiality as simultaneously having and being, which entails the unresolved distinction between essence and existence, is clarified with reference to Heidegger's deconstruction of substance dualism (being vs. becoming, being vs. appearance)[13] by way of retranslating *phusis* and *ousia*. As Walter Brogan writes, Heidegger sought "to avoid the more familiar translations—'substance' and 'essence' . . . *Ousia* is the way of being of natural beings that are constituted by movement . . . *Ousia* is the horizon in which we are to further grasp how it is that *kinēsis* constitutes natural beings. Thus, *kinēsis* is to be understood in terms of *ousia*. Since the traditional interpretation of *ousia* as substance or essence excludes movement from consideration, it misses its meaning completely" (Brogan, *Heidegger and Aristotle*, 47). Additionally, there is a salient doubling in the term *ousia*, which he says is first used as a term for one's possessions or property. In *Basic Concepts of Aristotelian Philosophy*, Heidegger says,

> The expression ουσια arose, as a term, out of an expression that was prevalent in everyday language and meant a definite being, namely beings with the character of property, possession, estate, etc. We want to take this customary meaning of ουσια as a clue insofar as we are asking whether in any sense, aspects of the customary meaning are already contained in the terminological meaning . . . What is characteristic of the customary meaning is that not only does it express a being, but a being *in the how of its being* . . . Thus, in the customary meaning of ουσια

lies a doubling: a being, but at the same time in the how of its being. (Heidegger, *Basic Concepts*, 20)

The introduction of the onticoontological difference between being and beings (i.e., how or in what *way* beings have their being) in the understanding of *ousia* is the necessary point of departure for any inquiry into movement as constitutive of the "how" or the "way." The short cut to the next step in this analysis is to relate the way of being to how Heidegger thinks *phusis*. Given that, for Heidegger, the inquiry into being pertains to beings that are produced by *phusis* and not *techne*, Brogan writes, "A natural being is not *phusis*; it is governed by *phusis* and 'in' *phusis*. Aristotle distinguishes between the presencing (*ousia*) of beings and beings that are present. He differentiates being and beings. It is only on this basis that he is able to think the sameness of a moving being with its being" (Brogan, *Heidegger and Aristotle*, 77). Brogan stresses that in the Heideggerian reading of Aristotle, being maintains itself "in" its sameness. In other words, it is never itself, but always in a relation to itself. This is key to understanding that *phusis* is not *in* a natural being:

Thus Aristotle says that fire, as a natural, elementary being, is directed toward the place to which it belongs. But its tendency is to be carried upward, the natural *kinesis* of fire, is not itself *phusis*. Nor is *phusis* in movement. Natural movement is rather *kata phusin*. This says simply that *phusis* is not the ontic movement of the sort we have discussed in the categories; nor is it itself a natural being such as fire. Rather, fire tends upward because it is in *phusis Phusis* draws it to itself and encloses it, while not itself being contained by it. (Brogan, *Heidegger and Aristotle*, 77)

Thus, if *kinēsis* or natural movement is the way natural beings are in *phusis*, then clearly for such entities their way of being is fundamentally *kinēsis* a "being moved." As Walter Brogan writes, "Heidegger cautions us about a basic confusion at the heart of this issue. It is not the particular motion from place to place that is under investigation, but rather how such beings that have the power to move of themselves are. For these beings to be, movement must belong to their very way of being" (Brogan, *Heidegger and Aristotle*, 26). In *Basic Concepts of Aristotelian Philosophy,* Heidegger clarifies that "it is really not a question of *defining* movement in some sense, but of *making* beings as moved *visible* in their being-there and holding fast to them . . . For Aristotle insofar as it is φύσει [phusei], and lives such that movement includes all that falls within the region of change: taking κίνησις [kinēsis] as μεταβολή [metabole change]. Propulsion across space is but an entirely determinate change: constant change of place" (Heidegger, *Basic Concepts*, 199). *Metabole*, then, is the fundamental movement that determines change. In his commentary on the *Physics,* Heidegger, referring to Aristotle's example of the activity of the carpenter, says, "Aristotle does not mean the 'movements' performed by the carpenter in handling the tools and the wood. Rather in the generation of the table, Aristotle is thinking precisely *of the movement of what is being generated itself and as such* Κίνησις is μεταβολή, the change of something into something, such that in the change the very act of change itself breaks out into the open, i.e., comes into appearance along with the changing thing" (Heidegger, *Pathmarks*, 217).

It is in this context of an inquiry into *phusis,* according to Brogan, that Aristotle (in *Physics* 193 a31-b6) "takes a radical new step in the path of his philosophy. He introduces the notion of potentiality *(dunamis)*" (Brogan, *Heidegger and Aristotle*, 92). Continuing in his discussion of Heidegger's 1939 commentary on Aristotle's *Physics* B1, Brogan shows that *dunamis* has to be understood as the force of the *presencing* of natural beings in their essential directedness toward their own form (or *morphē* with an aspect [*eidos*]). He writes,

> just as *hulē* belongs essentially to natural beings only when it is directed toward and governed by *morphē (eidos),* so also *dunamis* can only properly be said to belong to natural beings to the extent that it is a *dunamis* for the achievement of the being of these beings. Thus *dunamis* means being-appropriated toward *(Eignung nach)* . . . *Dunamis* is a constitutive moment (phase) in the structure of natural beings that achieve their presencing through *kinēsis.* If *dunamis* is translated as potentiality or possibility, then these terms need to be thought also as *hulē.* The being that is constituted by *dunamis* does not lose its potentiality (or its *hulē*) when it fulfills itself. (Brogan, *Heidegger and Aristotle*, 92–93)

Given this (hastily sketched) context, the notion of possibility that is contained in *dunamis* can be once and for all severed from its misunderstanding as will or choice (a distinction that Agamben is often at pains to establish). In *Basic Concepts*, Heidegger further clarifies, with reference to *Physics* Book Γ 201 a 19–27, that

> one and the same being can be determined both as δυνάμει ὄν and ἐνεργείᾳ ὄν: a definite being is at the same time a present being, 'cold,' and as a being present in this way, it is the possibility of 'warm.' Only what is cold has the possibility of the warm, not what is hard and red. Only a definite, distinctive presence of a being has at the same time the possibility of the warm. The possibility is not just any arbitrary one, but rather one that has a definite direction. This fact of the matter is the condition of the possibility of there being something like movement, connections in nature, working in relation to one another. (Heidegger, *Basic Concepts*, 196)

Brogan's commentary on this issue is further clarifying not only of the specific role that *dunamis* as a concept plays in Aristotle and Heidegger's thinking about *phusis* as the *"archē* of natural beings" (Brogan, *Heidegger and Aristotle*, 93) but also of the distinction between what Agamben indicates as generic and existing potentiality. Brogan writes,

> A natural being cannot be said to be if it is not yet what it is but only could be. Mere potentiality does not suffice to characterize the *dunamis* that *belongs* to natural beings. We have already seen that only the *hulē* that is incorporated in accord with the aspect toward which a natural being is directed can be considered the *hupokeimenon* of natural beings. Likewise, we see here that only the *dunamis* that is appropriated in accord with the aspect can be said to belong essentially to a being "that places itself together into a stand (*sunistamenios*) by *phusis*" (*Physics* 193 b1). *Dunamis* expresses more clearly this being-directed toward and in relation with the *eidos* than *hulē* does. The being that *is* is by shaping what is appropriated into its limits and containing it by holding itself together in the presencing of itself in its aspect . . . It is the look or outward appearance that something offers. (Brogan, *Heidegger and Aristotle*, 93)

Heidegger also underlines (in his commentary on the *Metaphysics* 1046a 19–29) that insofar as *dunamis* refers not only to what can be produced—to the producible or producibility (*poiein*)—but also to a certain bearing (suffering or *paschein*; Heidegger, *Aristotle's Metaphysics*, 87), Aristotle is nevertheless not enumerating various types of forces as if to arrive at the universal one. Rather, he is focused on the "divisive simple essence of force-being" (Heidegger, *Aristotle's Metaphysics,* 91). This insight then leads Heidegger in his perusal of Aristotle to the crucial discussion of "unforce" or what Agamben terms "impotenza" (or impotentiality) as another variation of force-being.

If we revisit Agamben's essay on potentiality, we note that he deliberately places maximum emphasis on this notion of "unforce" or impotentiality (rather than its relation to *entelechia* or the temporal presencing of completedness), thus appropriating the concept to serve his political philosophy. Agamben's approach is nevertheless Heideggerian in the sense that he introduces the problem of unforce with reference to "disposition" or a certain way of having a faculty for (*hexis*). In this case, it is the peculiarity that reigns in a living being having various sensory faculties that do not have sensations of their own. "The term faculty," Agamben here suggests, "expresses namely the way in which a certain activity is separated from itself and is assigned to a subject, the mode in which a living being 'has' its vital practice" (Agamben, *La Potenza,* 275). This kind of having, Agamben then goes on to say, "is not a simple absence, but has rather the form of a privation (in the vocabulary of Aristotle, *sterēsis,* 'privation,' it is in a strategic relation with *hexis*) namely of something that attests the presence of what is lacking in action. To have potentiality, to have a faculty signifies: to have a privation . . . Potentiality is, consequently, the *hexis* of a *sterēsis*" (*La Potenza,* 276).

Heidegger's discussion of *sterēsis* in his lecture course on the *Metaphysics* occurs within the context of the bearing (*paskhein*) and producing (*poiein*) that characterizes the force of presencing. He cites and translates Aristotle's text at 1046a 29–35. To focus here only on the first three lines 1046a 29–31, Heidegger renders this as

> And unforce (forcelessness) and consequently also the "forceless" is a withdrawal as what lies over and against δύναμις [*dunamis*] in the sense developed; hence every force, if it becomes unforce, that is, as unforce is in each case in relation to and in accordance with the same (with respect to that by which a force is a force, every force is unforce). Withdrawal, [*sterēsis*] however is stated and understood in multiple ways. (Heidegger, *Aristotle's Metaphysics,* 92)

He follows this translation with a commentary, wherein he says, "here it is stated: In addition to force there is unforce, 'im-potentia,' non-force. Yet this non- and this un- are not merely negations, but mean rather having withdrawn, '*being in a state of withdrawal* στέρησις [*sterēsis*]'" (Heidegger, *Aristotle's Metaphysics*, 92). Aiming to grasp the concept of στέρησις [*sterēsis*] in its essence, Heidegger suggests that listing the multiple ways in which privation appears serves only to show that the concept "meets with only partial success in Aristotle and antiquity in general" (Heidegger, *Aristotle's Metaphysics*, 93), but that its influence on the ensuing history of thought cannot be forgotten. As a "summarizing definition," then, he goes on to offer the following all-important interpretation:

> What relation, then, does στέρησις [*sterēsis*] hold to our complex of questions concerning δύναμις [*dunamis*]? Does this occur merely to show that there is, in addition to force, unforce as well? No. Aristotle wants instead to say something else. This receives a concise formulation in the sentence at line 30f: τοῦ αὐτοῦ καὶ κατὰ τὸ αὐτὸ πᾶσα δύναμις ἀδυναμία. "In relation to and in accordance with the same is every force unforce." And so the text is also clear; there is no need to improve it with the dative ἀδυναμίᾳ. What is emphasized here is the referring back of unforce upon the same thing by which force is force: what is emphasized is the constitutional belonging of unforce to the guiding meaning of force—as an inner variation of this, and even in differing respects that are already pre-given with the power to something, each according to its particular content. (Heidegger, *Aristotle's Metaphysics*, 93–94)

Continuing his commentary on these lines, Heidegger reiterates and underlines the salience of the relation between *dunamis* and *sterēsis*. He says,

> The decisive thesis reads (a30–31): "Every force is unforce with reference to and in accordance with the same thing." This states that unforce is nevertheless bound to the realm of force that remains withdrawn from it. That from which something has withdrawn is related in and through this withdrawal precisely to that which has withdrawn. And despite the negative character of the withdrawal, this withdrawing relation always produces its own positive characterization for that which is in the state of withdrawal commensurate with the way of withdrawal

215

(which itself is still different in relation to one and the same thing.) . . . The modification of force to un-force, from possessing and having to a withdrawal, is a more essential one in the field of force than in any other phenomena. *Δύναμις is in a preeminent sense exposed and bound to στέρησις.* (Heidegger, *Aristotle's Metaphysics*, 94–95)

Agamben, too, cites these lines from Aristotle (τοῦ αὐτοῦ καὶ κατὰ τὸ αὐτὸ πᾶσα δύναμις ἀδυναμία) and comments,

> *Adunamia* or impotentiality does not here signify absence of every potentiality, but potentiality that passes not into the act. The thesis defines, namely, the specific ambivalence of every human potential that in its original structure maintains itself in rapport with its own privation and always—and with respect to the same thing—potential to be and not be, to do and not do. And this relation that constitutes according to Aristotle the essence of potentiality. The living being that exists in the mode of its potentiality is capable of its own proper impotentiality and only in this way possesses proper potentiality. It is capable of being and doing because it holds onto a relation with its proper nonbeing and nondoing. In potentiality, the sense is constitutively anesthesia, thought nonthought, work worklessness.[14]

The importance of the thought of worklessness or inoperativity in Agamben's thought cannot be overestimated. It is the single most decisive insight that holds together the political and the ontological in all of his writings. Inoperativity is not some kind of ontical state of indolence or resignation. On the contrary, it pertains to the force that determines living being as living being. And insofar as this force can be only through its being bound to unforce as στέρησις, privation or lack, it is definitive of power as such. Thus, if we are to grasp Agamben's political ontology, we must trace the genealogy of power in its essential division. (Once again, we note here that insofar as Derrida fails to discover power and sovereignty as nonpresence or presencing and focuses the entire "force" of his deconstruction on presence, his politics cannot contend with the power that manifests or is effected as στέρησις.) What we have, then, is a politico-ontological concept series in Agamben, where the thought of living being as characterized by force in terms of unforce (potentiality and impotentiality) serves to disclose the essential structure of the sovereign decision on the state of exception. The ethical task, then, is to appropriate unforce from the decision, thereby bringing force as such to its fulfillment.

What does any of this have to do with the body and exceptional movement? How can the study of ontological movement offer anything of value to the politics of the body and bodily movement? In the following, I consider the relation (suggested by Agamben) of unforce as rest—being-at-rest—to gesture as the kernel of exceptional movement. This relation, then, leads to a political discovery—namely, that insofar as rest as such pertains to gesture, it opens the realm of pure means, means that refuse any perceptible ends. In other words, I suggest that rest and gesture are fully disclosed and exhibited only in exceptional movement or acrobatics, and this exhibition, which is nothing if not the appropriation of unforce as gesture, carries political force because it is essentially pure means—means without ends, or a mode of inoperativity. Furthermore, the ethics of this inoperativity is not merely the elimination of ends but the site where the care of the self is "possible."

Rest (ἠρεμία ēremia)

In *Basic Concepts of Aristotelian Philosophy*, Heidegger says, "*Rest* is only an *extreme case of movement*. Resting is only possible for something that in itself has the being-determination of being in movement or being able to be in movement." (Heidegger, *Basic Concepts*, 212). In the lecture course on Aristotle's *Metaphysics*, Heidegger cites Aristotle's *Physics* (at Δ 12, 221b12f) and translates, "For not everything unmoving is at rest; rather, we call the unmoving at rest only when it is unmoving through being robbed of movement, and in such a way that what has been robbed is suited, according to its inner essence, to being moved." Heidegger then goes on to elaborate that this thesis corresponds to other (sensory) realms whereby darkness is the privation of light and silence is the privation of speech and speech a *sterēsis* of noise (Heidegger, *Aristotle's Metaphysics*, 95). As a "distinctive *akinēsia* of force," rest (as loss and withdrawal) is at the essence of force *dunamis* and is possessed as and in its proper or own character. The structure of *dunamis* is thus revealed in this consideration of rest; for once rest is understood in this rigorous sense of being at hand, then the relation of codetermination between *dunamis* and *energeia* is also clarified. Ultimately, Heidegger's elaboration of the concept of rest finds an example in the stance of the sprinter. In his commentary on the *Metaphysics* 1047a 20–24, he says, "to take into account the difference between δύναμις and ἐνέργεια means to attempt not to replace immediately the actuality of δύναμις with ἐνέργεια, thereby doing away with δύναμις. It means instead to attempt to see that δύναμις has its own actuality and to see how this is so" (Heidegger, *Aristotle's Meaphysics*, 185–86). It is at this point that gesture enters the discussion in the example of walking and other bodily movements as *"modes of being in movement"* (Heidegger, *Aristotle's Metaphysics*, 186). Heidegger's beautiful example of the sprinter's gesture as the encapsulation of rest is worth citing in its entirety for it is directly relevant to the project at hand:

> Let us consider a sprinter who, for example, has (as we say) taken his or her mark in a hundred-meter race just before the start. What do we see? A human being who is not in movement; a crouched stance; yet this could be said just as well or even more appropriately about an old peasant woman who is kneeling before a crucifix on a pathway; more appropriately, because with the sprinter we do not simply see a kneeling human not in movement; what we call "kneeling" here is not kneeling in the sense of having set oneself down; on the contrary, this pose is much more that of being already "off and running." The particularly relaxed positioning of the hands, with fingertips touching the ground, is almost already the thrust and the leaving behind of the place still held. Face and glance do not fall dreamily to the ground, nor do they wander from one thing to another; rather, they are tensely focused on the track ahead, so that it looks as though the entire stance is stretched taut toward what lies before it. No, it not only looks this way, it is so, and we see this immediately; it is decisive that this be attended to as well . . . What exhibits itself to us is not a human standing still, but rather a human poised for the start; the runner is poised in this way and is this utterly and totally. (187)

This example of the concentrated bodily gesture that demonstrates the rest at the heart of movement as force is intended to clarify that *capability as such* is never exhausted in the act when the call "Go" is uttered and the sprinter is off and running, and that "capability" as that which makes the act possible is as such "incapable" because it is always only imminent, at hand, and therefore at "rest." Here, then, in this moment that is always *before* and *now*, (un)force, (im)potentiality, (a)*dunamia* is revealed as the element of time operative in the act. In other words, when force is understood and grasped in its essence as unforce, we arrive at the strange paradox of discerning the truth about temporality and repetition as fundamentally a "not-doing" or inoperativity, and of course inoperativity as time.[15]

AGILE

Let us take a second look at agile movement, separating it from the various institutions that have appropriated it and at some level degraded it in relation to their larger, socially sanctioned goals. I suggest that it is more to the point to consider acrobatic movement before it is incorporated into show business by the circus, gymnastics, sports, stunt performing, or even some forms of dance. Unlike sports stars or dancers, acrobats are usually anonymous. The lowly status of professional acrobatics notwithstanding, what is genuinely "common" about acrobatic movement is that it is a low-threshold skill that is characteristic of play and doing tricks distinguished from sports, games, or art, and that it is resistant to cultural nationalism. In other words, turning a cartwheel, juggling, or tightrope walking does not demand evaluation as aesthetic or competitive acts. In a sense, play as a practice is completely open activity that few, however, engage in. Insofar as play is play only when it is unregulated by scoring or judging, it is at one's whim whether or not to fold the body into a particular shape, turn a cartwheel, or juggle half a dozen oranges, be it in private or public. Acrobatics as play thrives on producing delight and surprise and resists appropriation by culture, nationalism, or history. While dance and sports always lend themselves to nationalistic and cultural appropriations, acrobatic movements have no inherent cultural identity. All over the world, people have walked and continue to walk on tightropes, to defy or play with gravity, juggle, balance, and fold their bodies, to defy the norm, to flirt with death. While certain nations and cultures may lay claim to excelling at such acts when they are institutionalized, the acts themselves have no historical or cultural origin in that no one culture can lay claim as inventor of the cartwheel, the backflip, or balancing on a rope, a pole, and so on.[16]

If acrobatics suffers from a lack of prestige, exceptional movement thrives on its association with illegality. More than ever in this
our great modern era of permissiveness (which should actually be
translated as hyper–security consciousness), such movement troubles
the law, trifles with criminality, and plays with death. As Philippe Petit, who calls himself an "artist criminal" has testified over the years,
merely walking on a tightrope in a public place or juggling tea cups is
liable to get one arrested. It is illegal to move one's body exuberantly
without license or to repurpose objects. Universal yet illegal, highly
skilled yet vulgar, disciplined yet disorderly, ancient yet nontraditional,
acrobatic movement is more often than not viewed as entertainment
for children and for a good reason—for they are children or adults at
play, doing things simply because they can, even though they should
not be doing them, and supposedly could not be doing them. And thus
they incite wonder. Wonder—that affect of intense openness experienced and shared by children and philosophers. But what is the body's
relation to such movement?

To apprehend the body as and in movement, its capability for
threshold existence, without reference to the institutions that have historically capitalized on it, I suggest we turn not to the professionals,
but to ourselves. The disclosure of the body's liminality is something
that most of us, whether we are able-bodied or not, have always already experienced, for instance, when once upon a time we tried to
climb a tree, do tricks on our bicycles, came sliding down a banister,
used our beds as trampolines, tried to walk on our hands, turn cartwheels, balance-walk on a wall, jump from high places, or fold our
limbs into impossible shapes. We can also add here all those forbidden and useless experiments we undertook with objects of ordinary
use (such as boxes, bottles, cans, paper, radios, and clocks) that were
either discarded or forbidden—the list can go on indefinitely as curiosity and inventiveness is endemic to exuberance. But alas, we no longer
do these things, as we were invariably disciplined. Discipline does not
tolerate such behavior. If we fell, hurt ourselves, broke the object or
our bones, we learned to interpret the ensuing pain as just retribution
for "the next time"—a lesson for future prudence. Or, if we were so
lucky as not to be punished, then we were certainly distracted, given
"safer" institutionalized outlets through Lego sets (build something),

sports (build team spirit), gymnastics (with its values of competition, glamour, prestige), and other forms of sane and healthful activity.[17] We were encouraged to "pursue our interests" safely, in an orderly and constructive way, and legitimately under sound adult supervision. In other words, the so-called outlets worked to transform our disorderliness, the body's free enjoyment, its exuberance, by investing it with right, as in the bestowed right to practice certain moves in designated places, submitting to standardization by learning the correct way to perform these moves, willing the body to obey and submit to externally imposed criteria, training exuberance to aim at the rewards and medals of conformity if only in order to put it to strong local or national competitive use. In short, the incalculable exuberance of the body is channeled into quantifiable and measurable expertise.

The fact that such exuberant behaviors when unchanneled by institutions are expressly forbidden, even prohibited, should give us pause. What is it about the body's exuberance, over and beyond the concern for safety (which has its own biopolitical implications), that flies in the face of authority? I suggest that the issue is not simply concern for broken bones or misuse or possible damage to property. Authority has a more essential objection that pertains to the question of waste—such horseplay is a waste of energy, a waste of time; it is useless behavior and is therefore potentially destructive. Exuberant exceptional movement, when free, unlocalized (by schools, gymnasiums, businesses), and unsupervised, is disorderly (i.e., without proper purpose or end). Underlying the capture and institutionalization of such movement is the normative status of the relation of means and ends, without which the law as such cannot function. In a sense, then, the relation between means and ends is the *dispositif* that is anterior even to the economic one of productivity. The *dispositif* of means and ends captures the body for a time that is purposive (a time that is significantly not "whiled" away), thereby providing the conditions for commodification and capitalization—processes that appropriate and trade objects indiscriminately for a market that is quintessentially indifferent to "singularities."

There can be little doubt that the relation of means to ends is as fundamental as it is normative. Ethical or ideological normativity necessarily implies the adjudication of the relation of means to ends.

In its most skeletal form, we can say that authority—whether it is parental; civil, as in schools and hospitals; or juridical—justifies itself by providing the rationale of purposive ends. As such, laws can be said to be effective only when they are able to reach their stated goals through legal means—that is, means that are available to them. The law's self-justification rests on this correlation. In other words, for a situation to be deemed lawful, a given end is legal only insofar as the means deployed to reach that end are also legal. While this correlation of legal means to legal ends pertains to the reach and limits of the law, it also points to the unquestioned supposition that a given act is considered to be justified and within the bounds of reason only insofar as its means and ends are correlated. When something is posited as an end, we understand that it is a good—a goal that carries a value for the individual or community striving to achieve it. Thus, it is possible to assert that some things are ends in themselves without utilitarian purpose, such as art or human life. For instance, in the realm of ethics and practical reason, we remember of course Kant's second categorical imperative that man is an end in himself and should never be used as a means. In fact, one of the modalities of ethical discourse at the kitchen table is to debate moral values by distinguishing what should be considered a mere means and what constitutes a proper end. For instance, is the acquisition of personal or national wealth an end in itself or should we consider it a means to a higher end? What about knowledge, education, religious devotion, or the practice of common virtues such as kindness, generosity, charity, temperance, and so on? All of the above questions connote territory that is conventional as the questions are familiar to common sense and our social existence. It is presupposed that all means are directed toward the purpose of achieving a good of some kind. While we understand the significance of an end in itself (thus, one ought to be kind and helpful without ulterior motive), the same cannot be said for something being a means in itself. What, then, are the implications of invoking the notion of pure means, means without end?

Gesture as Pure Means

Means without End: Notes on Politics is the title of a collection of pithy essays by Agamben. In the preface, he writes that "in the following pages, genuinely political paradigms are sought in experiences and phenomena that usually are not considered political or that are considered only marginally so" (Agamben, *Means without End*, IX). Among the paradigms he explores, the one that is of direct relevance to the project at hand is what he describes as "the sphere of gestures or pure means (that is, the sphere of those means that emancipate themselves from their relation to an end while still remaining means) posited as the proper sphere of politics" (Agamben, *Means without End*, X).

Gesture, common human gesture, as political! What, then, is gesture? And how do we understand exceptional movement as gesture? In what sense does such movement (understood as gesture) open "the proper sphere of politics"? In what lies the gesturality and political import of, for instance, walking on a tightrope, swinging on a trapeze, or juggling tea cups?

I have already noted that the exuberance of the body expressed in exceptional movement when not institutionalized is always forbidden; I also suggested that this prohibition pertains to authority's disapproval of purposeless action. Given that such purposeless behavior is precisely what Agamben discusses as the political realm of gesture as pure means, it behooves us to review his analysis.

Agamben begins by suggesting that in contemporary life, gestures (understood as the everyday miracle of the body walking, picking up something, turning one's head, etc.) "lose their ease under the action of invisible powers" and human beings lose all sense of "naturalness" (Agamben, *Means without End*, 53). We are reminded at once of the clockworked Charlie Chaplin in *Modern Times* who, upon exiting his factory job, cannot stop his hands from performing the mechanical action of using a wrench. Chaplin was, of course, satirizing the period of factory Fordism that attempted to transform organic human labor into an inorganic machine; however, Agamben implies that in the current era of late capitalism, "every single gesture becomes destiny" and in such a world, life as such becomes entirely "indecipherable" (Agamben, *Means without End*, 53). In other words, when bodily movement is

programmed for and tethered to an end and thereby becomes prede-
termined, it loses all expressivity and gesturality. Other, preeconomic
examples we could cite would perhaps be ceremonial gestures such
as the salute, the curtsy, and so on, demanded by power, or even specifically saturated signs that connote an obscenity or insult. Thus, the
task of "redeeming the gesture from its destiny" (Agamben, *Means
without End*, 54), Agamben suggests, acquires an unanticipated sense
of political urgency. In order to think through this task, Agamben
distinguishes dynamic historical gesture from the stiffened mythical
image. Following Benjamin's cue, Agamben turns to film as modernity's antidote to the stiffened image and loss of gesture. In film, he
writes, "there are no images but only gestures. Every image, in fact, is
animated by an antinomic polarity: on the one hand, images are the
reification and obliteration of a gesture (it is the *imago* as death mask
or as symbol); on the other hand, they preserve the *dynamis* intact (as
in Muybridge's snapshots or in any sports photograph)" (Agamben,
Means without End, 55). Gesture, then, is the pose-repose glimpsed in
the ever unfolding of being as *phusis*. In other words, it is the *dunamis*
of a presencing—the being that lingers or "whiles" in the time of its appearance. Gesture, we may say then, is the gathering up of movement
as rest, as standing still, that Heidegger suggests is the purest form of
kinēsis. Thus, Agamben suggests that we read paintings as not "im-
movable and eternal forms, but as fragments of a gesture or as stills of
a lost film" (Agamben, *Means without End*, 55–56). In one of his characteristic poetic flights, he suggests that images are under a paralyz-
ing spell from which they must be liberated (Agamben, *Means without
End*, 56).

But having established the normative enchaining of gesture to
ends or *actus*, we may well ask, "What is the significance of gesture?
And what about it specifically belongs to the 'realm of ethics and politics (and not simply to that of aesthetics)'" (Agamben, *Means without
End*, 56)? Agamben quotes the Roman scholar Varro to characterize
gesture as a sphere of action distinguished from making (*facere*) and
acting (*agere*). Rather, in gesture, which is a third category of action,
"nothing is being produced or acted, but rather something is being endured or supported. The gesture, in other words, opens the sphere of
ethos as the more proper sphere of that which is human" (Agamben,

Means without End, 57). Pursuing the notion of gesture as "event," Agamben offers a crucial clarification. He writes,

> If producing is a means in view of an end and praxis is an end without means, the gesture then breaks with the false alternative between ends and means that paralyzes morality and presents instead means that, *as such*, evade the orbit of mediality without becoming for this reason, ends.
>
> Nothing is more misleading for an understanding of gesture, therefore, than representing, on the one hand, a sphere of means as addressing a goal (for example, marching seen as a means of moving the body from point A to point B) and, on the other hand, a separate and superior sphere of gesture as a movement that has its end in itself (for example, dance seen as an aesthetic dimension). Finality without means is just as alienating as mediality that has meaning only with respect to an end. If dance is gesture, it is so, rather, because it is nothing more than the endurance and the exhibition of the media character of corporal movements. *The gesture is the exhibition of a mediality: it is the process of making a means visible as such.* It allows the emergence of the being-in-a-medium of human being and thus it opens the ethical dimension for them. (Agamben, *Means without End*, 58)

With this extraordinary passage, we find ourselves led once again to the thought of the threshold, the spacing between determinate entities, to the trace, and silence. Insofar as it is the sphere of a "pure and endless mediality" (Agamben, *Means without End*, 59), gesture encapsulates potentiality. "The gesture is, in this sense, communication of a communicability" (Agamben, *Means without End*, 59). As trace and spacing, its relation to language is fundamental in the sense that it discloses the "being-in-language of human beings" as pure means. This supplementary relation of gesture to language, then, places it in the eloquent realm of silence. Because this "being-in-language" cannot actually be said or expressed in so many words, Agamben writes that "the gesture is essentially always a gesture of not being able to figure something out in language; it is always a *gag* in the proper meaning of the term, indicating first of all something that could be put in your mouth to hinder speech, as well as in the sense of the actor's improvisation meant to compensate a loss of memory or an inability to speak" (Agamben, *Means without End*, 59). There is a silence, Agamben suggests, that is shared by gesture, cinema, and philosophy in that all three expose the "being-in-language of human beings." This ontological exposure, for Agamben, the disclosure of mediality—communicating communicability, "that I am communicating"—is something that cannot be captured as content and constitutes a political gesture. He ends with a thought fragment that trails into a silence: *"Politics is the sphere of pure means, that is, of the absolute and complete gesturality of human beings"* (Agamben, *Means without End*, 60). There can be no question that this seemingly gnomic pronouncement is critical to the theory advanced in the essay if not to his entire oeuvre.

Exuberant Ethics

Agamben's theory of gesture as pure means invites us to think the exuberant movements of the body as gesture that opens the sphere of political and ethical action. But how? There is, of course, the simple visual element: consider the body in a backflip as it leaps backward into air or the tightrope walker as he/she grasps a pole and sets one foot before another suspended over an abyss. Each second of that meaningless walk or leap is gesture in that it takes place in a time that is experienced as a slowing down and/or speeding up, a time that film would capture in slow motion where the gesturality of the body is disclosed in the *lapse* when one frame succeeds another. But "absolute and complete gesturality" as the sphere of politics cannot be equated with this visual aspect—for such gesture is surely prevalent and perceptible within such "stiffened" institutionalized settingsas sports, the circus, and so on. Thus, we cannot mistake all perceptible gesture as being political or all politics as only some kind of gesture. The cardinal point that raises gesture to the sphere of the political is simply that gesture is to be understood neither as gesticulation nor signing/indicating, but as pure means. It is the disclosure of mediality itself that opens the sphere of the political. Our task, in a sense, is to discern this disclosure of mediality in agile exceptional movement.

While exceptional movement can be understood as the "pure means" of gesture liberated from ends, the question of why such disclosure of mediality (or pure means) is political and ethical yet remains to be answered. If we are to locate exceptional movement as a third form of action—neither producing (means to an end) nor acting (end in itself) but persisting in the realm of pure means as gesture—and if we expose gesture as mediality and mediality as gesture that does nothing other than disclose the being in medium of human being, in what sense is it a site that opens the sphere of the political and the ethical? Why is this space, which, if you think about it, is really a self-reflexive space of impossible auto-affection, also that of political and ethical potentiality? The question can be rephrased as follows: what is the relation of the disclosure of mediality and pure means to Agamben's thought regarding political ontology? Is there, then, a political ontology implied in the concept of pure means?

Work

Agamben's validation of pure means as the site of human dwelling no doubt implies an ontology of action—a certain way of doing something. While his work is well known for offering a renewed understanding of the pervasiveness of biopower within the rule of law, it has not always been noted that his analysis of power (whether sovereign or disciplinary) cannot be separated from his theory of (not) doing as being. I refer here not only to the essay on Bartleby and the phrase "I prefer not to" but also to his interpretation of "the proper work of man." The concept of gesture as pure means leads to or proposes a notion of work that can be handily understood as a limb of the materialist critique of labor. I shall posit here as a necessary context for an understanding of Agamben's final sentence, *"Politics is the sphere of pure means, that is, of the absolute and complete gesturality of human beings"* (Agamben, *Means without End*, 60), the notion of estranged labor that founds Marx's critique of political economy.

As a central concept of historical materialism, the notion of estranged labor occurs in numerous instances in Marx's oeuvre from his early writings to the later ones, such as the *Grundrisse*. However, it is in the *Economic and Philosophical Manuscripts* of 1844 that Marx speaks in ontological terms about the human being's relation to practical activity. For Marx, humans are estranged from their work when it is externalized and commodified. By selling labor, the worker is alienated from both the production process and the product itself. The worker is, in a sense, "forced" to work and thus labor becomes "self-sacrifice" and "mortification" (Marx, "Economic and Philosophical Manuscripts," 326). The result of such "loss of self," Marx suggests, is that

> the worker feels that he is acting freely only in his animal functions—eating, drinking and procreating, or at most in his dwelling and adornment—while in his human functions he is nothing more than an animal.
>
> It is true that eating, drinking and procreating, etc. are also genuine human functions. However, when abstracted from other aspects of human activity and turned into final and exclusive ends, they are animal. (Marx, "Economic and Philosophical Manuscripts," 327)

The contemporary mode of production, Marx suggests, does not so much reduce human to animal as alienate and separate expressive life from participation in natural life. Thus, alienation here is fundamentally self-alienation, a caesura (to use one of Agamben's terms) that runs first and foremost within humans themselves. The lamentable aspect of such alienation, from the political and ethical point of view, is that it consigns and confines humans to the wretched task of laboring solely to preserve their individual existence. In other words, one works, sells one's labor, and submits oneself to the clock on the factory floor simply to satisfy physical needs—"to earn one's bread," "so one and one's children can eat." For Marx, this use of creative potential as a "means" to the "end" of individual survival constitutes an expropriation of man's generic power for self-expression. Marx's use here of the famous term *Gattungswesen,* usually translated as species-being (*Gattung* may well be translated as genus, genre, generic), refers, then, not so much to an individual essence but in fact to a generic potential that is in common. Far from an essentialist or even normative notion, *Gattungswesen* refers to a potential that is not for a particular act or a particular thing but to a potential for freedom in a sphere where one produces and acts without a specific end or purpose. Marx writes that what distinguishes human production from animal is the fact that while animals "produce only their own immediate needs or those of their young . . . man produces universally; they produce only when immediate physical need compels them to do so, while man produces even when he is free from physical need and truly produces only in freedom from such need" (Marx, "Economic and Philosophical Manuscripts," 329). It is important to understand the necessary communality of such potential to grasp the full implications of alienation in capitalism. Marx writes,

> Even if I am active in the field of science, etc.—an activity which I am seldom able to perform in direct association with other men—I am still *socially* active because I am active as a *man*. It is not only the material of my activity—including even the language in which the thinker is active—which I receive as a social product. My *own* existence *is* social activity. Therefore what I create from myself I create for society, conscious of myself as a social being.
>
> . . . It is above all necessary to avoid once more establishing 'society' as an abstraction over against the individual. The individual *is* the *social being*. His vital expression—even when it does not appear in the direct form of a *communal* expression, conceived in association with other men—is there an expression and confirmation of *social life*. Man's individual and species life are not two *distinct things*, however much—and this is necessarily so—the mode of existence of individual life is a more *particular* or more *general* mode of the species-life, or species-life a more *particular* or more *general* individual life. (Marx, "Economic and Philosophical Manuscripts," 350)

Thus, in the situation of alienated labor, human beings experience estrangement at several levels—from the product, from the act of production, from each other, and above all from themselves. Humans experience a fundamental alienation from their generic nature when their animal nature is confined to the private sphere and separated from their expressive, social, and creative potential. This separation first of all individualizes humans. As Foucault argues in several places, when human beings are rendered into psychological subjects, or atomized individuals separated from political life and economic activity, they are eminently prepped for subjectification and discipline.[18] This is perhaps more true of the contemporary class of career professionals than even the traditional working classes. In other words, alienated labor is the condition of possibility for social normalization. In this scenario, the human being's creative activity is alienated from the producer and captured for purposive ends.

Thus, we can posit Agamben's theory of pure means as a response to such alienation, as a form of action that is neither productive nor performative but that fundamentally resists the capture of all human action as labor directed at purposive ends (such as survival). It is also against this expurgation of free creativity that Agamben asks us to consider an ontological question: is there a work that is proper to human beings—that is, do humans as such have a work of their own? What is free human action? Let us clarify, however, that to ask, "what is a work that is proper to the human being?" is not to ask after the essence of human action. It is *not* to ask, "is there a mode of work that is proper to human beings, that is quintessentially human?" Rather, it is a way of asking, "what is the action that a human being undertakes that discloses his/her participation in a genre of being (*Gattungswesen*)?" Or, to put it differently, "are there genres of work that human beings participate in (such as composing poetry, investigating the world, promising, making pornography) that disclose their participation in certain genres of being, that may well be shared with other beings?" More precisely, it is the necessary circularity of asking, "what is the action that human beings perform in order to develop their capacity to do?"

In his essay "The Work of Man," which presents a series of close readings of Aristotle's *Nicomachean Ethics* and *De Anima* through Averroes and Dante, Agamben shows that the problem of defining human work in general, apart from social identities, is central to the thought of politics and the good. If Aristotle defines the specificity of human work as life itself—life lived in the logos as not merely a faculty or potentiality but always already a doing or action—Averroes and Dante read the very same proposition differently. The specificity of being in logos is reconfigured as a form of potentiality, as not quite act but *proximity* to the act: human work as pure possibility (a power) that can never be exhausted in the act. Once work is detached from economic necessity, then politics, too, is released from its foundation in work as purposive action. Politics, then, may be conceived as the thought of the end of work. In other words, not only "what kind of work?" but "what is work for?" Or, even more precisely, "why work?" Agamben writes,

In the modern era, Western politics has consequently been conceived as the collective assumption of a historical task (of a "work") on the part of a people or a nation. This political task coincided with a metaphysical task, that is, the realization of man as rational living being. The problematicity inherent in the determination of this "political" task with respect to the concrete figures of labor, action, and, ultimately, human life has gradually grown. From this perspective, the thought of Marx, which seeks the realization of man as a generic being (*Gattungswesen*), represents a renewal and a radicalization of the Aristotelian project. Hence the two aporias implicit in this renewal: (1) the subject of the work of man must necessarily be an unassignable class, which destroys itself insofar as it represents a particular activity (for example, the working class); (2) the activity of man in the classless society is impossible or, in any case, extremely difficult to define (hence the hesitations of Marx concerning the destiny of labor in the classless society and the right to laziness claimed by Lafargue and Malevich. (Agamben, "The Work of Man," 6)

I have quoted this passage at length, because here we glimpse, if somewhat fleetingly, something of Agamben's vision for what might constitute the "proper work" of humans. Let us briefly take up the two "*aporias*" that he discerns as necessary to his critique of work.

In his comment on Marx's *Gattungswesen* as the subject of work that has no substantial social identity, Agamben is here alluding to his long-standing interest in the question of vocation, a theme that invariably opens onto the heart of what he terms the messianic community.

In *The Time That Remains: A Commentary on the Letter to the Romans*, Agamben devotes a chapter ("The Second Day") to the Pauline word *klētos*, or "calling"—that is, messianic vocation. Here, he retraces and exhumes the principle governing the meaning of the word through a series of engagements with its use in the history of thought. I cannot here offer a summary of this chapter since his engagement with each of the thinkers of *klēsis* leads like the spokes of a wheel onto related themes such as use, exigency, parable, and so on. Instead, I note simply that here Agamben underlines the intimate Pauline relation between heeding the messianic call and professional "factical" calling. For Agamben, Max Weber's argument that Martin Luther secularized the notion of messianic vocation, which was marked by "eschatological indifference," misconstrues the meaning of the term vocation. Referring to the Pauline exhortation "Let every man abide in the same calling wherein he was called" (Agamben, *Time That Remains,* 19) but to do so henceforth "as not" (*hōs mē*) in the very juridical and factical status that one finds oneself, Agamben writes,

> *Klēsis* indicates the particular transformation that every juridical status and worldly condition undergoes because of, and only because of, its relation to the messianic event. It is therefore not a matter of eschatological indifference, but of change, almost an internal shifting of each and every single worldly condition by virtue of being "called." For Paul, the *ekklēsia,* the messianic community, is literally all *klēsis,* all messianic vocations. The messianic vocation does not, however, have any specific content; it is nothing but the repetition of those same factical or juridical conditions *in which* or *as which* we are called.
>
> . . . *Hōs mē,* "as not": this is the formula concerning messianic life and is the ultimate meaning of *klēsis.* Vocation calls for nothing and to no place. For this reason it may coincide with the factical condition in which each person finds himself called, but for this very reason, it also revokes the condition from top to bottom. *The messianic vocation is the revocation of every vocation.* In this way, it defines what to me seems to be the only acceptable vocation. What is a vocation, but the revocation of each and every concrete factical vocation? (Agamben, *Time That Remains,* 22–23)

Coming back to the question of *Gattungswesen,* Agamben agrees with Benjamin that there is a homology, even a continuity, between Marx's notion of the classless society and the Pauline notion of messianic time (Agamben, *Time That Remains,* 30). The transformation of "status" into "class," attendant upon the dissolution of all inherited rank and authority due to the domination of the bourgeoisie, can be read as a secularization of Pauline "re-vocation." In other words, the concept of vocation in both discourses emerges from a profound opposition to estranged work in order to heed human potentiality as belonging to the genre of creatures that has the development or care of "self" as its work.

In the previously cited quotation from "The Work of Man," Agamben asserts that Marx's project consisted of a radicalization of the Aristotelian thought of potentiality. In the text on Paul, which surely alters the inflection of potentiality, Agamben takes his analysis further to note some differences. He suggests that whereas in Marxism the proletariat is subsequently identified with a "determinate social class" or a "substantial social identity," thereby betraying Marx's historically contingent figure, in the thought of the messianic community, all social identity is nullified. However, the fact remains that whether it is Aristotle, Paul, Marx, or Agamben himself, there is a necessary indetermination of the subject of work, who can have no assignable identity, and the destiny of labor, which can never be prescribed or defined. The vocation that is proper to humans, then, is revocation of all vocation. To speak of the proper work of humans is to speak of potentiality, the proximity to work—the threshold of a doing that discloses this very condition of being at the threshold.

The second "aporia" that Agamben names pertains to the impossibility of defining the topos of work, or the proper activity of man in a classless society. However, there is an irresistible hint here of the direction in which such an inquiry might proceed, thanks to his mention of the Russian artist and innovator of suprematism, Kazimir Malevich, and the French communist Paul Lafargue. Agamben is alluding here to Malevich's 1921 essay "Laziness Practiced and Perfected" and Lafargue's *The Right to Be Lazy*, which was justly popular in its own day. In this essay, Lafargue argues that the work ethic is fundamentally aimed at keeping the proletariat in servitude while making leisure available for the wealthy few. Writing with a combination of humor and dead seriousness, Lafargue recommends that

> work ought to be forbidden and not imposed. The Rothschilds and other capitalists should be allowed to bring testimony to the fact that throughout their whole lives they have been perfect vagabonds, and if they swear they wish to continue to live as perfect vagabonds in spite of the general mania for work, they should be pensioned and should receive every morning at the city hall a five-dollar gold piece for their pocket money. Social discords will vanish. Bond holders and capitalists will be first to rally to the popular party, once convinced that far from wishing them harm, its purpose is rather to relieve them of the labor of over-consumption and waste, with which they have been overwhelmed since their birth. As for the capitalists who are incapable of proving their title to the name of vagabond, they will be allowed to

follow their instincts. There are plenty of disgusting occupations in which to place them. (Lafargue, *The Right to Be Lazy*, 62–63)

The workers themselves will be made to consume the goods and luxuries they produce instead of making do with rags and gristly meat. Instead of industrial overconsumption, which requires the destruction or adulteration of goods, Lafargue envisions a society in which men, women, and children will work for a very limited amount of time and regain their robust physiques and natural bonhomie and sanguinity. Lafargue reminds us that "the Greeks in their era of greatness had only contempt for work: their slaves alone were permitted to labor: the free man knew only exercises for the body and mind. . . . The philosophers of antiquity taught contempt for work, that degradation of the free man, the poets sang of idleness, that gift from the Gods *O Melibae Deus nobis haec otia fecit*" (Lafargue, *The Right to Be Lazy*, 24).[19]

It is important to grasp that the concept of laziness or leisure as envisioned by Agamben and the materialists is not reducible to inertia and entropy, which would connote an aversion toward life. As a critique of alienated labor, capitalist accumulation, and dominance of the economy, laziness or worklessness is a means of taking back one's generic capability to produce, to do, as a form of action that is expressive of being. In other words, it is the reclamation of a mode of doing that is neither productive nor performative but a disclosure of mediality—doing as gesture or pure means. Let us recall Agamben's dictum that *"Politics is the sphere of pure means, that is, of the absolute and complete gesturality of human beings"* (Agamben, *Means without End*, 60).

Work, then, has to be rethought in fidelity to this essential inoperativity or "worklessness" of humans—their being in potential—a potentiality that is not exhausted but conserved in action. Thus, humans as such have no proper essence, no proper work; what is proper to their *inessentiality* is, therefore, their essential worklessness or potentiality (the act of inaction), which must serve as the starting point or organizing principle of politics. Can there be any doubt that some of the most effective political movements in history have discovered and disclosed precisely this principle? We simply have to contemplate the great and simple gesture of Gandhi seated at his spinning wheel—a gesture of profound opposition to the might of the British Empire and its textile industry, but an opposition expressed in a manner that is neither passive nor active but merely exposes the being in medium of humanness by opting out of the political economy imposed by British rule.

The ethical force of this principle is simply that as potentiality, worklessness expresses the human being or brings us to our element; it connotes life, a political life that has "nothing at stake except living itself" and is thus a modality of happiness—what Agamben terms the happy life or the profane life. In such a polis, human action is not a means entirely consecrated to an end, whose potentiality is exhausted in action. (Thus, worklessness is not rest after work, like God on the seventh day of creation or Robinson Crusoe surveying his handiwork after a day of labor.) The liberation of pure means from ends serves as one of the salient moves by which we can conceive of "a figure if not of inaction, at least of a working that in every act realizes its own *shabbat* and in every work is capable of exposing its own inactivity and its own potentiality" (Agamben, "Work of Man," 10).

What does it mean for every act to realize its own *shabbat*? Given the seemingly recondite aspect of these words, we could, in this attempt to associate Gandhi at his spinning wheel with Philippe Petit on the tightrope, parse this sentence with the help of a Zen homily. As the contemporary Zen monk Thich Nhat Hanh puts it, "Happiness is possible when you are capable of doing the things and being the things you want to do and to be. When we walk for the sake of walking, when we sit for the sake of sitting, when we drink for the sake of drinking tea, we don't do it for something or someone else" (Thich Nhat Hanh, *Answers from the Heart*, 62). In other words, to simply act or do something—sit, stand, walk, and so on, not for someone or something but for itself and to be in the act—is to find the exuberance and the re-pose that is at the heart of action. In his famous "Theologico-Political Fragment" written the same year as the "Critique of Violence," Walter Benjamin says, "the order of the profane should be erected on the idea of happiness. The relation of this order to the Messianic is one of the essential teachings of the philosophy of history" (Benjamin, "Theologico-Political Fragment," 312). This and other passages from the fragment are often quoted by Agamben whenever he addresses the question of ethics. Commenting on this line in Benjamin, he clarifies that "the definition of the concept of 'happy life' remains one of the essential tasks of the coming thought (and this should be achieved in such a way that this concept is not kept separate from ontology, because 'being: we have no experience of it other than living itself')" (Agamben, *Means without End*, 113).

Agamben's insistence that we cannot define the concept of the happy life in isolation from ontology immediately raises the question not only of action but also of the body—the happy body, the profane body liberated from law and sovereignty or all the various discourses of discipline that seek to subjectify and manage its life and its form. As the foundation of a political philosophy, the happy life is "an absolutely profane 'sufficient life' that has reached the perfection of its own power and of its own communicability—a life over which sovereignty and right no longer have any hold" (Agamben, *Means without End*, 114–15). Is such a life possible? What is a life that even in action always retains its fundamental potentiality—its capability to do or not do? How can the human being free him/herself from the concept of free will or free choice, which refers humanness to the mastery of the cogito and reflective consciousness in its separation from body, and regain the far simpler sense of potentiality, of being able to? And in what sense is such a life manifested in its indifference to law? While Gandhi, Bartleby, and so on are stellar examples of a worklessness that is fundamentally *political* and philosophical, the attention of this chapter is focused on the potentiality of the body in agile movement as a liminal body between human and animal.

Free Movement

My citation of children's bodily exuberance, their willingness to do something simply to see if they can, as the adumbration of the ethical happy life that Agamben theorizes may seem arbitrary. But, in fact, I take my cue from Agamben himself, who, in his essay "In Praise of Profanation," situates play and children's games in terms of a being and an acting that exists in a completely liminal sphere of pure means freed from ends. Not unlike the incredible phonematic capacity of infants and very young children, who linguists say have the potential to make any sound before their tongues are hardened into native languages, play and free exceptional movement, too, are things that all human children can do more often through discovery than through conscious learning.

However, it is not such a simple matter to identify and grasp the freedom, the "immense happiness" that is the experience of such agile movement. The principles of the "task" of apprehending the ethico-political potentiality of free movement are not immediately obvious. There is no question that today we can no longer contrast children and adults in terms of their access to play and free movement. Such a realm of pure means seems more impossible than ever in contemporary modernity given the micromanagement of our bodies, especially children's games and pleasures. Given the ubiquity of discipline, we must perforce ask after its recess, "Where is free exceptional movement to be found? Where does free movement appear? What is a time that is free? How can it appear? Is it possible; does it exist?"

But first let us briefly review the context of agile exceptional movement in contemporary society in order to grasp the negation of free movement. I have already noted that our childhood capabilities are lost to us as discipline begins to invade and manage the body for productivity and to downgrade or institutionalize free movement. However, one could argue to the contrary that the institutions such as the sport of gymnastics in fact preserve and perfect such movement by raising it to the level of an art form. There is no question that as spectacle, gymnastics displays a pure athleticism that shows off the potentiality of the human body to perfection. But does the movement in gymnastics aim at freedom, at exuberance? Is it gesture? Does it open a time of recess within work?

Gymnastics is an institution controlled by the International Federation of Gymnastics, which sets sports standards and norms of competition. As a ferociously competitive sport, it is well known as a site of alienation, even oppression, insofar as it aims not simply to negate or transform but also to capture and institutionalize the generic exuberance of the human (especially the child's) body. The beautiful spectacles with their aura of glamour on the arena floor aside, we cannot in this ethical-political pursuit of exuberance and happiness ignore the broken bodies of children who are incorporated into gymnastic training. Joan Ryan's *Little Girls in Pretty Boxes* documented in painstaking detail the horrors wreaked on children—their enjoyment and the health of their bodies—by this competitive sport. Prior to the 2008 Beijing Olympics, the controversy over underage Chinese gymnasts exposed the abuse of children in this field. Can there be any doubt that competitive sports in general are in the same relation to physical movement as capitalist production is to labor? Once tethered to the goal of winning, all play becomes work. In other words, professional sports are entirely ruled by capital and are vocational activities, not re-vocation.

At the opposite pole from the glamorous sport of gymnastics, sociologists have documented the efflorescence of underground "movements" (in both senses of the term) that arise from traditionally deprived communities. The social protest stories embedded in agility genres such as capoiera, breakdancing or B-boying and B-girling, skateboarding, graffiti, and so on have been greatly valorized and analyzed within the academic and art communities—especially cultural studies. As extraordinarily acrobatic and working-class activities, critics have argued that these modes of movement repurpose space, objects, and bodies. This is no doubt true, but insofar as they are devoted solely to athletic mastery, they do not differ in essence from other sport forms and thus inherently lack resistance to the dominance of economic motives and its work ethic. It should come as no surprise that even as valorization brings rewards and publicity, each and every one of these so-called underground exceptional movements over time gets incorporated into the competitive, commodified structure of the means-end economy. The social protest element drained out of them, these forms are no longer just play but are transformed into lucrative entertainment, aerobic exercise, competitive art, sport, and so on.

What, then, is play—pure unmonetized play? How do we understand it as gesture, as a fundamentally political-ethical act—a harbinger of the happy life? When and how does true recess occur? My contention has been that if approached from a certain angle, any agile exceptional movement, such as walking on a tightrope, swinging from a trapeze, balancing, contortioning, juggling, and so on, can be said to harbor the kernel of human gesturality (as worklessness) that may well disclose the happy, profane life that is lived in the generic potentiality of the human body. But the question dogging and driving this inquiry has been "How can this kernel of inoperativity be disclosed; how can its ethicopolitical possibility be grasped? When does exceptional movement appear as the disclosure of pure means without end?" The body at play is the threshold body, and it is thought and experienced in a time that differs significantly from the time of production. Thus, we surely need a philosophy at the threshold to apprehend its appearance. Perhaps we cannot discern such movement without rethinking the presuppositions that govern normative notions regarding the body and its relation or separation from mind.

Profanation

Though the concept of play has always been a technical term in Agamben's vocabulary, its political and messianic aspects are not fully elaborated until his essay "In Praise of Profanation." The term profanation (unlike the term transgression) necessarily refers us to a theological paradigm. An object is declared sacred through an act that separates it from the profane world of common human use. Agamben, in fact, offers the insight that "not only is there no religion without separation, but every separation also contains or preserves within itself a genuinely religious core" (Agamben, *Profanations*, 74). Thus, if the consecration of a person or an object means that it is henceforth untouchable and considered as the property of the gods, to profane, Agamben writes, means "conversely, to return them to the free use of men" (Agamben, *Profanations*, 73). The profanation of a sacred object can be carried out in a number of ways: through contact or contagion, negligence (in the sense that one ignores the separation), and play. Significantly for Agamben, profanation cannot be understood as a process that is dialectically opposed to consecration, thereby producing a new synthesis, such as the secular. On the contrary, the twinned processes of consecration and profanation produce a residue (a trace), whereby there is always a profane element in the sacred and something sacred in the profaned. Concretely, what is occurring in this back-and-forth process is an alternation of the usability of the object in question through the power of separation. When something is set apart as untouchable and sacred, it is immediately vulnerable to being touched and profaned—it can move from being off limits and nonusable to free and usable. Underlining the relation between profanation and use, Agamben clarifies that "profanation does not simply restore something like a natural use that existed before being separated into the religious, economic, or juridical sphere" (Agamben, *Profanations*, 85). Rather, it makes possible a "new and possible use" for the object. The object, we could say, is re-purposed. It is freed from its inscription in a certain rule, which could be theological, economic, juridical, or even biological. Profanation dedisciplines an object; it uses it in a way that you are "not supposed to," and yet it does not abolish or destroy the rule. Rather, "to profane means not simply to abolish and erase separations but to learn to put them to a new use, to play with them" (Agamben, *Profanations*, 87). In other words, it is a completely unpresupposed use and is therefore the very opposite of consumption. It comes as no surprise, then, that the mode of profanation that Agamben privileges is that of play.

Agamben refers to Emile Benveniste, who "shows that play not only derives from the sphere of the sacred but also in some ways represents its overturning" (Agamben, *Profanations*, 75) because it evacuates a sacred ritual of its mythical content while retaining the empty rite (for instance, like the children in Bresson's film *Au Hasard Balthazar* playing at baptism with a little donkey, thereby completely emptying the ritual of its sacred significance). Agamben elaborates on this special mobility of play:

> This means that play frees and distracts humanity from the sphere of the sacred, without simply abolishing it. The use to which the sacred is returned is a special one that does not coincide with utilitarian consumption. In fact, the "profanation" of play does not solely concern the religious sphere. Children, who play with whatever old thing falls into their hands, make toys out of things that also belong to the spheres of economics, war, law, and other activities that we are used to thinking of as serious. All of a sudden, a car, a firearm, or a legal contract becomes a toy. What is common to these cases and the profanation of the sacred is the passage from a *religio* that is now felt to be false or oppressive to negligence as *vera religio*. This, however, does not mean neglect (no kind of attention can compare to that of a child at play) but a new dimension of use, which children and philosophers give to humanity. It is the sort of use that Benjamin must have had in mind when he wrote of Kafka's *The New Attorney* that the law that is no longer applied but only studied is the gate to justice. Just as the *religio* that is played with but no longer observed opens the gate to use, so the powers [*potenze*] of economics, law, and politics, deactivated in play, can become the gateways to a new happiness. (Agamben, *Profanations*, 76)

There are perhaps several significant implications in this view of play. It appears that play subverts right and authority simply by emptying it of its narrative and iterative content. But this process of subversion is ludic, parodic, profane, and playful. As pure and studious mischief, it not only undoes and rewires an object, perhaps rendering it unrecognizable and unserviceable, but also rejects the means-end logic that demands productivity. Not only is the exuberance of such profanation founded on creativity but "the activity that results from this thus becomes a pure means, that is, a praxis that, while firmly maintaining its nature as a means, is emancipated from its relationship to an end; it has joyously forgotten its goal and can now show itself as such, as a means without an end. The creation of new use is possible only by deactivating an old use, rendering it inoperative" (Agamben, *Profanations*, 86). A contemporary term for profanation may well be hacking, though this latter term has one too many significances, of which not all forms correspond with profanation.

Agamben makes it clear that play as profanation is not simply unregulated and antisocial behavior. On the contrary, it becomes a fully political task when we recognize that today, in the age of late capitalism, or the "society of the spectacle," "an absolute profanation without remainder now coincides with an equally vacuous and total consecration" (Agamben, *Profanations*, 81). In other words, we have a situation in which the separation of the sacred and the profane no longer functions meaningfully, whereby the alternation between serious content and play with forms can occur, sustaining and engendering the exuberance of creative activity. On the contrary, the sacred and the profane enter a "zone of indistinction" so that everything is separated as unusable and exhibited, fetishized, museumized, and everything is profaned in that everything is emptied of content insofar as it is a commodity with only monetary value. Paradoxically, then, it is only in capitalism that we experience a condition in which objects as commodities are completely unusable. "That is to say, use is always a relationship with something that cannot be appropriated; it refers to things insofar as they cannot become objects of possession. But this use also lays bare the true nature of property, which is nothing but the device that moves the free use of men into a separate sphere, where it is converted into a right" (Agamben, *Profanations*, 83). Further, he writes, "the classless society is not a society that has abolished and lost all memory of class differences but a society that has learned to deactivate the apparatuses of those differences in order to make a new use possible, in order to transform them into pure means" (Agamben, *Profanations*, 87). So what we have is a situation in which not only use is no longer possible, but profanation itself. Insofar as capitalism is a machine of incessant and ever-faster modes of profane separation, a setting apart without content or the sacred, it is, in a sense, an economic machine that attempts to create a world that is absolutely unprofanable. Thus it is that we now recognize that "to return to play its purely profane vocation is a political task" (Agamben, *Profanations*, 77). Though Agamben does not spell out how such a task should and can be carried out, we can perhaps justifiably surmise that it can only be undertaken through what Foucault terms the "care of self," through the practice of "ascetic" techniques upon the self—mind and body (i.e., through gesture).

It is at this point that we must return to the particular threshold at which Agamben's thought is situated—the threshold between being and doing, language and gesture, passivity and activity, exuberance and repose as "immense happiness"—that opens a door between philosophical traditions, Continental and Asian.

Askēsis

Whenever two nouns denoting different traditions are invoked, there are discursive habits that accompany the act, such as the comparative approach or, in the case of beliefs, an interfaith dialogue. My sense is that such habits of speech and interpretation cannot do justice to the particular threshold body that Agamben's thought invites us to perceive. Let us acknowledge that at first glance, there can be no doubt that on the theme of the mind-body relation, Asian thought (for instance Zen and Yoga philosophies) growing out of Buddhist and Hindu doctrines is by and large at profound variance with the dominant concepts that develop from Judeo-Christian culture (Descartes and Kant). The theorizing of these differences is entirely within the jurisdiction of experts and disciplinary ambassadors. Given my present concern, it would be of no use to delve into that archive, since it can at best only create friendly exchanges between determinate entities. To glimpse movement as the ethical and political expression of potential being, of gesturality, requires the clearing of a threshold where assigned identities dissolve. I shall then, at the risk of naiveté, simply note coincidences that are relatively commonplace details and are therefore presumably noncontroversial.

Attempting to specify the singular relation between mind and body that must necessarily found the inoperative kernel (the gesturality) of exceptional movement, let us turn briefly to the contemporary Japanese philosopher Yuasa Yasuo, who belongs to the famed Kyoto school, where comparative work between Continental and Asian thought was undertaken in the first part of the twentieth century. In his book *The Body: Towards an Eastern Mind-Body Theory*, Yuasa suggests that one of the distinguishing characteristics of South and East Asian (Hindu, Buddhist, Tao) philosophies is that the oneness of mind and body is not a simple fact to be discovered but must be understood as an achievement. In other words, the union of body and mind is a state that one strives toward to experience the truth of being. Thus, the emphasis in South and East Asian thought falls heavily on the *cultivation* of oneness through practices of the "self," or what might be termed "spiritual exercises." In his introduction, written expressly for the English translation, Yuasa situates the cultivation of mind-body oneness as a concept that runs through diverse physical activities (such as *Nō* drama or *Judo* and *Kendo*). "The oneness of the body-mind," Yuasa writes, "is an ideal for inward meditation as well as for outward activities" (Yuasa, *The Body*, 24). The question that he then goes on to pose is "How can the essence of meditation and activity be the same?" This paradox of action through inaction (*wu wei, tapas*), which is expressed through a number of antinomies (force and stillness, power and weakness, etc.), is a central question in South and East Asian forms of thought. No doubt, this question resonates powerfully with the concept of movement as gesture and potentiality. In subsequent chapters, Yuasa discusses the perspective of two modern Japanese thinkers, Tetsuro Watsuji (1889–1960) and Kitaro Nishida (1870–1945), and their debt to the great traditional Zen masters Dōgen (1200–53) and Kūkai (774–835). To attempt a discussion of the details of Yuasa's interpretations of these thinkers and their influential interpretations of Tao, Buddhist, and Hindu metaphysics would take me too far afield. In sum, however, it can be said that Yuasa underlines the fundamental threshold character of the countless spiritual disciplines and schools of thought that have developed from Buddhist, Hindu, and Tao philosophy insofar as they seem to emerge in the interstice between theoretical thinking and practical bodily cultivation, rationalism and empiricism, and, importantly, the "religious" and the metaphysical. Despite the immense diversity of Hindu, Buddhist, Tao, and other forms of Asian thought, Yuasa suggests that what is shared by the various schools, in contradistinction to the philosophical systems in the West, is the emphasis on self-cultivation.[20]

Yuasa's assertion is no doubt valid, as is his observation that though much comparative work between Japanese and Continental philosophical traditions is undertaken in Japan due to widespread familiarity with Western thinkers, the opposite is true in the West. Yuasa points out that in the West, interest in Asian thought is usually expressed by psychologists or Orientalists but very rarely by philosophers (Karl Jaspers and Rudolf Otto being mild exceptions). Yuasa does not mention the Western discipline of theology, where much comparative work is carried out. However, the fact is that the historical conflict between self-cultivation practices, or spiritual traditions and theology, that Foucault cites (Foucault, *The Hermeneutics of the Subject*, 27) as occurring between the fifth and seventeenth centuries in Europe greatly complicates the possibility of intellectual exchange between Western and Asian thinkers. Setting aside the significance and dangers of this power imbalance (which is a disciplinary question) for the moment, we cannot fail to remark on the contemporary trend within some strains of Continental thought that have turned away from the dominant tendency to isolate, privilege, and develop reason solely for the accumulation of knowledge toward the ethical, political, and even spiritual practices of self-cultivation. In his 1981–82 course lectures at the Collège de France on *The Hermeneutics of the Subject*,[21] Michel Foucault, in fact, suggests that "the entire history of nineteenth-century philosophy [German Idealism and Phenomenology] can, I think, be thought of as a kind of pressure to try and rethink the structures of spirituality within a philosophy that, since Cartesianism, or at any rate since seventeenth-century philosophy, tried to get free from structures. Hence the hostility . . . of all the 'classical' type of philosophers—all those who invoke the tradition of Descartes, Leibniz, etcetera—towards the philosophy of the nineteenth century that poses, at least implicitly, the very old question of spirituality and which, without saying so, rediscovers the care of the self" (Foucault, *The Hermeneutics of the Subject*, 28). No doubt, Foucault's summary antithesis between the so-called classical and neospiritual systems can be challenged. It is perhaps less controversial to assert that the broad questions of what constitutes an ethical life, what the sociopolitical conditions of possibility are for such a life, and how these conditions can be brought about to effect change in society, the environment, and consequently on oneself have acquired a sense of urgency. I cannot here touch on the rich historical circumstances that have prompted this turn to the ethicopolitical; instead, I can only note that within the individual evolution of each tradition, there is, despite the assertion of difference on all sides, a gathering of thought at the threshold—diverse strains of thought arriving somewhere between theory and practice, religion and metaphysics, knowledge and spirituality.

However, it is also the case that though social transformation preoccupies Western philosophers of most, if not all, stripes today, very few have actually ventured into the suspect "spiritual" territory of personal transformation, thereby reinforcing age-old and familiar divisions between the so-called individual and society, private and public, biological and sociopolitical, body and mind. But there are some exceptions to this trend, and in the following, I consider briefly the research undertaken into Western modalities of self-cultivation by Pierre Hadot and Foucault. The period that they focus on is Greek antiquity from the pre-Socratics on to imperial Rome as a phase, notwithstanding discontinuities and shifts, when philosophy was devoted to self-cultivation. Both philosophers unhesitatingly deploy the term "spiritual" in order to discuss the practical "modifications of existence" that have, according to them, always prevailed within Western culture since antiquity. Hadot writes,

> "Spiritual exercises." The expression is a bit disconcerting for the contemporary reader. In the first place, it is no longer quite fashionable these days to use the word "spiritual." It is nevertheless necessary to use this term, I believe, because none of the other adjectives we could use—"psychic," "moral," "ethical," intellectual," "of thought," "of soul"—covers all the aspects of the reality we want to describe. Since, in these exercises, it is thought which, as it were, takes itself as its own

subject-matter, and seeks to modify itself. (Hadot, *Philosophy as a Way of Life*, 81–82)

In his opening lecture, Foucault,[22] too, speaks of the modern suspicion in the West toward the "care of self" and goes on to assert the difference between Greco-Roman and modern philosophical norms in terms that very much echo Yuasa's distinction between Asian and Continental traditions. Here, the term "spiritual" is introduced and defined. If philosophy is "the form of thought that asks what it is that enables the subject to have access to the truth," "spirituality," Foucault says, refers to the "researches, practices, and experiences, which may be purifications, ascetic exercises, renunciations, conversions of looking, modifications of existence, etc., which are, not for knowledge but for the subject, for the subject's very being, the price to be paid for access to the truth" (Foucault, *The Hermeneutics of the Subject*, 15). He goes on to specify that what distinguishes modernity is the notion that "knowledge itself and knowledge alone gives access to the truth" (Foucault, *The Hermeneutics of the Subject*, 17). In other words, the modern notion that anyone may have access to the truth solely through using correct methods of reasoning without having to prepare or transform him or herself for its reception, Foucault says, is in sharp contrast to the ancients, who believed that access to the truth necessitated the subject's very being to be thrown into question, trained, and transformed. Foucault's opening lecture leaves us with little doubt that the horizon where one might perceive the convergence of parallel traditions (Asian and Continental) might well be that of a certain redemption. If Asian thought has long been dismissed by Western philosophers as being "merely" soteriological (better left to the theologians), then Foucault's genealogy of Western thought recuperates precisely this "Asian" element. In modernity, he says,

> knowledge will simply open out onto the indefinite dimension of progress, the end of which is unknown and the advantage of which will only ever be realized in the course of history by the institutional accumulation of bodies of knowledge . . . as such, henceforth the truth cannot save the subject. If we define spirituality as being the form of practices which postulate that, such as he is, the subject is not capable of the truth, but that, such as it is, the truth can transfigure and save the

subject, then we can say that the modern age of the relations between the subject and truth begin when it is postulated that, such as he is, the subject is capable of truth, but that, such as it is, the truth cannot save the subject. (Foucault, *The Hermeneutics of the Subject*, 19)

In "Forms of Life and Forms of Discourse," Hadot suggests that for the philosophers of antiquity, "the philosophical life will be an effort to live and think according to the norm of wisdom, it will be a movement, a progression, though a never-ending one, towards this transcendent state" (Hadot, *Philosophy as a Way of Life*, 59). Although Hadot believes that the practices of meditation in the Greco-Roman traditions were "unlike the Buddhist meditation practices of the Far East," which assumed a "corporeal attitude" (Hadot, *Philosophy as a Way of Life*, 59), he nevertheless asserts that the exercises were about progressing spiritually toward wisdom and were "analogous to the athlete's training or to the application of a medical cure" (Hadot, *Philosophy as a Way of Life*, 59). In other words, the subject's access to the truth was inescapably linked to a rethinking of the mind-body relation. For Hadot, an understanding of this spiritual tradition transforms as well our understanding of the Delphic oracle *gnothi seauton* ("know thyself"). In his lectures, Foucault develops this point to argue that *gnothi seauton* should be subsumed by another more important maxim, *epimeleia heautou,* or "care of the self" (Foucault, *The Hermeneutics of the Subject*, 4). Later in the same course, Foucault will go on to offer yet another formula: *tekhnē tou biou,* or the "art of existence" (Foucault, *The Hermeneutics of the Subject,* 447), as the general question that engenders the care of the self.

The genealogy that Foucault constructs for the discourses and systems of spiritual exercises is one that agrees with the work of several comparatists. If in Plato, the figure of Socrates enjoins the care of the self to those who seek to exert power and dispense justice (thereby making spiritual development a necessary component of justice), Foucault marks a shift in the Hellenic era. In this period (i.e., the first and second centuries), which Foucault designates as the golden age of the spiritual exercises, the care of the self was not confined to the elite, but was urged upon all (20 January 1982). In the later lectures, especially of 24 February, 3 March, and 24 March 1982, Foucault sharply distinguishes Christian monasticism from the philosophical *askēsis* of the Imperial era.[23] According to Foucault, the spiritual exercises of Christian monasticism were designed toward a self-renunciation as opposed to the ethic of self-realization. The vigilance exercised over the self was not directed toward the discovery of hidden powers but toward exorcism of concupiscence (Foucault, *The Hermeneutics of the Subject*, 299–300).

One can be carried away by Foucault's dazzling expositions, and so it behooves us to rein in a little and ask, "what is the relevance of Greco-Roman spiritual exercises, 'the care of self,' to the task at hand, which is to apprehend the kernel of repose at the heart of movement in its ethicopolitical potentiality?[24] When is agile exceptional movement resistant to the cooptation of bodily exuberance as means to a monetized or purposive end?"

We can derive the premise from the opening that Yuasa provides—that a given form of exceptional movement can disclose its ethicopolitical potential, its inherent inoperativity, only when it exceeds the exclusive focus on bodily development, as in sports or conventional acrobatics. In other words, it must be an exercise that alters the mind-body relation as obtained from a spiritual discipline. The disciplines of dance and sport make very particular demands on targeted muscles of the body in order to develop a single aptitude, a single faculty, thereby exploiting the generic ability of youth. A spiritual bodily practice, on the other hand, will make demands on all aspects of the anatomy from breath to muscle, bone, consciousness, and emotion that develop and balance all the functions that a body undertakes in its anatomical singularity and will continue throughout life as an accompaniment to old age. In fact, such a practice will necessarily be founded on a theory of the body (as evidenced in Asian medical technologies) that differs significantly from the discipline of scientific anatomy. I hazard, then, that exceptional movement can be the disclosure of pure means only when it is approached and understood as a practice that bears a relation to the original sense of the word "gymnastics." Hadot notes the working of a powerful analogy between the athlete and the philosopher in Plato, Porphyry, and Epictetus. Speaking of self-modification exercises, he underlines that both the athlete and the philosopher modify their respective objects (namely, the body and the soul) and ultimately their being through exercises. "The analogy seems all the more self-evident in that the *gymnasion*, the place where physical exercises were practiced, was the same place where philosophy lessons were given; in other words, it was also the place for training in *spiritual* gymnastics" (Hadot, *Philosophy as a Way of Life*, 102). In his discussion of the formula *epimeleisthai heautou*, or care of self, Foucault stresses that

> *Epimeleisthai* does not only designate a mental attitude, a certain form of attention, a way of not forgetting something. Its etymology refers to a series of words such as *meletan, melete, meletai* etcetera. *Meletan*, often employed and coupled with the verb *gumnazein*, means to practice and train. The *meletai* are exercises, gymnastic and military exercises, military training. *Epimeleisthai* refers to a form of vigilant, continuous, applied, regular, etcetera, activity much more than to a mental attitude. (Foucault, *The Hermeneutics of the Subject*, 84)

However, the precise extent to which physical exercises were also spiritual exercises, and spiritual exercises entailed physical training, is at best controversial and one that only historians of antiquity can settle. For instance, Jason König, in *Athletics and Literature in the Roman Empire*, begins with an epigraph from Galen speaking scathingly of acrobats and sports. To this, König then adds a lengthy inscription commemorating the athletic achievements of one Markos Aurelios Asklepiades to illustrate the "alluring challenges and difficulties which stand in the way in any attempt to analyse the athletics of the ancient world" (König, *Athletics and Literature in the Roman Empire*, 6). Foucault, too, reminds us of Seneca's contempt for gymnastics in letter 15 to Lucilius (Foucault, *Hermeneutics of the Subject*, 428). Though the analogy between athletic and spiritual exercises or philosophical *askēsis* is one that Foucault exploits to the maximum,[25] even he does not propose a blending between the two. On the other hand, the fact that most Asian movement techniques, from *haṭha yoga* to martial arts, are spiritual disciplines is almost too well known to require citation. So we have two approaches to spiritual exercises, as it were: the Western one, which largely believes in balancing the physical *and* the intellectual, and the Asian one, where the spiritual and the physical balance each other *through* each other in a relation of propinquity or *yoga*.

Given these two overlapping yet disjunct approaches to the relation between the intellectual and the physical, mind and body, thinking and training, being and doing, what we have is the sharing between ancient Greek and Asian traditions of a very general notion that access to the truth requires self-transformation, and self-transformation leads to self-realization. The differential assumptions about the body, ethics, motivations, that govern the practice of a given ascetic discipline and how these are to be understood are so textually intricate that no generalization is possible. Without seeking to totalize these highly differentiated schools of thought, we can yet note a few overlapping themes. Many of the features that Foucault identifies as being characteristic of the discourse of care of the self will have an element of déjà vu for those knowledgeable about spiritual disciplines in Asia. My point of reference hence will be to *yoga* philosophy, which Yuasa identifies as a pervading influence on East Asian systems. There are several kinds of yoga, such as Bhakti (devotion) yoga, Karma (inaction in action) yoga, Raja (sovereign) yoga, and so on. However, since the focus of this chapter is on exceptional movement, I shall refer only to the branch of *Rajayoga* (the yoga of sovereignty) called *haṭha yoga,* or the practice of "force."

The philological significance of *Yoga* is relevant here since it directly concerns the recognition and suspension of the logic and laws of separation, thereby relating it to Agamben's concept of profanation. According to Eliade,[26] it is derived from the root *yuj,* meaning to bind or yoke (related to *jungere, jugum* in Latin and *giogo* in Italian, *joug* in French). In other words, it is a bringing together of separated elements without necessarily sublating them into a new synthesis. Further, we could say that as a form of yoking, it is a philosophy fundamentally of a certain transcendental immanence. Paradoxical as that may seem, transcendental immanence is not the transcending of the body and its pathetic limitations. Rather, the body is within a transcendental field—a threshold of matter and space where the body *is* in immanence. Whether the process of disclosing and reposing in such a transcendental immanence or "transcendental empiricism" (to use a phrase associated with Gilles Deleuze) is a discoverable ethic in the ancient discourses of *epimeleia heautou* is open to question. However, there are *techniques,* if not metaphysical assumptions, about space, time, and matter that are shared between Foucault's interpretations of the Stoics, the Epicureans, the Therapeutae, and so on, and the practices of a *yogin*. Foucault is aware of this universality. He writes that "the idea that one must put a technology of the self to work in order to have access to the truth is shown in Ancient Greece, and what's more in many, if not all, civilizations, by a number of practices" (Foucault, *Hermeneutics of the Subject*, 46–47). For instance, in one of the earlier lectures, Foucault lists some of the recommended practices very schematically. First, there are the purification rites. These are followed by

> Techniques for concentrating the soul. The soul is something mobile. The soul, the breath, is something that can be disturbed and over which the outside can exercise a hold. One must avoid dispersal of the soul, the breath, the *pneuma* . . . One must therefore concentrate the *pneuma*, the soul, gather it up, condense it, and unite it in itself . . . [T]he technique of withdrawal (*retraite*), for which there is a word, which as you know will have a prominent future in all of Western spirituality, *anakhoresis* (withdrawal or disengagement from the world). Withdrawal is understood in these archaic techniques of the self as a particular way of detaching yourself and absenting yourself from the world in which you happen to be. (Foucault, *Hermeneutics of the Subject*, 47)

Withdrawal or *pratyahāra* is a ubiquitous concept in all six schools of ancient Indian philosophy, but it is nowhere more fully elaborated as a "technology" or a practice of the self than in the literature of yoga. For instance, every lay practitioner of yoga today is aware that the classic text of yoga philosophy, Patañjali's *Yoga Sutras*, recommends withdrawal (*pratyāhāra*) as one of the essential components of its praxis.[27] However, in his monumental work, *The Shape of Ancient Thought*, the classical philologist Thomas McEvilley discovers several correspondences between Socrates and Patañjali, particularly the Socrates of the Phaedo where "withdrawal of the mind from the senses is followed by 'concentrating itself on itself.' Similarly for Patañjali, pratyahara—the withdrawal of attention from sense objects and thoughts about them—is to be followed by dharana, concentration" (McEvilley, *The Shape of Ancient Thought*, 180). In a later chapter in the same work, McEvilley compares Stoic thought and spiritual exercises to concepts mentioned in Vedanta literature and also yoga philosophy. For instance, he writes that "parallelisms between *pneuma* and *prāṇa* are thoroughgoing" (McEvilley, *The Shape of Ancient Thought*, 545). I cannot do justice to the correspondences, not to mention predictable differences, that McEvilley discovers between Greek and Indian philosophies in his deeply researched work, but the archive opened by both Foucault and McEvilley is evidence that the principles by which we can grasp exceptional movement simultaneously as gesture and profanation will have to be forged from this threshold between traditions, as a practice sans tradition.

Besides withdrawal and concentration, Foucault also discusses the description of several other spiritual exercises in Marcus Aurelius and Epictetus in relation to diet, meditation, the observance of austerities, and so on. Once again, the almost uncanny similarity would be apparent to any lay practitioner of *hatha yoga*. Though *hatha yoga* is devoted to the development of all eight limbs of yoga, it is perhaps best characterized as specializing in the first four limbs, called the outer limbs (*yama, niyama, asana, pranayama, pratyahara*). In the later literature, the physical movement aspect that Patañjali calls *asana* (movement into repose, though usually translated as pose or posture, but also meaning seat, a place of resting) has been codified into a number of different system manuals. The *Haṭha Yoga Pradipika* of Swātarāma, a fourteenth- or fifteenth-century practitioner, is evidence of the highly developed and detailed discourses of the "care of the self" during this period. The text elaborates the finer points of diet, daily regimen, austerities, observances, avoidances, and of course various techniques for developing the intelligence of the body through movement into a pose and resting in it.

When *asana* is approached as a form of exceptional movement in which inaction is preserved as action—for it is nothing if not the discovery of repose in pose—then its correspondence, or more properly identity, with Agamben's concept of gesture is secured. In fact, it would be remiss not to mention that *asana* is impossible without *mudra*—the science of gesture. Let us now turn to the question of the political in such gesture.

The political direction of this inquiry into exceptional movement was initiated by the observation that agile movement, when unsanctioned by the apparatuses of the means-end economy and by discipline, tends to be illegal. In other words, it appears to threaten the law without actually overthrowing it. It seems to confound and interrupt the law or, at best, it is tolerated. But given that ascetic practices (Asian or Hellenic) were focused on care of the self, their address to the law is perhaps more incidental than primary. Foucault's interpretation is once again instructive.

> In the culture of the self of Greek, Hellenistic, and Roman civilization, the problem of the subject in his relation to practice leads, I believe, to something quite different from the question of the law. It leads to this: How can the subject act as he ought . . . In fact, neither of these two problems (of obedience to the law and of the subject's knowledge of himself) was really fundamental or even present in the thought of ancient culture. There was "spirituality of knowledge *(savoir)*," and there was "practice and exercise of the truth." This is how, I think, the question of *askesis* should be approached. (Foucault, *Hermeneutics of the Subject*, 319)

However, Foucault also acknowledges that apart from the Pythagoreans, groups such as the Stoics, Epicureans, and so on did not respect social distinctions between rich and poor, the powerful and the obscure. He writes that "these groups did not accept even the distinctions between a free man and a slave, in theory at least" (Foucault, *Hermeneutics of the Subject*, 118). Surprisingly, such "respect" for disrespect of the law is not alien to yoga philosophy, and the spiritual praxes often arrive as antidotes to the notorious rigidity of social distinctions in India and Asia in general.[28] Yoga, as previously discussed, is related to profanation in that it is the yoking of that which is separate and bringing them into a delicate balance. Thus, my sense is that agile movement, as a form of profanation, which incorporates spiritual exercises where mind-body relations are transformed and unified, can perhaps remain immune to the (capitalist) logic of ends and means. But is it possible for movement to retain the historical lowliness of acrobatics alongside the historical rigor of philosophical ascesis to expose human potentiality as pure means?

No doubt, not every tightrope walker or juggler is a political activist, a profaner, any more than every elite gymnast can be said to practice philosophical *askēsis*. The ethicopolitical significance of the body in agile exceptional movement is neither a function of specific physical moves nor of ideologies. It obtains rather from the practice of a potent restitution of the mind to the body and the body to the mind. On one hand, the *bricolage* of profanation "proper" is composed of those elements of ascetic practice that are shared by Western and East/ South Asian thought systems: chastity, emptiness of mind, silence, the view from above, indifference to rank, the death exercise, otium, and an ethic of happiness. On the other, profanation also includes characteristics of old-fashioned acrobatics: its lowliness, lack of national and cultural patrimony, purposelessness, noncompetitiveness, nomadism, dare devilry, nonprescriptiveness, spontaneity, exuberance, and joy. Profanation transforms spaces, the polis, and the self. It is playful, has no goal, not even that of the self, of winning, or reaching an aesthetic ideal. It is not transgressive in the sense that it does not simply break the law. Rather, it interrupts the law by tricking and confounding it. In order to conceptualize exceptional movement as having political and ethical valence, it must be at the threshold between traditional spiritual exercises (Greco-Roman and Asian) and athletic exercises, with their local traditions devoted only to the physique. As profanation, exceptional movement will be a *bricolage* that borrows freely as much from philosophical *askēsis* as from sport or crime, from stoicism as much as from the circus or dance, from children as much as from the truly old. But unlike all spiritual practices as well as competitive athletics, it will be empty of prescription, and empty of content. And unlike circus acrobatics, it will not purport to entertain nor will it devolve into a lucrative spectacle. It is merely a form of movement that exposes its own being in the movement.

My concrete example of such profanation is Philippe Petit, whose practice of agile exceptional movement is the absolute obverse of an elite gymnast.

Loitering

No doubt, then, exceptional movement is a mode of profanation and play, and is particularly interesting because in it a being is disclosed as a profaning animal. An example of such an animal is perhaps Philippe Petit. My reason for citing him is not that he is in some sense exemplary but merely that he provides a good idea of the possibility of such action, thereby permitting us to examine the theory more closely and concretely. I suggest that Petit the high-wire artist is perhaps best understood as a spontaneous situationist, one who troubles and interrupts the law. In his book *To Reach for the Clouds*, later reprinted as *Man on Wire*, Petit describes the meticulous plans and preparations for his illegal walk across the Twin Towers of the World Trade Center in New York in 1974. Petit writes joyfully about the interruption he caused, bringing the machine of the great city to a grinding halt. With the police, helicopters, rescue teams, and media thronging toward the towers, Petit blissfully loiters on the high-wire, sauntering up and down, and at one point even lying down and gazing up at the sky and communing with a lone seagull. "Taxi drivers abandon their cabs in the middle of the street to run and see. Morning traffic is paralyzed. Wall Street stops counting and looks up . . . The city has changed face. Its maddening daily rush transformed into a magnificent motionlessness. It listens. It watches. It ponders" (Petit, *Man on Wire*, 198–99). Loitering on the high-wire, loitering in general, is what Petit seems to do with rigor and determination, thereby exposing the peculiarity of a law that defines remaining in a public place without purpose as a crime. A citizen is subject to arrest if he or she does not "move on" when accused by an official to be loitering. The presumption of the law is that a loiterer has a secret and therefore illegal purpose. Thus, sitting for too long on a public bench, wandering around without purpose in any public space, particularly places of transportation, seem to excite the law, as does trespassing, which is usually understood as infringing on property rights. In New York, after his walk across the Twin Towers, Petit says, he was arrested and charged with "criminal trespass, disorderly conduct, endangering my life and that of others, working without a permit, disregarding police orders—a litany of misdemeanors" (Petit, *Man on Wire*, 213–14). Though eventually all charges were dismissed by the district judge, the immediate reaction of the police at Petit's descent was to treat him with rough and shocking violence. He was summarily handcuffed behind his back, shouted at, literally dragged to a prison cell and treated like a dangerous criminal or "a stinky vagrant mutt" (Petit, *Man on Wire*, 205).

As a mode of profanation, Petit seems to invoke the force of the law, which almost always arrives with all of its repressive and humorless power, but only so he can play with it. In fact, he did not hesitate to pick open his handcuffs with a paper clip, snatch the policeman's cap, and balance it on his nose (Petit, *Man on Wire*, 210–11). But as anyone who has perused his account will recognize, the mischief here is remarkably skillful, knowledgeable, and utterly without purpose. As Agamben emphasizes, not only is such play or profanation utterly indifferent to the separations and prohibitions of the law, but it is first and foremost *not* careless activity. On the contrary, it is concentrated, "studious," to use Agamben's favored term. In his essay on profanation, Agamben writes that "no kind of attention can compare to that of a child at play" (Agamben, *Profanations*, 76). It is not only his deliberate and ludic run-ins with the law that make Petit such a mirthful and fit example of Agamben's political ontology. Petit's self-description as a "criminal," his interest in pick-pocketing, lock-picking, feigning, and faking puts him more in the category of folkloric tricksters and con-artists who harbor forbidden skills and develop useless illegal technologies than a conventional artist who produces works that can be bought and sold. Though today, as artist-n-residence at the Cathedral of St. John the Divine in New York, he is considered something of a performance artist, what differentiates him from iconic performance art figures such as Yves Klein or Josef Beuys is his relation to art history. Given the fact that the con-arts he practices along with juggling and tightrope-walking cannot be said to participate in a national history of art in that they neither break nor continue tradition but only interrupt, his nonworks are necessarily excluded from the world of avant-garde art. Though it would be impossible to trace the origins of tightrope-walking, pick-pocketing, juggling (he even mentions owning a "counterfeiting kit"), and so on, one could no doubt trace the genealogy of these practices in specific locations. For instance, Robert Isherwood documents the popularity of funambulism in the fairs held in Paris during the eighteenth century.[29] On the other hand, a great card shark such as Ricky Jay has researched histories of the personalities through the centuries who have practiced mostly in anonymity the lowly arts of card tricks, funambulism, fire eating, and so on. However, my sense is that to place Petit in this history of the circus arts (where he arguably does belong) or in the history of the avant-garde is to not attend to the significance of his acts to history. In other words, it would be to elide the political and profanatory potential of his acts. We can perhaps do justice to the relation of Petit's playful acts to history only if we consider it through the lens of play as such and its relation to history.

History

If we raise the question of history in relation to profanation, we must, if we wish to avoid an ideological argument (along the lines of Bakhtin),[30] necessarily turn to play itself. In an early essay entitled "In Playland," included in *Infancy and History*, Agamben examines the relation of play and ritual to time and history by suggesting that they share an inverse yet interdependent relation. Ritual, he says, occurs in synchronic time. Fundamentally, religious rituals reenact, reaffirm, and secure the calendar. On the other hand, play occurs in diachronic time and it serves to break the time of the ritual calendar to introduce what he calls "human time" (Agamben, *Infancy and History*, 70). Further, he suggests that in general, rituals are marked by their ability to transform an event into structure, whereas in play, structures are turned into events (Agamben, *Infancy and History*, 74). Agamben underlines that these two processes never appear independently of each other; rather, they belong to a single binary system. Ritual and play appear, rather, as two tendencies operating in every society; although the one never has the effect of eliminating the other, and although one might prevail over the other to a varying degree, they always maintain a differential margin between diachrony and synchrony. History, human time, Agamben then goes on to suggest, emerges from this binary machine as the differential. "The object of history is not diachrony [play], but the opposition between diachrony and synchrony [ritual] which characterizes every human society" (Agamben, *Infancy and History*, 75). However, the transformation enacted by ritual and play, of synchronic signifiers into diachronic and vice versa respectively, never fully coincides nor is it accomplished without leaving a disturbing residue, a trace. These unstable signifiers, then, are always experienced as a threat. Agamben cites the example of funeral rituals that convert the dead into ancestors, thereby neutralizing the terrifying appearance of the ghost as a signifier of the synchronic into living time. Conversely, birth rites also serve to convert the uncanny newborn into the properly living, thereby neutralizing the threatening signifier of the unborn. While these unstable or threshold signifiers mark on the one hand the difference and the discontinuity between the two worlds, their significance lies in the fact that they serve to reproduce the system of exchange between them, thereby guaranteeing the transmission of signifiers. Agamben writes that "true historical continuity cannot pretend to discard the signifiers of discontinuity by confining them to a Playland or a museum for ghosts . . . but by 'playing' with them, accepts them so as to restore them to the past and transmit them to the future" (Agamben, *Infancy and History*, 86).

Though the basic structure of play as the emptying of ritual is retained (though only ritual seems to do all the work of historical transformation in the above examples), we can note a significant shift in Agamben's thinking with regard to history and language in the later essay on profanation. Rather than sounding a resonance with Derrida's theme of history as trace, here the influence of Benjamin and the messianic thought of "redeemed humanity" is the context in which play and profanation find their niche. To discuss the details of this shift in emphasis, one would no doubt have to engage with his 1983 essay "Language and History." I cannot here do justice to the concerns of that essay or the build-up of the argument but shall merely refer to the relevant bits.

In this signal essay, which is concerned with the historicity of transmission as such (i.e., what is transmitted in history), history is no longer thought as the trace of the continuous transaction between synchrony and diachrony that renders all history into "writing" or makes for the infinite task of hermeneutic interpretation. Rather, Agamben writes, "Benjamin explicitly states that the language of redeemed humanity has 'burst the chains of writing' and is a language that is 'not written but festively celebrated'" (Agamben, *Potentialities*, 57–58). In other words, Agamben's deployment of the concept of play here is not in service of the infinite and continuous transmission of history as heritage but rather toward its fulfillment. The noncoincidence between the diachronic and the synchronic or between history (event, play) and language (structure, ritual) "now disappears and gives way to a perfect identity of language and history, praxis and speech . . . Here language disappears as an autonomous category; it is possible neither to make any distinct image of it nor to imprison it in any writing. Human beings no longer write their language; they celebrate it as a holiday without rites, and they understand each other 'just as those born on Sunday understand the language of birds'" (Agamben, *Potentialities*, 61).

I have not checked to see if Philippe Petit was born on a Sunday, but that he understands the language of birds could not possibly be doubted. The relation of his acts to history is best understood not in continuity with the circus arts or prestigious avant-garde art but with a certain vision of the end of history as the transmission of heritage. To cite Agamben again, we may say that "it has no past to transmit, being instead a world of 'integral actuality'" (Agamben, *Potentialities*, 61). Studious play as profanation interrupts history by freeing it (even if momentarily) as property. This is perhaps the widest context in which we can situate and apprehend agile exceptional movement, which thereby discloses in their interrelation the critiques of property rights, the law, and vocation. Envisioning the messianic fulfillment of time when the law will be rendered inoperative, Agamben writes, "One day humanity will play with law just as children play with disused objects, not in order to restore them to their canonical use but to free them from it for good. What is found after the law is not a more proper and original use value that precedes the law, but a new use that is born only after it. And use, which has been contaminated by law, must also be freed from its own value. This liberation is the task of study, or of play. And this studious play is the passage that allows us to arrive at that justice that one of Benjamin's posthumous fragments defines as a state of the world in which the world appears as a good that absolutely cannot be appropriated or made juridical" (Agamben, *State of Exception*, 64).

Thus, it follows that Petit's use of his mastery of the con-arts to infringe on the sacred notion of property rights (rigging and wire-walking without a permit) is necessarily tied to his undisguised disdain for commerce, middle-class prestige, and the entertainment media. In other words, his critique of the dominance of the economy is practical. As he says, "either we do a bank robbery, or we do a film about a bank robbery. We cannot do both . . . I have decided to do a bank robbery" (Petit, *Man on Wire*, 62). And so we are told that he repeatedly turns down offers from impresarios who want to manage his "career," advertising agents who want to recruit him to sell fast food and sugar substitutes, talk show hosts, and Hollywood actors, extracting from them, however, free meals at fine restaurants under the guise of discussing the deal. When he is low on cash, he prefers to draw a circle in the street, juggle, do a few tricks, and pass his ripped top hat around.

Otium

On the track of ethicopolitical movement, the trajectory of this chapter has been a traversal of concepts on the wheels of specific interlinks. Reading movement as *kinēsis* and potentiality led to the discovery of "gesture" as a condensed moment of everything that can be comprehended by the concept of potentiality, especially the idea of pure means, or means without end. The disclosure of a form of life that has only pure means as its generic possibility also implied a certain critique of the work ethic and a valorization of worklessness. Movement as worklessness is, of course, not mere inertia, but "profanation," an ethicopolitical act that is akin to a philosophical ascesis, "care of the self," and Asian thought, such as *yoga* philosophy.

The gesturality of Petit's loitering lies in the fact that what the act discloses is nothing if not potentiality—the fact that a human being can do this, walk on the tightrope between two towers. Here, loitering was disclosed as loitering. What does the example of Petit clarify about the theme of pure means as potentiality or worklessness (*otium*) that is at the heart center of this inquiry into exceptional movement?

Agile play is fundamentally ascetic insofar as it necessitates a disclosure of the intelligence of the body, where the ancient dichotomies of mind and matter, consciousness and instinct, language and nonlanguage, human and animal are neither reconciled nor overcome. Rather, what happens when we leap into mid-air is, to cite Agamben's *The Open: Between Man and Animal*, a "reciprocal suspension of the two terms, [and] something for which we perhaps have no name and which is neither animal nor man settles in between nature and humanity and holds itself in the mastered relation, in the saved night" (Agamben, *The Open*, 83; 85).

In-Conclusion

LET ME THEN TELL A STORY—A PARADIGMATIC STORY OF HOSPITALITY drawn from the *Bhaghavata Purana*, book 10, cantos 80–81. It is the story of Krishna and Sudama, also known as Kuchela (a surname or epithet). It is a surprisingly simple story, enigmatic in its lack of didacticism and moral allegorization. Sudama or Kuchela is a learned but impoverished Brahmin. His good and long-suffering wife suggests that he visit his old school friend Krishna, who is now the king of Dwaraka and married to Rukmini, known as the incarnation of Lakshmi, the goddess of fortune. Sudama agrees, and takes a heap of puffed rice borrowed from a neighbor as a gift for Krishna. Sudama arrives at Krishna's glittering palace and, surprisingly, no one bars his way. When Krishna sees Sudama, he embraces him warmly, reminisces about their school days and eagerly partakes of the puffed rice that Sudama is too ashamed to offer. When Sudama returns to his village, he finds that his humble hut has been transformed into a luxurious palace and that he and his family have been provided with every material necessity. The text says he was liberated from labor. Sudama dedicates his life to living happily, teaching, and practicing austerity and humility, and eventually attains salvation.

It was not until I was familiar with other meaning contexts—such as the tale of the poor fisherman and his greedy wife or the parable of Lazarus and the rich man—that I recovered the strangeness of this tale. How should one understand this story, which seems uncritical of the complaining wife, the luxury of the rich, and even equates reward with material wealth? Let us try again by contemplating the story as it unfolds:

This time I shall call the story
Eating the Nothing
I see this:

Despair, a pathless future, a deep poverty, an unquantifiable crisis of body and soul grips the young scholar. His wife offers a solution: try to remember—only recall, she says, for all knowledge and all having are wrought by the power of memory. Reflecting quietly, under the shade of a Bodhi tree, the scholar recalls the time of a friendship. A friend during the days of learning, and that friend was he who could eat the nothing. The scholar smiles as he realizes that this time of friendship is neither the past nor the future. It comes about; it merely comes about around nothing. Thus called to a time within time, the poor scholar gathers together in a piece of clean sari torn from his wife's shoulder a heap of puffed rice, itself borrowed from a kindly neighbor—emptiness itself, rice with kernels removed, with nothing inside. And this he sets out to give to him, the friend who had the great capacity to receive.

A long and arduous journey, a pilgrimage, a prayer later, the poor scholar arrives at the gates of the friend. No questions are asked as one magnificent door leads to another. The doors stand wide open within the dazzling palace; no one bars his way and no questions are asked of him. The scholar's path brings him to the innermost sanctum, where the friend dallies with fortune itself. Spying the scholar hesitating at the doorway, the friend hastens and embraces him with delight. There is no hesitation, no uncertainty, no surprise. Only delight, sheer delight. No questions are asked: How are you, when did you come, why did you come, how long has it been, but have you not changed? Just delight, sheer delight. The poor scholar finds his tired feet washed by the friend, as the brilliant one who bestows fortune fans him and offers him fresh fruit, nuts, and honey. Nevertheless, the friend is ashamed—viriditta, avan mukah (literally—a face without words). For he is bare (Kuchela), emaciated, unkempt. "ku-cailaṁ malinaṁ kṣāmaṁ; dvijaṁ dhamani-santatam" (10.80) He cannot escape himself; he stands exposed in an "ultimate intimacy," a nakedness that is not only his bare body, his empty belly, but also the nakedness of his very being. He cannot cover himself before his friend. The friend only smiles. He speaks of their school days and the time when they lost their way together in a dark forest during a rainstorm. Remember—the crack of lightning, the thunder, the tall dark trees, the whistling storm, the flood. Discovering them at dawn, the teacher had blessed them. For what? For having lost their way together. The friend and the scholar reflect in silence on the words of that blessing from Sāndipani, their teacher. *Then the friend smiles and asks a question: Did you bring me anything from home, dear one? Hospitality confounds giving and receiving, host and guest, agent and patient. But Kuchela is* avan mukah*—a face bereft of words; he hangs his head in shame. What must he do? The friend spies the poor bundle of puffed rice; he gamely grabs it from the naked and emaciated scholar—he who has come to give* because he has nothing. *Is it audacity, or is it love, this giving nothing, giving what he does not have? The friend sinks his palm in the heap of rice and, opening his mouth wide, eats a fistful with sheer delight of the emptiness and the nothing, and reaches for more, and yet more, until fortune gently stays his hand. It is enough, she says, it is more than enough, for he is already liberated:* "karma-bandhād vimucyate" *(10: 81.41) freed from the bondage of material work.*

And as the friend empties the emptiness within the puffed rice, the scholar feels himself filling up. His satisfaction is immeasurable. Incalculable happiness and fortune accrue to him, the more he gives of what he does not have, the more he finds himself receiving what he could not imagine. Can something come out of nothing? Is it possible to give, eat, and be full of the nothing? Is this the meaning of grace? And is this also the time of hospitality? Is hospitality a time, a fortunate time, rather than a something that is given or received? Does hospitality simply happen when or, rather, because we lose our way together?

Later, the scholar recalls that he had asked nothing; indeed he needs nothing. And once again, he loses his way—his hut has disappeared, his bare belongings have disappeared, nothing has disappeared, and for this he is again blessed.

Notes

1. First Words on Silence

1. Throughout this book, dual page numbers refer to the English translation first, followed by the original French or Italian. Derrida and Roudinesco, *For What Tomorrow*.

2. Derrida and Mallet, *The Animal That Therefore I Am*.

3. Besides the pioneering work of the utilitarian philosopher Peter Singer, see Kelly Oliver, *Animal Lessons*; Cary Wolfe, *Animal Rites*; Leonard Lawlor, *This Is Not Sufficient*; Mary Midgeley, *Beast and Man*; Gary Steiner, *Anthropocentrism and Its Discontents;* Matthew Calarco, *Zoographies;* Stephen R. L. Clarke, *Animals and Their Moral Standing*; Catherine Osborne, *Dumb Beasts and Dead Philosophers*; Stanley Cavell et al., *Philosophy and Animal Life*; Peter Steeves and Tom Regan, *Animal Others*; Singer, Calarco, and Atterton, *Animal Philosophy*; Cary Wolfe, *Zoontologies*, and so on.

4. See, for instance, Peter Singer, Tom Regan, Paola Cavalieri, and so on.

5. "The Difficulty of Reality and the Difficulty of Philosophy," in Cavell et al., *Philosophy and Animal Life*, 43–89.

6. For a useful discussion of the various debates within linguistics on language origin, see Christine Kenneally, *The First Word: The Search for the Origins of Language,* especially 154–74 on "structure."

7. Derrida, *The Beast and the Sovereign*. My references throughout to this seminar will be to the original paragraph numbers.

8. Naas, "'One Nation . . . Indivisible': Jacques Derrida on the Autoimmunity of Democracy and the Sovereignty of God," 18.

9. One must here recall Foucault's oft-quoted words that "power must be understood in the first instance as the multiplicity of force relations immanent in the sphere in which they operate and which constitute their own organization. . . . Power's condition of possibility, or in any case the viewpoint which permits one to understand its exercise, even in its more 'peripheral' effects, and which also makes it possible to use its mechanisms as a grid of intelligibility of the social order, must not be sought in the primary existence of a central point. . . . The omnipresence of power: not because it has the privilege of consolidating everything under its invincible unity, but because

it is produced from one moment to the next, at every point, or rather in every relation from one point to another" (*History of Sexuality*, vol. 1: 93).

10. In "Différance," Derrida writes, "the trace relates no less to what is called the future than to what is called the past, and it constitutes what is called the present by this very relation to what it is not, to what it absolutely is not; that is, not even to a past or future considered as a modified present. In order for it to be, an interval must separate it from what it is not; but the interval that constitutes it in the present must also, and by the same token, divide the present in itself, thus dividing, along with the present, everything that can be conceived on its basis, that is, every being in particular, for our metaphysical language, the substance or subject. Constituting itself, dynamically dividing itself, this interval is what could be called spacing; time's becoming-spatial or space's becoming temporal (temporalizing)" (143).

11. "How to conceive what is outside a text? That which is more or less than a text's own, proper margin? . . . It is certain that the trace escapes every determination, every name it might receive in the metaphysical text. It is sheltered and therefore dissimulated, in these names. It does not appear in them as the trace 'itself.' But this is because it could never appear itself, as such. Heidegger also says that difference cannot appear as such. There is no essence of différance; it (is) that which not only could never be appropriated in the as such of its name or its appearing, but also that which threatens the authority of the as such in general, of the presence of the thing itself in its essence" ("Différance," 25–26).

12. References are to the paragraph numbers, which are the same in the original and the translation.

13. Derrida, *The Animal That Therefore I Am* (52; 79).

14. Agamben, *The Open*, 33–38; 38–43.

15. "È un insieme eterogeneo, che include virtualmente qualsiasi cosa, lingusitico e non-linguistico allo stesso titolo: discorsi, instituzioni, . . . Il dispositivo in se stesso è la rete che si stabilisce tra questi elementi" (*Che cose un dispositivo?*, 7).

16. See also Deleuze's short essay "What Is an Apparatus?" in Armstrong, *Michel Foucault, Philosopher*.

17. Agamben's theory of economic theology is elaborated in Agamben, *Il regno e la gloria*.

18. Roland Barthes's essay "From Work to Text" was first published as "De l'ceuvre au texte'" in *Revue d'esthitique 3* (1971). It appears in *Image/Music/Text*, trans. Stephen Heath (London: Fontana Press, 1977).

19. Budick and Iser, *Languages of the Unsayable*, xi–xii.

20. Foucault, "The Discourse on Language," published as an appendix in *The Archaeology of Knowledge.*

21. Consider, for example, the present function of the media and its ability to "manufacture consensus."

22. Consider, for example, Edward Said's Foucauldian critique of the discipline of *Orientalism.*

23. Brown, "In the 'Folds of Our Own Discourse': The Pleasures and Freedoms of Silence."

24. Agamben rethinks Jean-Luc Nancy's term from the inoperative community in several places. In *The Open* he discusses the term "desouvrement" in its original coinage by Bataille. Agamben's elaboration of the concept refers the term back to Benjamin, Kojeve, Blanchot, and a pair of paintings by Titian. In *The Time That Remains*, the term "inoperativity" appears in relation to Paul's letter to the Romans as messianic time. See also *The State of Exception, Homo Sacer, Il regno e la gloria,* and *Nudita.*

25. Arendt, *Origins of Totalitarianism.*

26. Jakobson, *Russian and Slavic Grammar: Studies 1931–1981,* 151–60.

27. In the recently discovered Orangery manuscripts published as *Writings in General Linguistics,* Saussure says that where morphological analysis is concerned, "the appearance of the zero sign is indistinct from a positive sign" (45).

28. Poyatos, *New Perspectives in Nonverbal Communication.*

29. Dauenhauer, *Silence.*

2. THE SECRET OF LITERARY SILENCE

1. See George Steiner's collection of essays, first published in 1958, *Language and Silence: Essays on Language, Literature, and the Inhuman,* especially "Silence of the Poet" (36–54).

2. Besides Steiner, see, for instance, Susan Sontag, "The Aesthetics of Silence"; Ihab Hassan, *The Literature of Silence: Henry Miller and Samuel Beckett;* Ernestine Schlant, *The Language of Silence: West German Literature and the Holocaust;* Elisabeth Loevlie, *Literary Silences in Pascal, Rousseau, and Beckett;* Karmen MacKendrick, *Immemorial Silence.*

3. First published in 1966 in the series *Théorie,* edited by Louis Althusser as *Pour une théorie de la production littéraire* and translated into English as *A Theory of Literary Production* by Geoffrey Wall, Macherey continues to be more influential in the Anglophone world as a literary theorist than as a philosopher who has written extensively on Hegel and Spinoza.

4. See, for instance, the essays in *Silence: The Currency of Power*, edited by Maria-Luisa Achino-Loeb.

5. "La Littérature au secret: une filiation impossible," in *Donner la mort*, translated by David Wills as *The Gift of Death, Second Edition and Literature in Secret*.

3. Law, "Life/Living," Language

1. The version that appears in *The Conjure Woman, and Other Conjure Tales* is based on two drafts of the story in the Charles Waddell Chesnutt Papers at Fisk University Library. The earlier and more complete of these drafts is a twenty-one-page typescript that is missing its second page; the other typescript version, consisting of eight pages, represents a later stage of revision but is fragmentary and incomplete. The Duke edition is a composite text based on these typescripts, following the later typescript wherever it exists and using the first typescript for the remainder of the story. "The Dumb Witness" was revised and incorporated with an altered ending into chapters 19 and 35 of Chesnutt's novel *The Colonel's Dream* (1905).

2. See, for instance, George M. Stroud, *A Sketch of the Laws Relating to Slavery in the Several States of the United States of America* (1856) (New York: Negro Universities Press, 1968).

3. On the hidden play of words between *subditus* (subjection to authority) and *subjectum* (substratum) in the notion of the modern subject, see Etienne Balibar, "Subjection and Subjectivation," in *Supposing the Subject*, ed. Joan Copjec (New York: Verso, 1994), 1–15. Balibar writes, "Why is it that the very *name* which allows modern philosophy to think and designate the *originary freedom* of the human being—the name of 'subject'—is precisely the name which *historically* meant suppression of freedom, or at least an intrinsic limitation of freedom, i.e. *subjection*? We can say it in other terms: if freedom means freedom *of the subject*, or subjects, is it because there is, in 'subjectivity', an originary source of spontaneity and autonomy, something irreducible to objective constraints and determinations? Or is it not rather because 'freedom' can only be the result and counterpart of liberation, emancipation, *becoming free*: a trajectory inscribed in the very texture of the individual, with all its contradictions, which starts with subjection and always maintains an inner or outer relation with it?" (8–9). Balibar takes up these themes also in "The Subject" in *(U)mbra: A Journal of the Unconscious*; "Ignorance of the Law," 2003, 9–23; see also his *Politics and the Other Scene* and *Masses, Classes, Ideas: Studies on Politics Before and After Marx*, especially chapters 2 and 9.

4. See the chapters "Force of Law" (32–40) and "Gigantomachy Concerning a Void" (52–64) in *State of Exception*.

5. Agamben, *The Time That Remains*, 32.

6. I have omitted the corresponding original page reference as the text is bilingual and the original is on the facing page.

7. Derrida, *Foi et Savoir* (Paris: Éditions Seuil, 1996), translated in 1998 as "Faith and Knowledge: The Two Sources of 'Religion' at the Limits of Reason Alone" in *Acts of Religion*, 40–101.

8. Page references are to original paragraph numbers. Perhaps an early indication of this "disagreement" is found in Derrida's criticism of Levi-Strauss in *Of Grammatology*. Discussing the latter's condemnation of writing as associated with power and corruption, Derrida writes, "In this text, Levi-Strauss does not distinguish between hierarchization and domination, between political authority and exploitation. The tone that pervades these reflections is of an anarchism that deliberately confounds law and oppression. The idea of law and positive right, although it is difficult to think them in their formality—where it is so general that ignorance of the law is no defense—before the possibility of writing, is determined by Levi-Strauss as constraint and enslavement. Political power can only be the custodian of an unjust power. A classical and coherent thesis, but here advanced as self-evident, without opening the least bit of critical dialogue with the holders of the other thesis, according to which the generality of the law is on the contrary the condition of liberty in the city" (132; 191).

9. Philology aside, the distinction between *bios* and *zōē* in relation to Artistotle's *Nicomachean Ethics* is one that Heidegger makes in *Basic Conceps of Aristotelian Philosophy*, 52 (paragraphs 72–75). Arendt repeats this point in *The Human Condition*, 24.

10. Ultimately, the true point of difference between the deconstructive and biopolitical perspectives perhaps has everything to do with the ways each thinker "inherits" Nietzsche. Foucault and Agamben are perhaps much more indebted to Heidegger's reading of Nietzsche's thought of the will to power than Derrida, but I cannot engage this underlying philosophical discussion here. See *Of Grammatology*, 19, and also *Spurs*.

11. The original 1993 edition does not contain the notes added to the 1994 English translation.

12. See also his *Of Hospitality*.

4. BETWEEN DERRIDA AND AGAMBEN

1. Parenthetical page numbers following quotations are for the French text, *La voix et le phénomène*, followed by those for Allison's English translation. In places where reference is made to a turn in the argument without quotation, the parenthetical page numbers refer to the English translation only.

2. Derrida writes, "For Husserl, historical progress always has as its essential form the constitution of idealities whose repetition, and this tradition, would be assured *ad infinitum*, where repetition and tradition are the transmission and reactivation of origins. And this determination of being as ideality is properly a *valuation*, an ethico-theoretical act that revives the decision that founded philosophy in its Platonic form. Husserl occasionally admits this; what he always opposed was conventional Platonism. When he affirms the nonexistence or nonreality of ideality, it is always to acknowledge that ideality *is* a way of being that is irreducible to sensible existence or empirical reality and their fictional counterparts. In determining the *ontōs on* as *eidos*, Plato himself was 'affirming the same thing'" (59; 52–53).

3. As I understand it, Derrida's critique of Husserl here itself interestingly repeats Heidegger's critique of Kant in *Kant and the Problem of Metaphysics*. In his influential analysis of the first critique, Heidegger discusses Kant's proposition that time and the "I think" are the same. Heidegger writes, "It is at once obvious, therefore, that time as pure self-affection is not found 'in the mind' 'beside' pure apperception. On the contrary, as the basis of the possibility of selfhood, time is already included in pure apperception and first enables the mind to be what it is . . . time and the 'I think' are no longer opposed to one another as unlike and incompatible; they are the same" (197). I owe this reference to Dennis Schmidt, who included this work in his reading list for the *Collegium Phaenomenologicum* 2007.

4. For a useful discussion of Heidegger's use of the term ontotheology and its subsequent impact, see Iain Thompson, "Ontotheology? Understanding Heidegger's *Destruktion* of Metaphysics."

5. In *Of Grammatology*, Derrida, discussing the proximity of Hjemslev's linguistic theory to grammatology, with the caveat that the latter could not admit the experience of arche-writing within his system, writes, "As for the concept of experience, it is most unwieldy here. Like all the notions I am using here, it belongs to the history of metaphysics and we can only use it under erasure [*sous rature*]. 'Experience' has always designated the relationship with a presence, whether that relationship had the form of consciousness or not . . .

That is not so at all in the case of experience as arche-writing. The parenthesizing of regions of experience or of the totality of natural experience must discover a field of transcendental experience. This experience is only accessible insofar as . . . one asks the question of the transcendental origin of the system itself, as a system of the objects of a science . . . It is because I believe that there is a short-of and a beyond of transcendental criticism. To see to it that the beyond does not return to the within is to recognize in the contortion the necessity of a pathway [*parcours*]. The pathway must leave a track in the text. Without that track, abandoned to the simple content of its conclusions, the ultra-transcendental text will so closely resemble the precritical text as to be indistinguishable for it. We must now form and meditate upon the law of this resemblance" (61; 89–90).

6. The concept of potentiality is taken up in modest detail in chapter 7, "HumAnimal Acts: Potentiality or Movement as Rest."

5. THE WILD CHILD

1. Originally published in *Cahiers de chemin* 29 (January 15 1977): 19–29. English translation in Foucault, *Power: The Essential Works of Foucault*, 157–75.

2. See especially his *Monolingualism of the Other.*

3. See *Speech and Phenomena* and *Of Grammatology*, 140.

4. See, however, Michael Nass's eulogy to Derrida, *"Alors, qui êtes-vous?: Jacques Derrida and the Question of Hospitality,"* in *SubStance* 106, 34, no.1 (2005): 6–17.

5. Richard Kearney writes, "In the *Timaeus* 48e-53b, Plato enquires into the primordial origin from which all things come. In what must be one of the most intriguing passages in his entire oeuvre, Plato struggles to identify the fundamental condition of possibility of the being a world. He calls this *khōra*, a virtually untranslatable term referring to a kind of placeless place from which everything that is derives. Deploying a number of allusive metaphors—nurse, mother, a perfume base, space, winnowing sieve, receptacle—Plato acknowledges *khōra* challenges our normal categories of rational understanding" (Kearney, *Strangers, Gods, and Monsters*, 193).

6. THE WILD CHILD AND SCIENTIFIC NAMES

1. According to Stephen Jay Gould, the reason for the Linnaean system's continued success is its uncanny consistency with "evolutionary topology." Gould offers a useful explanation regarding Linnaeus's "binomial

nomenclature": "the formal name of each species includes two components: the generic designation, given first with an initial uppercase letter (*Homo* for us, *Canis* for dogs, etc.); and the so-called 'trivial' name, presented last and in fully lowercase letters (*sapiens* to designate us within the genus *Homo*, and *familiaris* to distinguish dogs from other species within the genus *Canis*—for example the wolf, *Canis lupus*) . . . We regard the 1758 version of *Systema Naturae* as the founding document of modern animal taxonomy because, in this edition and for the first time, Linnaeus used the binomial system in complete consistency and without exception" (Gould, *I Have Landed*, 292–93).

2. See Banton, *Racial Theories*.

3. The characteristics Linnaeus attributed to the races in the 1758 edition are as follows: "Americanus: reddish, choleric, and erect; hair black, straight, thick; wide nostrils, scanty beard; obstinate, merry, free; paints himself with fine red lines; regulated by customs. Asiaticus: sallow, melancholy, stiff; hair black; dark eyes; severe, haughty, avaricious; covered with loose garments; ruled by opinions. Africanus: black, phlegmatic, relaxed; hair black, frizzled; skin silky; nose flat; lips tumid; women without shame, they lactate profusely; crafty, indolent, negligent; anoints himself with grease; governed by caprice. Europeaeus: white, sanguine, muscular; hair long, flowing; eyes blue; gentle, acute, inventive; covers himself with close vestments; governed by laws."

4. See, for instance, Patricia Fara, *Sex, Botany, and Empire: The Story of Carl Linnaeus and Joseph Banks* (New York: Columbia University Press, 2003), 10; Philip R. Sloan, "The Buffon-Linnaeus Controversy," *Isis* 67, no. 238 (spring 1976): 356–75; Douthwaite, *The Wild Girl, Natural Man, and the Monster*, 17; Richard Nash, *Wild Enlightenment: The Borders of Human Identity in the Eighteenth Century* (Charlottesville: University of Virginia Press, 2003), 16.

5. See Gunnar Broberg, "Linnaeus' Classification of Man," in *Linnaeus: The Man and His Work*, ed. Tore Frangsmyr, Sten Lindroth, Gunnar Eriksson, and Gunnar Broberg (University of California Press, 1983), 156–94.

6. It is interesting in this context to note that Gould mentions that later physicists characterized Linnaean taxonomy and paleontology as "philately"—mere stamp-collecting with little relevance to true science. See his *We Have Landed*, 288–89.

7. However, in *The Open: Between Man and Animal*, Giorgio Agamben writes that Linnaeus's decision to "classify man among the *Anthropomorpha*, the 'man-like' animals" indicates clearly that "*Homo* is constitutively nonhuman" (30) and that this central nonhumanity of man was already adumbrated three centuries earlier in the preeminent work of Renaissance humanism, Pico's *Oration on the Diginity of Man*.

8. I was led to both the Digby and the Connor sources by Michael Newton, *Savage Girls and Wild Boys*, 18–23. Digby's *Two Treatises* is available online at http://gateway.proquest.com/openurl?ctx_ver=Z39.88–2003 &res_id=xri:eebo&rft_id=xri:eebo:image:59612. Connor's *History of Poland* (1698) is available online at http://gateway.proquest.com/openurl?ctx_ver =Z39.88–2003&res_id=xri:eebo&rft_id=xri:eebo:image:52719:201.

9. For accounts of Peter, see Newton, *Savage Girls and Wild Boys*, 24–52. See also *"An enquiry how the wild youth, lately taken in the woods near Hanover, (and now brought over to England) could be there left, and by what creature he could be suckled, nursed, and brought up . . ."* (London: H. Parker, 1726) and Daniel Defoe, "Mere Nature Delineated," ed. Andrew Wear (1726) in Defoe, *Writings on Travel, Discovery, and History*, eds. W. R. Owens and P. N. Furbank (London: Pickering and Chatto, 2001–2).

10. Despite her relatively fluent French, Lord Monboddo, who was famed for his view that Orang Outang's are a variety of human, classified her as the closest relation to Homo sapiens. Monboddo, in fact, classified Peter the Wild Boy below an Orang Outang and Marie Angelique as above the latter and next to the fully human. Of course, he never bothered with the inconsistent logic of classifying the singular case of Peter or Marie Angelique with a species of ape, let alone the fact that he also aimed to discover her racial or national origins.

7. HumAnimal Acts

1. Perhaps it is folklore that best grasps the body as movement when it speaks of "shape-shifting"—that is, the body's ability to change shape, to undefine its form, and thereby render all forms temporal. If "metamorphosis" is traditionally understood as the shedding of an old form for a new one, shape-shifting throws all shapes and forms into question. The patron god here may well be Proteus, who changes shape to avoid foretelling the future, thereby rendering knowledge of the truth uncapturable. For an interesting discussion of shape-shifting in Ovid's *Metamorphosis*, see Elaine Fantham, *"Sunt quibus in plures ius est transire figuras*: Ovid's Self-Transformers in the 'Metamorphoses,'"* in *The Classical World* 87, no. 2 (November–December 1993): 21–36. Fantham discusses the few instances of voluntary shape-shifting in Ovid, selecting among them the figures of Thetis, Mestra, and Vertumunus. As is well known, Ovid does not retell the story of Proteus, though he is of course invoked periodically in his text.

2. *Irish Cinema Times*, "Interview: The Man on Wire," http://www.movies .ie/interviews/Interview__The_Man_On_The_Wire.

3. There are significant omissions and discrepancies (also some errors in Aristotle citations) between the original and the English translation. The latter attributes the original to an unpublished lecture delivered in Lisbon in 1986, whereas the Italian edition dates a lecture also at Lisbon in 1987. Translations are mine when followed by the original in the text.

4. The following ambiguous paragraph placed in parentheses appears in the English translation but does not correspond to a passage in the original: "(It is often said that philosophers are concerned with *essence*, that, confronted with a thing, they ask 'What is it?' But this is not exact. Philosophers are above all concerned with *existence*, with the *mode* [or rather, the *modes*] of existence. If they consider essence, it is to exhaust it in existence, to make it exist" (179).

5. "Aristotele risponde, nella Metafisica, alla tesi dei Megarici, che affermavano . . . che la Potenza esiste solo nell'atto (energē monon dynasthai, hotan de mē energē ou dynasthai, 1046b 29–30). Se ciò fosse vero, obietta Aristotele, noi non potremmo considerara architetto l'architetto anche quando non costruisce, né chiamare medico il medico nel momento in cui non sta esercitando la sua arte. In questione è, cioè, *il modo di essere* della Potenza, che *esiste* nella forma della *hexis*, della signoria su una privazione. Vi è una forma, una presenza di ciò che non è in atto, e questa presenza privative è la Potenza. Come Aristotele afferma senza riserve in un passo straordinario della *Fisica*: 'La *sterēsis*, la privazione, è come una forma [*eidos ti*, una specie di viso: *eidos* da *eidenai*, 'vedere']' (193b 19–20)" (277).

6. *"Il vivente, che esiste nel modo della Potenza, può la propria impotenza, e solo in questo modo possiede la propria Potenza. Egli può essere e fare, perché si tiene in relazione col proprio non-essere e non-fare"* (281).

7. "'Ciò che è potente [*to dynaton*] può [*endechetai*] non essere in atto [*mē energein*]. Ciò che è potente di essere può tanto essere che non essere. Lo stesso è, infatti, potente di essere e di non essere [*to auto ara dynaton kai einai kai mē einai*]' Dechomai significa 'accolgo, ricevo, ammetto.' Potente è ciò che accoglie e lascia avvenire il non essere e questa accoglienza del non essere definisce la Potenza come passività e passion fondamentale." Heller-Roazen's translation is as follows: "what is potential is capable (*endekhetai*), Aristotle says, both of being and of not being. *Dekhomai* means 'I welcome, receive, admit.' The potential welcomes non-Being, and this welcoming of non-Being *is* potentiality, fundamental passivity" (182).

8. *"Se una potenza di non essere appartiene originalmente a ogni Potenza, sarà veramente potente solo chi, al momento del passaggio all'atto, non annullerà semplicemente la propora potenza di non, né la lascerà indietro rispetto all'atto, ma la farà passare integralmente in esso come tale, potrà, cioè, non-non passare all'atto."*

Heller Roazen's translation is as follows: "*if a potentiality to not-be originally belongs to all potentiality, then there is truly potentiality only where the potentiality to not-be does not lag behind actuality but passes fully into it as such.* This does not mean that it disappears in actuality; on the contrary, it preserves itself as such in actuality. What is truly potential is thus what has exhausted all its impotentiality in bringing it wholly into the act as such" (183).

9. The translation adds the following sentence: "This is why freedom is freedom for both good and evil" (183).

10. See Agamben, *Il regno e la gloria*, for an elaboration of how will was made to supersede potentiality first and foremost by attributing the creation to God's will rather than to his power.

11. Agamben's references to Heidegger's lecture course on Aristotle's *Metaphysics Book Theta*, though missing in the translation, can be found in the original Italian version of his essay in "La Potenza del Pensiero," translated as "On Potentiality" (284). Note that the translation erroneously cites the title of Heidegger's translated course as *Aristotle's Metaphysics Book Omega 1–3*.

12. In a brief response to Antonio Negri in June 2005, Agamben spoke of "movement" as a term that has been left undefined for too long and therefore constitutes one of the great "unthought" and overused concepts of our time requiring critical attention. Given the context of "social movements," the formation of which is understood as a politically decisive instance in Negri's work, Agamben then goes on to outline the spare intellectual history of the concept by mentioning Lorenz Von Stern, Hannah Arendt, Freud, and finally Carl Schmitt. It is Schmitt's attempts to define the concept that eventually propel his argument. Agamben suggests that for Schmitt, a movement constituted the politicized element of 'the people' who were as such considered by him to be unpolitical. Agamben then goes on to extrapolate that the condition of possibility of "movement" is undemocratic in the sense that it depoliticizes and introduces a caesura within "the people," thereby disclosing the biopolitical force of the movement as such. In other words, the nonpolitical and excluded elements from the movement are necessarily reduced to "populations." How, then, he asks, must we rethink this concept if we are to continue to use it? Agamben says it is a long-term research project but goes on to offer some indications. Characteristically, he turns to Aristotle and reminds us of the centrality of the concept of *kinēsis* in its relation to potentiality and actuality. He offers two bullet points: (1) that for Aristotle, *kinesis* is always imperfect act (the thought of potentiality as potentiality), and (2) that it sustains a relation to privation and is therefore unfinished. In concluding, Agamben says, "The movement is always constitutively the relation with its lack, its absence of end, or *ergon*, or *telos* and *opera*. What I always disagree with Toni

[Antonio Negri] about is this emphasis placed on productivity. Here we must reclaim the absence of *opera* as central. This expresses the impossibility of a *telos* and *ergon* for politics. Movement is the indefiniteness and imperfection of every politics. It always leaves a residue . . . The movement is that which if it is, is as if it wasn't, it lacks itself (*manca a se stesso*), and if it isn't, is as if it was, it exceeds itself. It is the threshold of indeterminacy between an excess and a deficiency which marks the limit of every politics in its constitutive imperfection."

13. See, in particular, Heidegger, *Introduction to Metaphysics*, chapter 4, "The Limitation of Being," especially 193–96.

14. "Adynamia, 'impotenza,' non significa qui assenza di ogni Potenza, ma Potenza di non (passare all'atto), dýnamis mē energein. La tesi definisce, cioè, l'ambivalenza specifica di ogni potenza umana, che, nella sua struttura originaria, si mantiene in rapporto con la propria privazione, è sempre— e rispetto alla stessa cosa—potenza di essere e di non essere, di fare e di non fare. È questa relazione che constituisce, per Aristotele, l'essenza della potenza. Il vivente, che esiste nel modo della potenza, può la propria impotenza, e solo in questo modo possiede la propria potenza. Egli può essere e fare, perché si tiene in relazione col proprio non-essere e non-fare. Nella potenza, la sensazione è constitutivamente anestesia, il pensiero non-pensiero, l'opera inoperosità" (281). Daniel Heller-Roazen's translation reads as follows: "'Impotentiality, [*adynamia*],' we read in the first, 'is a privation contrary to potentiality. Thus all potentiality is impotentiality of the same and with respect to the same' (*tou auto kai kata to auto pasa dynamis adynamia*) (1046 e 25–32) [sic.] What does this sentence mean? It means that in its originary structure, dynamis, potentiality, maintains itself in relation to its own privation, its own *stēresis*, its own nonbeing. This relation constitutes the essence of potentiality. To be potential means to be one's own lack, *to be in relation to one's own incapacity*. Beings that exist in the mode of potentiality *are capable of their own impotentiality*, and only in this way do they become potential. They *can be* because they are in relation to their own nonbeing. In potentiality, sensation is in relation to anesthesia, knowledge to ignorance, vision to darkness" (181–82).

15. In his book on Paul's letter to the Romans, Agamben refers to the paradox of "operational time" as the noncoincidence of thought and the self-presence of consciousness and therefore the noncoincidence of the thought of time and the representation of time. He suggests that the noncoincidence takes on the "form of time" that is nevertheless not added from the outside to chronological time. "Rather, it is something like a time within time—not ulterior but interior—which only measures my disconnection with regard to it, my being

out of synch and in noncoincidence with regard to my representation of time, but precisely because of this, allows for the possibility of my achieving and taking hold of it" (67).

16. Consider also "national" forms such as capoiera, which was once banned in Brazil. In many parts of the world, "acrobatic" movement is practiced by nomadic groups such as gypsies and tribal peoples, who are traditionally viewed as tricksters, con-artists, and have little to no protection from the law. Neither do they possess a fixed venue, usually performing in makeshift tents or out in the commons.

17. Nadia Comaneci, the legendary gymnast, writes eloquently about the transformation of her surplus energy as a child into the discipline of gymnastics under the tutelage of the now famous coach Bela Karolyi. See her memoir, *Letters to a Young Gymnast*.

18. See, for instance, Foucault, *Society Must Be Defended* and Foucault, *Discipline and Punish*.

19. "O Melibaeus: A God has granted us this ideleness!" From Virgil, *Bucolics*.

20. However, contemporary Indian philosopher Daya Krishna has disputed this view, citing the diversity and heterogeneity of Indian thought. See his *Indian Philosophy: A Counterperspective* (Delhi: Oxford Univeresity Press, 1991), cited in Thomas MacEvilley, *The Shape of Ancient Thought: Comparative Studies in Greek and Indian Philosophies*, 177–78.

21. Foucault, *The Hermeneutics of the Subject: Lectures at the Collège de France 1981–82*.

22. Hadot's work made a strong impact on Foucault, and the basis of many of the propositions he made in his 1982 lectures at the Collège de France (*Hermeneutics of the Subject*) can, despite some differences, be traced back to Hadot, *Exercices Spirituels et Philosophie Antique*, parts of which have been translated in Hadot, *Philosophy as a Way of Life*.

23. See especially 322 and 482–85.

24. Given that Foucault's genealogy of Christian monasticism is a contradiction to the theory of potentiality and its validation of will, I shall not be referring anymore to it.

25. "Consequently, you see that what we should think about is, of course, an athletic kind of concentration . . . We are much closer here to the famous archery exercise, which, as you know, is so important for the Japanese for example" (222). The footnote to this passage reads "Foucault, we should recall, was a great reader of E. Herrigel: see, by this author, *Le Zen dans l'art chevaleresque du tir à l'arc* (Paris: Dervy, 1986) [English translation by R. F. C. Hull, *Zen in the Art of Archery* (London: Routledge and Kegan Paul, 1953)]" (227).

26. Eliade, *Yoga: Immortality and Freedom*, 4.

27. Patañjali's identity is in dispute. Some scholars identify him with the second-century BCE grammarian and author of the *Mahā Bhāsya*, while others believe he lived in the second century CE and was deeply influenced by prevailing Buddhist thought. The type of *yoga* that Patañjali elaborates is *Rajayoga*. The author describes it as a practice of "citta vritti nirodah" (1:2) or transformation of consciousness. Thus, in sutra 2:29 he says that as a practice, *rajayoga* has eight branches: *yama* or the five ethical disciplines, *niyama* or the five personal disciplines, *asana* or mindful movement and rest (*asana* usually translated as pose or posture), *pranayama* or the numerous disciplines of the breath, *pratyahara* or withdrawal of the sense, *dharana* or concentration of the mind, *dhayana* or meditation where the flux of the mind which is logos is pacified, and finally *samadhi* or experience of ecstasis. Given that each of these terms has several subgroupings that require a lifetime to master, yoga philosophy is necessarily a spiritual discipline that is also a knowledge system that one must study only with the help of a teacher.

28. Sects such as Aghoris and Kapalikas, whose yoga practice is deeply Tantric in nature, are necessarily transgressors of the law—religious laws as well as juridical ones. Transgression, of course, is not the same as profanation, and thus these sects are given a place by the law as legitimate outlaws who have ostensibly renounced the world. See Eliade, *Yoga: Immortality and Freedom*, chapter 8, especially 296–301.

29. See Robert Isherwood, "Entertainment in the Parisian Fairs in the Eighteenth Century," *Journal of Modern History* 53 (March 1981): 24–47.

30. See Bhaktin, *Rabelais and His World*.

Bibliography

Achino-Loeb, Maria-Luisa, ed. *Silence: The Currency of Power.* New York: Berghahn Books, 2006.

Agamben, Giorgio. *The Coming Community.* Translated by Michael Hardt. Minneapolis: University of Minnesota Press, 1993. Original: *La comunità che viene.* Torino: G. Einaudi, 1990.

———. *Homo Sacer: Sovereign Power and Bare Life.* Translated by Daniel Heller-Roazen. Stanford, Calif.: Stanford University Press, 1998. Original: *Homo sacer. Il potere sovrano e la nuda vita.* Turin: G. Einaudi, 1995.

———. "'I Am Sure That You Are More Pessimistic Than I Am.'" *Rethinking Marxism* 16 (2004): 115–24.

———. *Idea of Prose.* Translated by Sam Whitsitt and Michael Sullivan. Albany: State University of New York Press, 1995. Original: *Idea della prosa.* Milano: Feltrinelli, 1985.

———. *Infancy and History: On the Destruction of Experience.* Translated by Liz Heron. London: Verso, 2007. Original: *Infanzia e storia: Distruzione dell'esperienza e origine della storia.* Torino: Einaudi, 1979.

———. *Language and Death: The Place of Negativity.* Translated by Karen Pinkus and Michael Hardt. Minneapolis: University of Minnesota Press, 1991. Original: *Il linguaggio e la morte. Un seminario sul luogo della negatività.* Torino: Einaudi, 1982.

———. *The Man Without Content.* Translated by Georgia Albert. Stanford, Calif.: Stanford University Press, 1999. Original: *L'uomo senza contenuto.* Milano: Rizzoli, 1970.

———. *Means without End: Notes on Politics.* Translated by Vincenzo Binetti and Cesare Casarino. Minneapolis: University of Minnesota Press, 2000. Original: *Mezzi senza fine. Note sulla politica.* Turin: Bollati Borlinghieri, 1996.

———. *Nudità.* Rome: Nottetempo, 2009.

———. *The Open: Man and Animal.* Translated by Kevin Attell. Stanford, Calif.: Stanford University Press, 2004. Original: *L'aperto. L'uomo e l'animale.* Turin: Bollati Boringhieri, 2002.

———. *Potentialities: Collected Essays in Philosophy.* Translated by Daniel Heller-Roazen. Stanford, Calif.: Stanford University Press, 1999.

Bibliography

————. *La potenza del pensiero. Saggi e conferenze*. Vicenza: Neri Pozza, 2005.

————. *Profanations*. Translated by Jeff Fort. New York: Zone Books, 2007. Original: *Profanazioni*. Rome: Nottetempo, 2005.

————. *Il regno e la gloria. Per una genealogia teologica dell'economia e del governo*, Vicenza: Neri Pozza, 2007.

————. *Remnants of Auschwitz: The Witness and the Archive*. Translated by Daneil Heller-Roazen. New York: Zone Books, 2000. Original: *Quel che resta di Auschwitz. L'archivio e il testimone*. Turin: Bollati Bolligheri, 1998.

————. *The Sacrament of Language: An Archaeology of the Oath*. Translated by Adam Kotsko. Stanford, Calif.: Stanford University Press, 2010. Original: *Il sacramento del linguaggio. Archeologia del giuramento (Homo sacer II, 3)*. Rome: Laterza, 2008.

————. *The Signature of All Things: On Method*. Translated by Luca D'Isanto and Kevin Attell. New York: Zone Books. Original: *Signatura rerum. Sul metodo*. Turin: Bollati Boringhieri, 2008.

————. *State of Exception*. Translated by Kevin Attell. Chicago: University of Chicago Press, 2005. Original: *Lo stato di eccezione*. Turin: Bollati Boringhieri, 2003.

————. *The Time That Remains: A Commentary on the Letter to the Romans*. Translated by Patricia Dailey. Stanford, Calif.: Stanford University Press, 2005. Original: *Il tempo che resta. Un commento alla lettera ai Romani*. Turin: Bollati Boringhieri, 2000.

————. "What Is an Apparatus?" In Agamben, *What Is An Apparatus? And Other Essays*, 1–24. Original: *Che cos'e un dispositivo?* Rome: Nottetempo, 2006.

————. *What Is An Apparatus? And Other Essays*. Translated by David Kishik and Stefan Pedatella. Stanford, Calif.: Stanford University Press, 2009.

————. "What Is the Contemporary?" In Agamben, *What Is An Apparatus? And Other Essays*, 26–39. Original: *Che cos'e il contemporaneo?* Rome: Nottetempo, 2008.

————. "The Work of Man." Translated by Kevin Attell. In *Giorgio Agamben: Sovereignty and Life*, edited byMatthew Calarco and Steven DeCaroli, 1–10. Stanford, Calif.: Stanford University Press, 2007.

Arendt, Hannah. *The Human Condition*. Chicago, Ill.: University of Chicago Press, 1998.

————. *The Origins of Totalitarianism*. New York: Harcourt, Brace & World, 1966.

Armstrong, Timothy J. *Michel Foucault, Philosopher: Essays Translated From the French and German*. New York: Routledge, 1992.

Bakhtin, Mikhail. *Rabelais and His World*. Translated by Helene Iswolsky. Bloomington: Indiana University Press, 2009.

Balibar, Etienne. *Masses, Classes, Ideas: Studies on Politics and Philosophy Before and After Marx.* New York: Routledge, 1994.

———. *Politics and the Other Scene.* London and New York: Verso, 2002.

Banton, Michael. *Racial Theories.* Cambridge and New York: Cambridge University Press, 1998.

Benjamin, Walter. "The Critique of Violence." In *Reflections: Essays, Aphorisms, Autobiographical Writings,* translated by Edmund Jephcott, 277–300. New York: Schocken Books, 1978.

———. "Theologico-Political Fragment." In *Reflections: Essays, Aphorisms, Autobiographical Writings,* translated by Edmund Jephcott, 312–13. New York: Schocken Books, 1978.

———. "Theses on the Philosophy of History." In *Illuminations: Essays and Reflections,* translated by Harry Zohn, 253–64. New York: Schocken Books, 1968.

Bennington, Geoffrey, and Jacques Derrida. *Jacques Derrida.* Chicago: University of Chicago Press, 1993.

Brogan, Walter A. *Heidegger and Aristotle: The Twofoldness of Being.* Albany: State University of New York Press, 2006.

Brown, Wendy. "In the 'Folds of Our Own Discourse': The Pleasures and Freedoms of Silence." *University of Chicago Law School Roundtable* 3 (1996): 185–97.

Budick, Sanford, and Wolfgang Iser. *Languages of the Unsayable: The Play of Negativity in Literature and Literary Theory.* New York: Columbia University Press, 1989.

Butler, Judith. *Bodies That Matter: On the Discursive Limits of "Sex."* New York: Routledge, 1993.

Calarco, Matthew. *Zoographies: The Question of the Animal from Heidegger to Derrida.* New York: Columbia University Press, 2008.

Calarco, Matthew, and Peter Atterton. *Animal Philosophy: Essential Readings in Continental Thought.* London and New York: Continuum, 2004.

Cavell, Stanley. *The Claim of Reason: Wittgenstein, Skepticism, Morality, and Tragedy.* New York: Oxford University Press, 1999.

Cavell, Stanley, Cora Diamond, John Mcdowell, Ian Hacking, and Cary Wolfe. *Philosophy and Animal Life.* New York and Chichester: Columbia University Press, 2009.

Chesnutt, Charles W. *The Conjure Woman, and Other Conjure Tales.* Edited by Richard H. Brodhead. Durham, N.C.: Duke University Press, 1993.

Clark, Stephen R. L. *Animals and Their Moral Standing.* London and New York: Routledge, 1997.

Coetzee, John Maxwell. *Foe.* London: Penguin Books, 1987.

Bibliography

Comăneci, Nadia. *Letters to a Young Gymnast.* New York: Basic Books, 2004.

Dauenhauer, Bernard P. *Silence, the Phenomenon and Its Ontological Significance.* Bloomington: Indiana University Press, 1980.

Derrida, Jacques. *Acts of Literature.* Edited by Derek Attridge. New York: Routledge, 1992.

———. *Acts of Religion.* Edited by Gil Anidjar. New York: Routledge, 2002.

———. *Adieu to Emmanuel Levinas.* Translated by Pascale-Anne Brault and Michael Naas. Stanford, Calif.: Stanford University Press, 1999.

———. *Aporias: Dying—Awaiting (One Another At) the "Limits of Truth."* Translated by Thomas Dutoit, Stanford, Calif.: Stanford University Press, 1993. Original: *Apories: Mourir—s'attendre aux "limites de la vérité."* Paris: Galilée, 1996.

———. *The Beast and the Sovereign.* Translated by Geoffrey Bennington. Chicago: The University of Chicago Press, 2009. Original: *Séminaire la bête et le souverain, Volume II, 2002–2003.* Paris: Galilée, 2009.

———. *The Ear of the Other: Otobiography, Transference, Translation: Texts and Discussions with Jacques Derrida.* Translated by Peggy Kamuf. New York: Schocken Books, 1985.

———. "Eating Well: Or the Calculation of the Subject." In *Who Comes After the Subject?* Translated by Peter Connor and Avital Ronnell. Edited by Eduardo Cadava, Peter Connor, and Jean-Luc Nancy, 96–119. New York: Routledge, 1991.

———. *Edmund Husserl's Origin of Geometry, An Introduction.* Lincoln: University of Nebraska Press, 1989.

———. "Force de Loi: Le 'Fondment Mystique de L'Autorité'"/"Force of Law: 'Mystical Foundation of Authority.'" Translated by Mary Quaintance. *Cardozo Law Review* 5–6 (July–August 1990): 920–1045.

———. *The Gift of Death, Second Edition and Literature in Secret.* Translated by David Wills. Chicago, Ill.: University of Chicago Press, 2008. Original: *Donner la mort.* Paris: Galilée, 1999.

———. *Khōra.* Paris: Galilée, 2006.

———. *Margins of Philosophy.* Translated by Alan Bass. Chicago: University of Chicago Press, 1982. Original: *Marges de la philosophie.* Paris: Éditions de Minuit, 1972.

———. *Of Grammatology.* Translated by Gayatri C. Spivak. Baltimore, Md.: Johns Hopkins University Press, 1998. Original: *De la grammatologie.* Paris: Éditions de Minuit, 1967.

———. *On the Name.* Translated by Thomas Dutoit. Stanford, Calif.: Stanford University Press, 1995.

———. *The Problem of Genesis in Husserl's Philosophy.* Translated by Marian Hobson. Chicago: University of Chicago Press, 2003.

———. *Psyche: Inventions of the Other.* Edited by Peggy Kamuf and Elizabeth Rottenberg. 2 vols. Stanford, Calif.: Stanford University Press, 2007 and 2008.

———. *Rogues: Two Essays on Reason.* Translated by Pascale-Anne Brault and Michael Naas. Stanford, Calif.: Stanford University Press, 2005. Original: *Voyous: Deux essais sur la raison.* Paris: Galilée, 2003.

———. *Sovereignties in Question: The Poetics of Paul Celan.* Edited by Thomas Dutoit and Outi Pasanen. New York: Fordham University Press, 2005.

———. *Specters of Marx: The State of the Debt, the Work of Mourning, and the New International.* Translated by Peggy Kamuf. New York: Routledge, 1994. Original: *Spectres de Marx: L'état de la dette, le travail du deuil et la nouvelle internationale.* Paris: Éditions Galilée, 1993.

———. *Speech and Phenomena, and Other Essays on Husserl's Theory of Signs.* Translated by David B. Allison. Evanston, Ill.: Northwestern University Press, 1973. Original: *La voix et le phénomène: Introduction au problème du signe dans la phénoménologie de Husserl.* Paris: Presses Universitaires de France, 2009.

———. *Spurs: Nietzsche's Styles –Éperons.* Translated by Barbara Harlow. Chicago: University of Chicago Press, 1996.

———. *The Work of Mourning.* Translated by Pascale-Anne Brault and Michael Naas. Chicago: University of Chicago Press, 2001.

———. *Writing and Difference.* Translated by Alan Bass. Chicago: University of Chicago Press, 1978. Original: *L'écriture et la différence.* Paris: Seuil, 1967.

Derrida, Jacques, and Anne Dufourmantelle. *Of Hospitality.* Translated by Rachel Bowlby. Stanford, Calif.: Stanford University Press, 2000. Original: *De l'hospitalité.* Paris: Calmann-Lévy, 1997.

Derrida, Jacques, and Maurizio Ferraris. *A Taste for the Secret.* Edited by Giacomo Donis and David Webb. Translated by Giacomo Donis. Malden, Mass.: Polity, 2001.

Derrida, Jacques, and Marie-Louise Mallet. *The Animal That Therefore I Am.* Translated by David Wills. New York: Fordham University Press, 2008. Original: *L'animal que donc je suis.* Paris: Galilée, 2006.

Derrida, Jacques, and Elisabeth Roudinesco. *For What Tomorrow . . . A Dialogue.* Translated by Jeff Fort. Stanford, Calif.: Stanford University Press, 2004. Original: *De Quoi Demain . . .* Paris: Flammarion, 2003.

Derrida, Jacques, and Michel Wieviorka. *Foi et savoir: suivi de le siècle et le pardon.* Paris: Seuil, 2000.

Bibliography

Diamond, Cora. "The Difficulty of Reality and the Difficulty of Philosophy." In *Philosophy and Animal Life*, by Stanley Cavell, Cora Diamond, John Mcdowell, Ian Hacking, and Cary Wolfe, 43–89. New York: Columbia University Press, 2008.

Douthwaite, Julia. *The Wild Girl, Natural Man, and the Monster: Dangerous Experiments in the Age of Enlightenment.* Chicago: University of Chicago Press, 2002.

Eliade, Mircea, *Yoga: Immortality and Freedom*. Translated by Willard R. Trask. Princeton, N.J.: Princeton University Press, 1990.

Foucault, Michel. *The Archaeology of Knowledge and the Discourse on Language.* Translated by A. M. Sheridan Smith. New York: Pantheon Books, 1972.

———. *The Birth of Biopolitics: Lectures at the Collège de France, 1978–1979.* New York: Picador, 2010.

———. *The Birth of the Clinic: An Archaeology of Medical Perception.* Translated by A. M. Sheridan Smith. New York: Vintage Books, 1994.

———. *Discipline and Punish: The Birth of the Prison.* Translated by Alan Sheridan. New York: Vintage Books, 1995.

———. *The Hermeneutics of the Subject: Lectures at the Collège de France, 1981–1982.* Translated by Graham Burchell. New York: Palgrave-Macmillan, 2005.

———. *The History of Sexuality, Volume I: An Introduction.* Translated by Robert Hurley. New York: Random House, 1990.

———. *The Order of Things: An Archaeology of the Human Sciences.* New York: Vintage Books, 1994.

———. *Power: The Essential Works of Foucault, 1954–1984, Volume 3.* Edited by James D. Faubon. Translated by Robert Hurley and others. New York: New Press, 2000.

———. *Society Must Be Defended: Lectures at the Collège de France, 1975–1976.* Translated by David Macey. New York: Picador, 2003.

———. *Security, Territory, Population: Lectures at the Collège de France, 1977–1978.* Translated by Graham Burchell. New York: Picador, 2007.

Genovese, Eugene D. *Roll, Jordan, Roll: The World the Slaves Made.* New York: Vintage Books, 1976.

Gould, Stephen Jay. *I Have Landed: The End of a Beginning in Natural History.* New York: Harmony Books, 2002.

Hadot, Pierre. *Philosophy as a Way of Life: Spiritual Exercises from Socrates to Foucault.* Edited by Arnold Davidson. Translated by Michael Chase. Malden, Mass.: Blackwell, 1995.

Hartman, Saidiya V. *Scenes of Subjection: Terror, Slavery, and Self-Making in Nineteenth-Century America.* New York: Oxford University Press, 1997.

Hassan, Ihab Habib. *The Literature of Silence: Henry Miller and Samuel Beckett.* New York: Knopf, 1968.

Haverkamp, Anselm. "Notes on the 'Dialectical Image' (How Deconstructive is it?)." In "Commemorating Walter Benjamin," special issue, *Diacritics* 22, no. 3/4 (Autumn–Winter 1992): 69–80.

Heidegger, Martin. *Aristotle's Metaphysics:* Θ 1–3: On the Essence and Actuality of Force. Translated by Walter Brogan and Peter Warnek. Bloomington: Indiana University Press, 1995.

———. *Basic Concepts of Aristotelian Philosophy.* Translated by Robert D. Metcalfe and Mark B. Tanzer. Bloomington: Indiana University Press, 2009.

———. *Introduction to Metaphysics.* Translated by Ralph Manheim. New Haven: Yale University Press, 2000.

———. "On the Essence and Concept of Φύσις in Aristotle's *Physics* B, I (1939)." Translated by Thomas Sheehan. In *Pathmarks*, edited by William McNeill, 183–230. Cambridge and New York: Cambridge University Press, 1998.

———. *Ontology—The Hermeneutics of Facticity.* Translated by John Van Buren. Bloomington: Indiana University Press, 2008.

Herrigel, Eugen. *Zen in the Art of Archery.* New York: Vintage Books, 1999.

Itard, Jean Marc Gaspard. *The Wild Boy of Aveyron.* Translated by George and Muriel Humphrey. Appleton and Lange, 1962.

Jakobson, Roman. *Russian and Slavic Grammar: Studies, 1931–1981.* Edited by Linda R. Waugh and Morris Halle. New York: Mouton Publishers, 1984.

Kearney, Richard. *Strangers, Gods and Monsters: Interpreting Otherness.* New York: Routledge, 2002.

Kenneally, Christine. *The First Word: The Search for the Origins of Language.* New York: Penguin Books, 2008.

König, Jason. *Athletics and Literature in the Roman Empire.* Cambridge: Cambridge University Press, 2008.

Kurzon, Dennis. *Discourse of Silence.* Amsterdam and Philadelphia: J. Benjamins, 1998.

Lafargue, Paul. *The Right to Be Lazy.* Translated by Charles H. Kerr. Chicago: Revolutionary Classics, 1989.

Lawlor, Leonard. *This Is Not Sufficient: An Essay on Animality and Human Nature in Derrida.* New York: Columbia University Press, 2007.

Lévi-Strauss, Claude. *Tristes Tropiques.* New York: Penguin Books, 1992.

Loevlie, Elisabeth Marie. *Literary Silences in Pascal, Rousseau, and Beckett.* Oxford and New York: Clarendon Press, 2003.

Macherey, Pierre. *A Theory of Literary Production.* Translated by Geoffrey Wall. London: Routledge and Kegan Paul, 1978.

MacKendrick, Karmen. *Immemorial Silence*. Albany: State University of New York Press, 2001.

Marx, Karl. "Economic and Philosophical Manuscripts." Translated by Gregor Benton. In *Early Writings*, edited by Lucio Colletti, Rodney Livinstone, and Gregor Benton. New York: Penguin Books, 1992.

McEvilley, Thomas. *The Shape of Ancient Thought: Comparative Studies in Greek and Indian Philosophies*. New York: Allworth Press, 2002.

Midgley, Mary. *Beast and Man: The Roots of Human Nature*. London and New York: Routledge, 2002.

Naas, Michael. "'One Nation . . . Indivisible': Jacques Derrida on the Autoimmunity of Democracy and the Sovereignty of God." *Research in Phenomenology* 36, no. 1 (2006): 15–44.

Newton, Michael. *Savage Girls and Wild Boys: A History of Feral Children*. New York: Picador, 2004.

Oliver, Kelly. *Animal Lessons: How They Teach Us to Be Human*. New York: Columbia University Press, 2009.

Osborne, Catherine. *Dumb Beasts and Dead Philosophers: Humanity and the Humane in Ancient Philosophy and Literature*. Oxford: Oxford University Press, 2009.

Petit, Philippe. *Man on Wire*. New York: Skyhorse Pub, 2008.

Plato. *Cratylus*. Translated by C. D. C. Reeve. Indianapolis: Hackett Publishing Company, 1998.

Poyatos, Fernando. *New Perspectives in Nonverbal Communication: Studies in Cultural Anthropology, Social Psychology, Linguistics, Literature, and Semiotics*. New York: Pergamon Press, 1983.

Richardson, William S. J. *Heidegger: Through Phenomenology to Thought*. 4th ed. New York: Fordham University Press, 1993.

Ryan, Joan. *Little Girls in Pretty Boxes: The Making and Breaking of Elite Gymnasts and Figure Skaters*. New York: Warner Books, 2000.

Said, Edward. *Orientalism*. New York: Vintage Books, 1979.

Sallis, John. *Being and Logos: Reading the Platonic Dialogues*. Bloomington: Indiana University Press, 1996.

Saussure, Ferdinand de. *Course in General Linguistics*. Translated by Roy Harris. Chicago: Open Court, 1972.

———. *Writings in General Linguistics*. Translated by Carol Sanders and Matthew Pires. Oxford and New York: Oxford University Press, 2006.

Schlant, Ernestine. *The Language of Silence: West German Literature and the Holocaust*. New York: Routledge, 1999.

Schmitt, Carl. *Political Theology: Four Chapters on the Concept of Sovereignty*. Translated by George Schwab. Chicago: University of Chicago Press, 2006.

Singer, Isaac Bashevis. *The Collected Stories of Isaac Bashevis Singer.* New York: Noonday Press, 1996.

Singer, Peter. *Animal Liberation: The Definitive Classic of the Animal Movement.* New York: Harper Perennial, 1975.

Sontag, Susan. "The Aesthetics of Silence." In *A Susan Sontag Reader,* 181–204. New York: Vintage Books, 1983.

Steeves, H. Peter. *Animal Others: On Ethics, Ontology, and Animal Life.* Albany: State University of New York Press, 1999.

Steiner, Gary. *Anthropocentrism and Its Discontents: The Moral Status of Animals in the History of Western Philosophy.* Pittsburgh, Pa.: University of Pittsburgh Press, 2005.

Steiner, George. *Language and Silence; Essays on Language, Literature, and the Inhuman.* New York: Atheneum, 1967.

Thomson, Iain. "Ontotheology? Understanding Heidegger's Destruktion of Metaphysics." *International Journal of Philosophical Studies* 8, no. 3 (2001): 297–327.

Thich Nhat Hanh. *Answers from the Heart.* Berkeley, Calif.: Parallax Press, 2009.

Wolfe, Cary. *Animal Rites: American Culture, the Discourse of Species, and Posthumanist Theory.* Chicago: University of Chicago Press, 2003.

———. *Zoontologies: The Question of the Animal.* Minneapolis: University of Minnesota Press, 2003.

Yuasa, Yasuo, and Thomas P. Kasulis. *The Body: Toward an Eastern Mind–Body Theory.* Albany: State University of New York Press, 1987.

Index

Abraham: covenant and, 60, 61; God
and, 46, 47, 51
absence, silence as, 36–40
accountability, 26, 75, 144, 167, 168
acrobatics, 197, 198, 199, 217, 219,
238, 254; exceptional movement
and, 220
actions: human, 230; ontology of,
227; words and, 152
actuality, 218, 259; impotentiality
and, 206; potentiality and, 105,
203, 204
actus, 205, 224; *potentia* and, 204
Adam, 141, 148, 153
aesthetics, 200, 224, 225, 245, 254
"Aesthetics of Silence, The"
(Sontag), quote from, 63
africanus niger, 182
Agamben, Giorgio, xi, 16, 72, 80,
85, 86, 87, 110, 120, 123, 139, 233,
260; on Adamic language, 169;
alienation and, 228; on animals,
173; anthropological machine
and, 27; antinomianism and,
83; Aristotle and, 200, 205, 206,
208, 216; on as not, 104–5; auto-
affection and, 133; be just and,
96, 97; Benjamin and, 169, 170,
258; biopolitics and, 69; Derrida
and, xvi, 79, 87, 106, 110, 125,
126, 131, 134, 135, 168; difference
and, 134; *dispositifs* and, 28, 29;
economic theology and, 266n17;

emptiness and, 94; ethics and,
103, 145, 159; exception and, 70;
on *facies/enfants sauvages,* 189;
facticity and, 209; on faculty,
214; on faith/law, 104; Foucault
and, 89, 90, 139; gesture and, 224,
225, 226; on *gramma,* 121; happy
life and, 236; Heidegger and,
204, 209; historical continuity
and, 258; on history, 171; human
action and, 230; on humanity,
259; identity and, 25–26; image
and, 101; impotenza and,
214; infancy and, 171–72, 178;
inoperativity and, 105, 142,
267n24; integral actuality and,
259; justice and, 83; on Kafka,
81–82; *kinēsis* and, 200, 209;
language and, 5, 95, 96, 124, 150,
169, 170, 171, 173, 174; law and,
5, 17, 71, 87, 96, 150, 152; logos
and, 123; means and, 227, 230;
mediality and, 226; messianic
time and, 81; metalanguage and,
124; name/naming and, 145; on
norm, 70; obfuscations of, xvii;
on opposition man/animal,
human/inhuman, 27; parody
and, 131, 132–33, 135; passivity
and, 199; on Paul/messianic
power, 105; perspectives of, 109;
on philosophy, 124, 152–53; play/
children's games and, 236;

KALPANA RAHITA SESHADRI is associate professor of English at Boston College. She is the author of *Desiring Whiteness: A Lacanian Analysis of Race* and the coeditor, with Fawzia Afzal-Khan, of *The Pre-Occupation of Postcolonial Studies.*

(continued from page ii)